MYSTIC SEAPORT®

A New England Table

edited by Ainslie Turner

Published by:
Mystic Seaport Museum Store
75 Greenmanville Avenue
Mystic, CT 06355

www.mysticseaport.org

©2000 Mystic Seaport, Inc.
Second Printing 2003

ISBN 0-939510-69-3

Printed in Canada
Designed by Trish Sinsigalli LaPointe

Additional copies of this book may be obtained by
using the order form in the back of the book, by writing
to the address listed above, or by calling
1.800.331.BOOK. To order *A New England Table*
for re-sale purposes, call 1.800.248.1066.

**Your purchase supports the maritime preservation work
of Mystic Seaport, The Museum of America and the Sea.**

Contents

Introduction

New England is truly the corner of the continent where American cooking first began. Can you imagine how the early colonizers struggled to adapt their Old World kitchen traditions to such strange new foods as wild turkey, corn, clams, cod, pumpkins, beans, and cranberries? Both Pilgrims and Indians shared the joys of the harvest, creating dishes whose titles speak of history itself... Joe Froggers, blueberry buckle, Johnnycakes, steamed puddings, Cape Cod chowders, rich brown breads and Boston Baked Beans. The bounty that came from the primitive Pilgrim hearth (tended, of course, by a good colonial housewife), was indeed a mixture of simplicity and frugality. Roasting, broiling, boiling and baking in the often-blistering temperatures of a wide kitchen fireplace was an all-day affair. Tending to spits, heat reflectors, trivets, drip pans, griddles, Dutch ovens, hanging pots, cranes ... what a challenge!

Updated Yankee cooking is far more simple, yet still revolves around the kitchen as the center of family life; a place to gather, sit by the fire, dine, listen to music, do homework, or just hang around waiting for the main event. From these roots, this unique recipe collection brings us a return to our beginnings, drawing a wide range of favorites from the past and present, each with some history of its own. Whether watching mother prepare a traditional Saturday pot of stew or helping a favorite uncle dig, shuck and grind clams for his famous chowder, picking the prized berries for a shortcake, harvesting a pumpkin pie, or rolling Christmas cookies with Grandma, all are memories to cherish.

So, guarantee smooth sailing at your next family dinner. Gather a few friends and relatives together and experience a taste or two from our true New England Table, remembering always that it is:

> "Better to eat vegetables with people you love than to eat the finest meat where there is hate; better to eat a dry crust of bread with a piece of mind, than have a banquet in a house of trouble." **Proverbs 15:17**

Ainslie Turner

Contributors

A special thank you to all the members of Mystic Seaport who made this cookbook possible.

Binti Ackley
Georgene Albrecht
Hon. John R.M. Alger
Cynthia Allyn
Evelyn Anderson
Patricia Apgar
Eileen Archer
Christopher Atwood
Susan Austin
Janet Avery
Elaine Banks
Betsy Jane Bartholet
Richard Beauchemin
Mrs. Alan P. Bentz
Carol Bergeron
Harriet Boedecker
Stephanie Bradshow
Nancy Brooks Marculewicz
Marylin C. Brown
Mr. and Mrs. Maynard
    Brown, Jr.
Edythe Burdick
Amy Bush
Joan Butler
Mr. and Mrs. Powell Cabot
James Capone
Mike Cardillo, Jr.
Patricia Carey
Susan Carney
Karen Carreira
Lisa Carruthers
Charles Cattanach
Diana Charnok
Jill Chessman
Diane Chupas
Liz Church
Anne Clapp
Joan Cohn
Kathleen Cole
Leslie and Peter Collins
Shirley Congdon
Carol Connor
Joan Corcoran
David Coursey
Clorinda Cuomo
Nic Damuck
Luella Daniels Landis
Jill Dannin Spear
Anne Darling
Phyllis Datlefs
Diane Davis

Jane Davis
Joan Davis
Connie Dayton
Sandra Defilippo
Steven Demick
Anne Denson
Mary Deveau
Mrs. Francis Dixon
Bevery Dobbin
Susan Drover
Dorothy Dsupin
Glen Dunham
Patricia Edwards
Frances Everett
Fanny Mason Farmstead
Mr. and Mrs. Dudley Fay
Deborah Febish
Mary Ferrier
Alvonia Fitzhugh
Bruni Fletcher-Koch
Marilyn Foster
Henry Fredella
Joyce Furlane
Sheila Gelsthorpe
Dr. Joseph B. Geraci
Elizabeth Glasfeld
Audrey Golub
Nancy Gould
Karen Graves
Janice Gross
Karen Gypson
Linda Sue Hall
Alan Hall
Jeanne Hamilton
Cindy Hardy
Heidi Hare
Debbie Harris
Mary Harrison
Joyce Hern Burdick
Peter Hobson
Frances Hoffman
Taffy Holland
Lorraine Homola
Betsy Honey
Virgil Huntley
Sonja Hveem
Eleanor Jamieson
Anka Jurkova Fitzgerald
Madelyn Kavanaugh
Carol Keemon

Anne Kennedy
Mrs. Peter Knapp
Sandra Kress
Janice Laats
Marta Lane
Barbara Langworth
Prudence Langworthy Parris
Julie Lanier
Joan Lawrence
Lynn Leech
Susan Lloyd
Mandy Loutrel
Jeanne Lovejoy
Barbara Lukens
Barbara Mahany
Marjorie Major
Gloria Malley Beauchamp
Pat Maloney
Joa Martinson
Corine Matarasso
Nancy Maynard
David and Margaret
    McCandless
Marguerite McGugan
Joyce McKay
Nancy Meitzler
Joan Merrill
Robert Merritt
Carol Miller Pekrul
Dianne Mirabito-Hough
Karen Morgan
Jennifer Morgenthau
Diantha Morse
Carol Murkett
Peggy Nalle
Winifred Newbury
Joan Newell
Ellen Nosal
F. Barbara O'Connell
Alice Olsen Rowley
Antonia Osgood
Marilyn Osowiski
Oxford House Inn
Dorothy Paige
Abby Parkinson
Polly Pasternack Huntington
Jane Paynter
Bonnie Pedersen
Alouise Pelletier
Chenoa, Tashawna and
    Adam Pierce

Andy Price
Kay Print Janney
Rosealie Ramadei
Mildred Reed
Irene Rioux
Dorothy Robart
Suzanne Robinett
Barbara Robinson
Judy Rosbe
Jean Ryan
Joan Ryan
Pam Ryley
Jonetha Sander
Peggy Sapphire
Joe Sauer
Judith Sauer
Elizabeth Savage
Dawne Scarlott
Patricia Shea McGrath
Jim Sherman
Jeanne Sinsigalli
Marilyn Sly
Jacquelyn Smakula
Sandra Smith
Tim Snider
Susan Sokoloski
Carolyn Stanley
Brian Suiter
Mary Tarbell
Lisa Tasi
Patricia Taylor
Steven Telsey
Roxana Terwilliger
Gail Thomas
Margaret Thoms
Tidewater Inn
Elinor Townsend
Roberta Turner
Suzanne Virgulak
Mary Waldau
Melinda Walsh
Donald Weaver
Nancy Wells
Kathy Wheeler
Patricia Ann White
Florence Wilson
Valerie Winston
Dave Wollman
Victoria Yolen

Some recipe titles may have been changed. If similar recipes were submitted, credit may be given to both parties.

First
Bites

Crab Bites With Lemon-Caper Sauce

Serves about 30

½ cup mayonnaise
2 eggs, lightly beaten
2 tablespoons Dijon mustard
2 tablespoons chopped fresh parsley
2 teaspoons Worcestershire sauce
1 pound crabmeat, drained well and picked over to remove any shell
24 saltine crackers, finely ground

1. Whisk mayonnaise, eggs, mustard, parsley and Worcestershire sauce in a large bowl to blend. Gently mix in crabmeat and crackers. Roll mixture into 1-inch balls and place on 2 baking sheets that have been sprayed with nonstick spray.
2. Preheat broiler. Broil Crab Bites until brown and cooked through, turning once. Watch these closely to avoid over-browning. Serve with the sauce.

LEMON-CAPER SAUCE

1 cup mayonnaise
4 tablespoons drained capers
4 tablespoons chopped scallions
2 tablespoons chopped chives
4 tablespoons fresh lemon juice
1½ teaspoons grated lemon rind

Mix all ingredients in a medium bowl to blend. Chill until cold. May be prepared 1 day ahead.

Joe And Mary's Toasted Crab Dip

Serves 10

From my sister in Baltimore… where they are as passionate about crabs as New Englanders.

1 pound crabmeat (lump or claw)
2 8-ounce packages cream cheese at room temperature
½ pint sour cream
5 tablespoons mayonnaise
juice of ½ lemon
1 teaspoon dry mustard
1 tablespoon Worcestershire sauce
1 tablespoon fresh chopped parsley
¼ teaspoon garlic salt
Old Bay Seasoning to taste (½ to 1 teaspoon)
½ cup grated cheese, Parmesan or cheddar

Carefully pick over crabmeat to remove any cartilage. Mix all ingredients except grated cheese; add crabmeat last so as not to break it up too much. Spray a 1-quart baking pan with nonstick cooking spray and pour in crab mixture. Sprinkle grated cheese on top and dust with paprika. Bake in a 325° oven for 30 minutes until top is browned. Serve hot with corn chips or Triscuits.

Hot Toasted Crab Dip

Serves 10

Such a simple and delicious dip – always asked to bring it along to parties.

1 6-ounce can crabmeat, drained and cartilage removed
1 8-ounce container whipped cream cheese
2 tablespoons milk
2 tablespoons finely chopped onion
1 teaspoon grated horseradish
$\frac{1}{3}$ cup sliced almonds
1 tablespoon chopped fresh parsley

Mix together all ingredients except almonds and parsley, being careful not to break up the crabmeat too much. Spread in a pie plate or small flat baking pan, sprinkle with almonds and bake for 45 minutes at 350° until bubbly. Sprinkle with parsley and serve hot with crackers or chips.

Creamy Crab Dip

Serves 8 to 10

2 8-ounce packages cream cheese, at room temperature
$\frac{1}{2}$ cup sour cream
$\frac{1}{4}$ cup mayonnaise
2 tablespoons white wine or cream
2 tablespoons grated onion
1 tablespoon Dijon mustard
1 teaspoon minced fresh garlic
Tabasco sauce
1 $6\frac{1}{2}$-ounce can crabmeat, drained
$\frac{1}{4}$ cup minced fresh parsley
$\frac{1}{4}$ cup minced scallions
$\frac{1}{2}$ cup toasted slivered almonds
paprika

Mix cream cheese, sour cream, mayonnaise, wine, onion, mustard, garlic and Tabasco sauce to taste in a medium saucepan. Fold in crabmeat, parsley and scallions. Warm over medium heat, stirring gently until just hot; do not boil. Spoon into a warm chafing dish or fondue pot, sprinkle with almonds and paprika and serve with crackers or toasted French bread.

Luxurious Lobster Mold

Serves 12 to 16

1 envelope unflavored gelatin
$\frac{1}{4}$ cup water
1 can cream of tomato soup, heated –
  do not dilute
2 tablespoons chopped scallions
4 tablespoons chopped celery
2 tablespoons chopped pimento
2 tablespoons chopped fresh parsley
1 8-ounce package cream cheese
1 12-ounce can lobster meat, rinsed
  and squeezed dry
salt and Tabasco sauce to taste

1. Dissolve gelatin in water, combine
   with heated soup and mix well. Add
   scallions, celery, pimento, parsley and
   cream cheese. Gently fold in lobster
   meat and season to taste with salt and
   Tabasco sauce.

2. Pour mixture into a lightly oiled
   decorative 4-cup mold; a lobster or
   fish shape is great if you have one.
   Refrigerate for at least 6 hours or
   best overnight. To unmold: place the
   bottom of the mold in a sink of warm
   water until you can shake it slightly
   free from the sides. Place your serving
   platter on top and flip – voilà! Tuck
   lettuce leaves around the edges and
   serve with crisp crackers.

Hot Toasted Crab Crisps

Yields 4 dozen rounds

1 cup mayonnaise
$\frac{1}{2}$ cup chopped scallions
1 cup freshly grated Parmesan cheese
4 drops Tabasco sauce (or more to taste)
1 tablespoon fresh lemon juice
$\frac{1}{4}$ teaspoon curry powder
8 ounces fresh crabmeat
2 baguettes, thinly sliced

Combine mayonnaise, scallions, cheese,
Tabasco sauce, lemon juice and curry
powder. Gently fold in crabmeat. Place
bread rounds on a cookie sheet and crisp
for 10 minutes in a 350° oven. Spread crab
mixture on rounds, increase oven to 375°
and bake for 15 minutes until bubbly and
lightly browned.

Marinated Shrimp And Artichokes

Serves 8 to 10

2 13$\frac{3}{4}$-ounce cans artichoke hearts, drained and quartered
1$\frac{1}{2}$ pounds medium shrimp, peeled and cooked
5 tablespoons minced chives
$\frac{1}{2}$ cup olive oil
$\frac{1}{2}$ cup white wine vinegar
1 egg (or $\frac{1}{4}$ cup egg substitute)
2$\frac{1}{2}$ tablespoons Dijon mustard
2 teaspoons fresh rosemary, minced
$\frac{1}{2}$ teaspoon salt
$\frac{1}{2}$ teaspoon freshly ground black pepper

Layer artichokes, shrimp and chives in a large bowl. Combine remaining ingredients in a blender and mix until it is the consistency of heavy cream. Pour marinade over shrimp, toss lightly and refrigerate at least 6 hours or overnight. Serve as a first course on Bibb lettuce garnished with cherry tomatoes or stuffed into hollowed-out vine-ripened tomatoes as a luncheon dish.

Steamed Clams With Bacon And Beer

Serves 4
You may substitute littlenecks, soft-shell clams, or mussels. Cooking times will vary.

4 slices bacon, diced
1 small onion, diced
3 pounds littlenecks, scrubbed
$\frac{1}{2}$ to 1 bottle of beer (about $\frac{3}{4}$ cup or water or chicken broth)
1 loaf of crusty bread

1. In a large saucepan, cook bacon until golden. Add onion and cook for 4 more minutes until onion is tender and bacon is brown.
2. Add clams and beer to saucepan, cover and cook until clams are open, about 6 to 7 minutes. Serve hot, in bowls with crusty bread to soak up the great broth.

**"No longer the slave of ambition
I laugh at the world and its shams
As I think of my pleasant condition
Surrounded by acres of clams.
*The Old Settle***

5

Coecles Harbor Oysters

Serves 6 as a first course or 4 as an entrée

8 ounces country ham or Canadian bacon
6 ounces fresh spinach
   (about 2 cups, packed)
2 large shallots, finely chopped
2 garlic cloves, finely chopped
2 tablespoons butter
$\frac{1}{2}$ cup dry white wine
$\frac{1}{4}$ cup Pernod or other anise-flavored
   liqueur
2 cups heavy cream
3 dozen shucked oysters
salt and freshly ground black pepper
   to taste
chopped fresh parsley

1. Cut ham into thin matchstick-size pieces, to measure 1 cup. Tear spinach into bite-size pieces.

2. In a large heavy skillet, cook ham, shallots and garlic in butter over moderate heat, stirring until shallots are softened. Add wine and Pernod and boil until most of liquid is evaporated. Add cream and simmer, stirring occasionally until liquid is reduced by half, about 8 minutes.

3. Stir in spinach and oysters and simmer, stirring gently, until oysters are cooked through, about 3 minutes. Season with salt and pepper and serve on toast or in puff pastry shells.

Blue Hill Bay Mussels

Serves 4

The collection process of this recipe is as important as the end product. We use it as a "guest activity" at our house in Maine. Waiting for the right tide, picking the best mussels from the beds and watching the glistening sun on the water from the deck – then on to the kitchen.

4 dozen mussels, cleaned and debearded
2 tablespoons chopped shallots
2 tablespoons butter (or olive oil)
2 tablespoons fresh chopped parsley
$\frac{1}{2}$ cup dry white wine
melted butter for dipping
salt and pepper

1. After cleaning mussels, leave in salt water until ready to cook. When ready to cook, drain and refresh with another rinse of water; fresh water is fine.

2. In a large saucepan, melt butter and sauté shallots for 3 minutes. Drain mussels, add to the saucepan with parsley and wine. Cover, cook over medium-high heat for 5 minutes until mussels open. Shake pan several times while cooking. Taste broth, season to your liking with salt and pepper and serve mussels in big bowls with extra broth on the side and plenty of melted butter for dipping.

One South Café Grilled Mussels

Serves 6
From a fine Stonington watering hole.

4 pounds mussels
2 tablespoons hot red pepper flakes
$1\frac{1}{2}$ cups white wine
1 pound butter, softened
1 tablespoon chopped garlic
3 tablespoons chopped fresh parsley
pinch white pepper, and salt
4 cups unseasoned bread crumbs
2 tablespoons dried parsley flakes
1 tablespoon garlic powder
$\frac{1}{8}$ teaspoon white pepper
lemon wedges

1. In a large saucepan, soak mussels, covered with water, mixed with hot pepper flakes for 15 minutes. Debeard the mussels and drain. Add the white wine to the saucepan, cover and steam for 6 to 8 minutes until open. Discard any shells that do not open. Drain and let cool. Remove and discard one half shell from each mussel.

2. While mussels are cooking, combine butter, garlic, fresh parsley, salt and pepper. In another bowl, combine bread crumbs, parsley flakes, garlic powder and remaining white pepper.

3. Spread each mussel with garlic butter mixture, dip each mussel into seasoned crumbs and place in a single layer on a baking sheet. (They may be frozen at this time.) Preheat broiler and cook for 3 to 4 minutes until golden brown. Pile on hot plates and serve with lemon wedges.

Clam Stuffed Clam Shells

Serves 8
With high approval from the Boston University Cook's Committee.

30 Ritz crackers, crumbled
1 10-ounce can whole baby clams, drained, juice reserved
3 tablespoons minced onion
2 cloves garlic, minced
3 tablespoons Worcestershire sauce
$\frac{1}{3}$ cup melted butter
salt and pepper to taste
8 lemon wedges
8 clam shells

Mix crackers, clams, onion, garlic, Worcestershire sauce and butter; season with salt and pepper. Add enough reserved clam juice to make a moist mixture. Fill clam shells (or ovenproof ramekins) and bake at 350° for 25 to 30 minutes until browned. Serve each with a lemon wedge.

Clam Stuffed Baked Clams

Serves 6 as an appetizer, 4 as an entrée
A double dose of clams in these.

20 Littleneck clams
4 cloves garlic, minced
4 whole bay leaves
1 tablespoon whole peppercorns
2 cups white wine
6 tablespoons bacon fat
1 shallot, minced
1 red bell pepper, minced
1 pint chopped clams, drained
$\frac{1}{2}$ cup Ritz Crackers, crumbled
2 tablespoons chopped parsley
2 tablespoons chopped basil
1 teaspoon Worcestershire sauce
$\frac{1}{4}$ teaspoon Tabasco sauce
1 tablespoon lemon juice
$\frac{1}{2}$ teaspoon Dijon mustard
$\frac{1}{8}$ teaspoon ground black pepper
3 tablespoons unsalted butter
lemon wedges

1. Steam clams until open in large, covered saucepan with $\frac{1}{2}$ garlic cloves, bay leaves, peppercorns and white wine. Remove clams from their shell and chop coarsely. Reserve shells.

2. Heat bacon fat in sauté pan over medium-high heat. Sauté shallot and red pepper until soft, 5 to 7 minutes. Add remaining garlic and chopped clam meat and sauté 1 to 2 minutes more.

3. Remove pan from heat and add rest of ingredients; mix thoroughly.

4. Fill cleaned clamshells with stuffing mixture. Dot with butter and bake at 350° for 15 minutes until lightly browned. Serve hot with lemon wedges.

Deviled Clams Evie

Makes 2 dozen
As a child, scavenging for the clamshells to make these was half the fun. Now at our summer house in Old Lyme, Connecticut, we buy clams, make a batch of chowder first and save the shells for this special treat.

20 milk or Pilot crackers, crushed fine
2 $6\frac{1}{2}$-ounce cans minced clams, drained
1 teaspoon salt
$\frac{1}{2}$ teaspoon pepper
$\frac{1}{2}$ cup parsley, finely chopped
$\frac{1}{2}$ cup red or green pepper, finely chopped
$\frac{1}{2}$ pound butter
24 medium clam shells
lemon wedges

1. Melt butter, cool slightly. Combine the cracker crumbs, clams, salt, pepper, parsley and red or green pepper. Pour butter slowly over crumb mixture and mix lightly with a fork until well blended.

2. Lightly butter clam shells or spray with nonstick cooking spray. Pile mixture into shells, being careful not to pack down too hard. (They can be refrigerated or wrapped and frozen at this point.) Place on a cookie sheet and bake at 375° for 20 to 25 minutes until lightly browned. Serve with lemon wedges.

Bay Street Shrimp Toasts

Makes 3 dozen
From the kitchen of a Mystic Seaport neighbor.

1 pound small shrimp, peeled and deveined
1 teaspoon salt
black pepper
1 tablespoon sherry
1 whole scallion, chopped
1 egg, beaten
6 water chestnuts, chopped
1 tablespoon cornstarch
12 slices white bread
peanut oil

1. Coarsely chop the shrimp. Combine with salt, black pepper to taste, sherry, scallion, egg, water chestnuts and cornstarch. Refrigerate for 15 minutes.
2. Trim crusts from bread. Cut each slice diagonally into 4 triangles. Spread 1 tablespoon of shrimp mixture evenly over bread. Heat oil in wok or frying pan until hot. Add bread, shrimp side down, and fry until golden brown, turning once. Drain on paper towels and serve with:

SWEET AND SPICY SAUCE
Makes 2 cups

4 tablespoons soy sauce
$\frac{3}{4}$ cup catsup
$\frac{3}{4}$ cup water
2 tablespoons vinegar
$\frac{1}{2}$ cup brown sugar
1 small onion, finely diced
1 clove garlic, minced
1 teaspoon grated fresh ginger

Combine all ingredients in a small saucepan. Simmer for 5 minutes until onion is tender. Refrigerate. This sauce is also excellent for basting grilled swordfish or shrimp.

Quarter Deck Smoked Bluefish Pâté

Makes 2 cups

$\frac{1}{2}$ pound smoked bluefish
4 ounces cream cheese, softened
8 tablespoons ($\frac{1}{2}$ cup) unsalted butter, softened
1 tablespoon minced onion
1 teaspoon Cognac
$\frac{1}{2}$ teaspoon Worcestershire sauce
2 tablespoons fresh lemon juice

In a food processor, purée all the ingredients, scraping down the side of the bowl several times. Transfer the pâté to a small bowl and serve it with crackers. The pâté keeps, covered with plastic wrap and chilled, for 3 days.

New England Mini Lobster Rolls

Makes 4 to 6 dozen

This recipe usually goes home with one or more guests every time my daughters and I serve these at a party.

$\frac{1}{2}$ cup butter
$\frac{1}{2}$ pound mushrooms, chopped
3 tablespoons flour
$\frac{3}{4}$ teaspoon salt
1 cup light cream
2 teaspoons minced chives
1 teaspoon lemon juice
8 ounces cooked lobster meat, coarsely chopped
salt and pepper
1 loaf thin-sliced bread (prefer fresh Sunbeam)
3 eggs, beaten
oil

1. Melt butter and sauté mushrooms until tender, about 5 minutes. Blend in flour and salt. Stir in cream and whisk over medium heat until thick. Add chives, lemon juice and lobster meat; season to taste with salt and pepper.

2. Cut crusts off of bread and roll each slice as thin as possible. As you work, cover the slices with a damp towel to keep from drying out.

3. Fill each slice with 1 teaspoon of filling and roll into a cylinder, brush with beaten egg. Heat a small amount of oil, about $\frac{1}{3}$ cup in a heavy skillet and fry rolls, turning, until golden brown. Remove from pan and drain on paper towels.
Rolls may be left whole or cut in half for serving. They also may be frozen and reheated in a 325° oven for 5 minutes when thawed.

Marblehead Shrimp Mousse

Serves 10

From a husband and wife cooking team.

1 envelope unflavored gelatin
$\frac{1}{4}$ cup cold water
8 ounces cream of mushroom soup
1 8-ounce package cream cheese, softened
1 cup mayonnaise
$\frac{3}{4}$ cup finely chopped celery
1 $6\frac{1}{2}$-ounce can medium shrimp, drained
1 tablespoon grated onion
$1\frac{1}{2}$ teaspoons Worcestershire sauce
parsley sprigs

1. Soak gelatin in cold water to soften, until dissolved. In a medium saucepan, heat soup, add gelatin and mix thoroughly. Add cream cheese and mayonnaise, beat until smooth. Cool. Add celery, shrimp, onion and Worcestershire sauce.

2. Pour mixture into a lightly oiled mold and chill for at least 6 hours or best overnight. Unmold onto a bed of fresh greens, garnish with fresh parsley and serve with crackers or Melba Toast.

Silver Lake Shrimp Dip

Makes 2 cups

In 1975, when my husband was stationed in Orlando, Florida, I spent my first Christmas away from home. My cousin, Sue, invited us to join them nearby in Mount Dora, where we were served this delicious shrimp dip. Every time I prepare this for guests, I think back to that Christmas which was so special for both of us.

1 package unflavored gelatin
1 tablespoon hot water
$\frac{1}{2}$ 10-ounce can tomato soup
1 8-ounce package cream cheese, softened
$\frac{3}{4}$ cup mayonnaise
1 5-ounce can tiny shrimp, drained
2 tablespoons chopped onion
$\frac{1}{4}$ cup chopped green pepper
salt and pepper to taste

1. Dissolve gelatin in hot water. Over low heat (or in a microwave), combine soup and cream cheese, cook until well blended; add the gelatin mixture. Cool for 15 minutes.

2. Gently blend in the mayonnaise, shrimp, onion and green pepper. Season to taste with salt and pepper and pour into a decorative bowl. Refrigerate until set, about 2 hours or overnight. Serve with corn chips or our favorite, Bugles.

Shaw's Cove Shrimp Sizzlers

Makes 24 to 28 hors d'oeuvres

1 pound (about 32) medium shrimp, peeled
$\frac{1}{4}$ cup coarsely grated cheddar or Monterey Jack cheese
2 tablespoons freshly grated Parmesan cheese
$\frac{1}{4}$ cup heavy cream
1 tablespoon sherry
2 tablespoons minced scallions
12 to 14 slices white bread, thinly sliced, crusts trimmed
$\frac{1}{4}$ cup ($\frac{1}{2}$ stick) unsalted butter, melted

1. Into a large saucepan of boiling salted water, plunge shrimp and simmer until just cooked through, 1 to 2 minutes. Drain shrimp in a colander and rinse under cold water. Pat shrimp dry and chop fine.

2. In a bowl, stir together shrimp, cheeses, cream, sherry, and scallions. With a rolling pin, flatten each bread slice into a $3\frac{1}{2}$-inch square. Put about 2 tablespoons shrimp mixture on each bread slice and roll up tightly. Put rolls, seam sides down, on a baking sheet and brush all over with butter. Chill rolls, covered loosely, at least 1 hour and up to 4. Preheat oven to 425°. Cut shrimp rolls in half and arrange on a baking sheet, seam sides down. Bake rolls until golden, about 12 minutes, and cool slightly. Serve warm.

Ram Island Salmon Mousse

Makes 4 cups
An after the "around the island race" yacht club favorite.

1 7-ounce can salmon, water packed, boneless
1 7-ounce can white tuna, water packed
1 tablespoon gelatin (1 envelope)
3 hard cooked eggs
$\frac{1}{2}$ cup chunky salsa
$\frac{1}{2}$ medium red onion, finely chopped
$\frac{1}{4}$ cup capers
1 tablespoon Worcestershire sauce
1 dill pickle, chopped
2 tablespoons lemon juice
black pepper to taste
2 tablespoons minced fresh dill, plus sprigs for garnish
1 cup mayonnaise

1. Drain salmon and tuna, reserving liquid; there should be $\frac{1}{2}$ cup. Discard any extra. In a small bowl, sprinkle gelatin into salmon-tuna liquid and let soften. Cover with plastic wrap and microwave on high power for 30 seconds or until gelatin is dissolved. (Or put gelatin mixture in a small saucepan, cook over low heat until dissolved.) Set aside.
2. In the bowl of a food processor, combine eggs, salmon, tuna, salsa, onion, capers, Worcestershire sauce, pickle, lemon juice and pepper. Process until blended but still chunky. Add gelatin mixture and process 10 seconds; add mayonnaise, process 10 seconds. Place mixture in a serving bowl and refrigerate, covered, for at least 2 hours. Garnish with fresh dill sprigs and serve with crackers or Melba Toast rounds.

Block Island Smoked Bluefish Dip

Makes about $2\frac{1}{4}$ cups
Serve with a platter of crudités and toasted slices of baguette.

$\frac{1}{2}$ cup sour cream
$\frac{1}{2}$ cup cream cheese (about 4 ounces), room temperature
2 tablespoons whipping cream
$1\frac{1}{2}$ tablespoons fresh lemon juice
3 garlic cloves, finely chopped
1 tablespoon chopped fresh dill
$\frac{1}{2}$ teaspoon Worcestershire sauce
$\frac{1}{2}$ teaspoon freshly ground black pepper
$\frac{1}{2}$ teaspoon Old Bay seasoning
4 drops hot pepper sauce
1 pound smoked bluefish or smoked whitefish chubs, skin and bones removed, flaked with fork
2 tablespoons chopped fresh chives
assorted crudités
toasted baguette slices

Beat first 10 ingredients in large bowl until well blended. Fold all but $\frac{1}{4}$ cup fish into dip. Transfer to serving bowl. Garnish dip with reserved $\frac{1}{4}$ cup fish and chives.

Stonington Scallop Puffs

Makes 32 puffs

$\frac{1}{2}$ pound sea scallops
$\frac{1}{4}$ cup mayonnaise
$\frac{1}{4}$ cup freshly grated Gruyère
$\frac{1}{2}$ teaspoon Dijon mustard
1 teaspoon fresh lemon juice
1 tablespoon finely chopped fresh parsley
   leaves
salt and pepper to taste
1 large egg white
8 slices of homemade-style white bread,
   toasted lightly, the crusts trimmed and each
   slice cut into 4 squares

1. In a saucepan, combine the scallops with
    enough salted water to cover them
    completely; bring the water to a simmer,
    and poach the scallops for 5 minutes.
    Drain the scallops well and cut them into
    $\frac{1}{2}$-inch pieces. In a bowl, whisk together
    the mayonnaise, Gruyère, mustard,
    lemon juice, parsley, and salt and pepper
    to taste, and the scallops. Toss the mixture
    well. In a small bowl, beat the egg white
    until it just holds stiff peaks and fold it
    into the scallop mixture gently but
    thoroughly.

2. Top each bread square with a heaping
    teaspoon of the scallop mixture, arrange
    the puffs 1 inch apart on baking sheets,
    and broil them under a preheated broiler
    about 6 inches from the heat for 1 to 2
    minutes, or until the toppings are bub-
    bling and lightly golden (do not allow
    the edges of the toasts to burn).

Sausage Bites With Apples And Raisins

Makes 4 dozen
**This recipe was passed on to me by a
friend who is a caterer. They are moist
and flavorful, also may be frozen.**

1 pound bulk pork sausage
2 cups Bisquik
1$\frac{1}{2}$ cups grated apple with peel
   (about 3 apples)
1 cup raisins
$\frac{1}{2}$ cup chopped pecans

In a medium mixing bowl, combine uncooked
sausage, Bisquik, apples, raisins and pecans;
mix well. Roll into 1-inch balls and bake in a
preheated 350° oven for 15 to 20 minutes
until browned. Turn once while baking. Drain
on paper towels if necessary and serve immediately, or freeze, then thaw and reheat
before serving.

Green Eggs And Ham

Makes 2 dozen
A favorite storybook-inspired hors d'oeuvre.

6 ounces thinly sliced country ham
12 large hard-cooked eggs
1 ripe avocado, peeled and mashed
2 tablespoons finely chopped onion
1 clove garlic, minced
2 tablespoons mayonnaise or salad
  dressing
$1\frac{1}{2}$ to 2 tablespoons fresh lime juice
1 teaspoon hot sauce
1 small tomato, peeled, seeded, and finely
  chopped
paprika

1. Cook ham in a nonstick skillet over
   medium heat 5 minutes or until lightly
   browned, turning once. Drain and
   finely chop.

2. Cut eggs in half lengthwise, and
   carefully remove yolks. Mash yolks
   with a fork; add avocado and next 5
   ingredients, stirring well. Fold in
   tomato, and spoon into egg whites.
   Top with ham and sprinkle with
   paprika.

Stuffed Portabello Capone

Serves 4
**An Old World recipe with a new world touch
– the veggie stuffing creates a delicious
appetizer that your guests will savor.**

4 large Portabello mushrooms, stems
  removed
2 tablespoons extra virgin olive oil
1 large red pepper, chopped
1 medium red onion, chopped
4 large cloves garlic, minced
2 tablespoons chopped fresh parsley
1 cup cooked spinach (fresh or frozen),
  well drained and chopped
$\frac{1}{4}$ cup seasoned breadcrumbs
6 tablespoons Parmesan cheese, grated
$\frac{1}{4}$ teaspoon salt
freshly ground black pepper

1. Heat the olive oil in a skillet, add red
   pepper and sauté for 3 minutes. Add
   onion and garlic, sauté for 2 minutes,
   stir in parsley and remove from heat.

2. Place spinach in a bowl, add sautéed
   vegetables, breadcrumbs and 4
   tablespoons Parmesan cheese. Toss to
   mix. Brush the tops of the mushrooms
   lightly with olive oil and place, cap side
   down, on a lightly greased baking sheet.
   Stuff mushrooms and bake at 400° for
   10 to 12 minutes until tops are browned.
   Before serving, sprinkle with remaining
   2 tablespoons cheese and serve hot.

Reuben Melt

Makes 2 cups

Serve this dip with a basket of rye crackers or mini rye bread slices for dipping.

4 ounces sliced corned beef, shredded
$\frac{1}{2}$ cup grated Swiss cheese
1 3-ounce package cream cheese
$\frac{1}{4}$ cup sour cream
$\frac{1}{3}$ cup sauerkraut, drained
2 to 3 tablespoons milk
paprika

In a saucepan, combine corned beef, Swiss cheese, cream cheese, sour cream and sauerkraut. Cook over low heat, stirring until cheeses melt. Thin with milk to a dipping consistency. Serve hot, sprinkled with paprika.

Cape Cod Meatballs Piquant

Makes 6 dozen meatballs

2 pounds ground beef
2 eggs
$\frac{1}{4}$ cup water
1 cup bread crumbs
1 small onion, finely chopped
$1\frac{1}{2}$ teaspoons salt
$\frac{1}{8}$ teaspoon black pepper
1 16-ounce can jellied cranberry sauce
1 12-ounce jar chili sauce
3 tablespoons brown sugar
2 tablespoons lemon juice
fresh chopped parsley

1. Combine beef, eggs, water, bread crumbs, onion, salt and pepper. Shape into walnut-size balls and set aside.

2. In a large Dutch oven or deep saucepan, combine remaining ingredients (except parsley). Bring to a boil, reduce heat and simmer until cranberry sauce has melted. Add meatballs and simmer for 45 minutes, gently stirring to make sure none stick to the bottom. Serve hot in a chafing dish sprinkled with parsley.

Hot Artichoke Nibbles

Makes 3 dozen squares
Always a hit at the Stonington Antiques Show Preview Party at the Community Center.

2 6-ounce jars marinated artichoke hearts
1 small onion
1 clove garlic
4 eggs
$\frac{1}{4}$ cup bread crumbs
$\frac{1}{4}$ teaspoon salt
$\frac{1}{4}$ teaspoon thyme
black pepper
$\frac{1}{2}$ pound sharp cheddar cheese, grated
$\frac{1}{2}$ cup fresh parsley, chopped

1. Drain marinade from artichokes, reserving half. In a food processor, coarsely chop onion and garlic; add artichoke hearts and process until they have just broken up.
2. Heat reserved marinade in a saucepan and sauté artichoke-onion mix until onion is soft, about 3 to 4 minutes.
3. In a large bowl, beat eggs until fluffy. Add crumbs, seasonings, cheese and parsley. Fold in artichoke mixture and turn into a greased 9-by-9-inch baking pan. Bake at 350° for 30 minutes and cut into cubes. These may be frozen and popped into freezer bags for use later.

Islandia II Best Bites

From the kitchen of a wonderful Jensen Beach hostess.

CURRY BITES
Makes 32 bites

4 English muffins, split
1 cup sharp cheddar cheese, grated
$\frac{1}{4}$ cup mayonnaise
$\frac{1}{4}$ cup ripe olives, chopped
$\frac{1}{4}$ teaspoon curry powder

Mix all ingredients and spread generously on muffins. Cut into fourths, place on a cookie sheet and broil 2 minutes until hot and bubbly.

BLUE CHEESE PUFFS
Makes 40 puffs

1 10-ounce package refrigerated buttermilk biscuits
$\frac{1}{2}$ cup butter or margarine
1 4-ounce package blue cheese, crumbled
caraway or sesame seeds

Preheat oven to 400°. Cut biscuits into fourths and place in a 7-by-11-inch baking pan. Melt butter or margarine in a saucepan, add cheese and remove from heat. Spoon over biscuits and bake 10 to 15 minutes, turning puffs over after 7 minutes and sprinkling with seeds.

Jezebel

Makes 3 cups

I first sampled this while on a rafting trip to the Grand Canyon – watch out, it's hot and addictive!

8 ounces apricot preserves
8 ounces apple jelly
1 4-ounce can French's mustard powder
1 6-ounce jar horseradish
cream cheese

Mix all ingredients and spoon over cream cheese, serve with crackers. This is even better after it has been refrigerated.

Hot Brandied Cheese Dip

Serves 12 to 20

Serve this heavenly dip, piping hot with pita bread wedges.

1 8-ounce package cream cheese, softened
1 8-ounce container sour cream
$1\frac{1}{2}$ cups Gouda or Fontina cheese (or a combination), shredded
3 tablespoons brandy
$\frac{1}{2}$ cup chopped walnuts

Combine cream cheese, sour cream, shredded cheese and brandy. Spread in a decorative 8- or 9-inch pie pan. Sprinkle with walnuts and bake in a 350° oven for 30 minutes.

Toasted Mushroom Spread

Serves 6 to 8

A Cambridge tradition, serve hot with bagel chips, rye bread or crackers.

2 tablespoons butter
1 pound mushrooms, sliced
$1\frac{1}{2}$ cups mayonnaise
1 large onion, finely chopped
10 strips bacon, fried crisp and crumbled
$\frac{1}{4}$ teaspoon seasoned salt
$\frac{1}{2}$ cup grated cheese, cheddar, Gruyere, or Emmental

In a large skillet, melt butter, add mushrooms and sauté for 3 to 5 minutes. Combine with mayonnaise, onion, bacon and salt. Spread in a flat ovenproof baking dish, sprinkle with cheese and bake at 350° for 20 to 25 minutes until bubbly.

Sweet Spice Blend

Makes $\frac{1}{2}$ cup

1 tablespoon orange peel powder
1 tablespoon ground ginger
1 tablespoon ground nutmeg
2 tablespoons ground cinnamon
1 tablespoon ground cloves

Mix thoroughly to blend. Stir spice into ice cream, yogurt, fruit, oatmeal or add 2 to 3 tablespoons to cake or quick bread batters.

Aunt Clara's Chili Sauce

Makes 5 cups
Particularly good on burgers and dogs, also a great alternative to salsa.

3 green peppers
5 medium onions
1 22-ounce can crushed tomatoes
1 teaspoon salt
1 teaspoon cinnamon
$\frac{1}{2}$ teaspoon ground cloves
$\frac{3}{4}$ cup vinegar
1 cup sugar

Grind or finely chop peppers and onions. Place onions and peppers and the remaining ingredients into a large saucepan. Simmer for one hour uncovered, stirring occasionally. Place in clean jars with screw tops. Keeps refrigerated for several months.

Herbal Unsalt

Makes 1 cup
A few herbal secrets from the pantry.

3 tablespoons dried basil
1$\frac{1}{2}$ tablespoons dried sage
2 tablespoons dried savory
1 tablespoon powdered kelp
2 tablespoons celery seed
1 tablespoon dried marjoram

Powder the herbs together in a spice grinder or blender. Transfer to a shaker when blended. Set alongside the salt and pepper at the table.

Jeanne And Amy's Caramel Corn

Serves 10
Try not to eat too much during the cooking process!

1 cup (2 sticks) unsalted butter
2 cups light brown sugar, firmly packed
$\frac{1}{2}$ cup light corn syrup
1 teaspoon salt
$\frac{1}{2}$ teaspoon baking powder
1 teaspoon vanilla
1 cup EACH: almonds and pecans (optional)
3 quarts popped corn

1. Melt butter in a 4-quart or larger saucepan, stir in brown sugar, syrup and salt. Bring to a boil stirring constantly; then boil for 5 minutes without stirring. Remove from heat and stir in baking powder and vanilla. This will rise <u>at least double</u> in volume and can burn you easily.

2. Pour over the popped corn and nuts. Pour into a large, shallow pan and bake at 250° for 1 to 1$\frac{1}{4}$ hours. Stir/toss well every 15 minutes. Remove from oven and cool completely. Break up any "fused" chunks. Store in air tight container.

NOTES:
I usually double or triple the recipe. If tripling, make caramel in 2 batches. I also use a large (2 if tripled) disposable turkey roasting pan. Stores for months in airtight containers and makes a wonderful gift.

Cooks
Caldron

Stay-Cool Summer Tomato Soup

Serves 6

In the oven first thing in the morning and it is ready to be served, hot or chilled, for lunch.

12 medium-large ripe tomatoes
1 head garlic, unpeeled, separated into
   cloves
2 medium onions, unpeeled
2 tablespoons olive oil
cracked black pepper
dash of kosher salt
4 cups chicken stock
4 tablespoons minced fresh basil
2 tablespoons minced fresh mint
2 tablespoons minced fresh parsley

Preheat the oven to 325°.

1. Place the tomatoes, garlic, and onions in a baking pan, drizzle with olive oil, black pepper, and salt. Bake for 45 minutes until tomatoes are soft and onions and garlic are golden.

2. Remove from oven and let sit for 15 minutes. Squeeze the garlic from their skins, peel the onions and coarsely chop.

3. In a food processor, purée the onion and garlic mixture, tomatoes and half the stock until smooth but still a little chunky. Transfer the soup to a saucepan; add the remaining stock, basil and mint. Adjust seasonings and simmer for 5 minutes. Garnish with parsley.

Chilled Cucumber Soup

Serves 10 to 12

Make this all summer long to ease an over-abundant cucumber crop.

4 large cucumbers, peeled, seeded, and
   chopped
1 small mild onion, chopped
1 tablespoon butter
1 quart chicken or vegetable stock
1 8-ounce container sour cream
2 8-ounce containers plain yogurt
10 fresh dill sprigs (or more if desired)
1 cup buttermilk
salt to taste
dash of Tabasco sauce

1. In a skillet, slowly cook half the cucumbers and onions in butter for about 15 minutes, or until tender.

2. Combine with the remaining ingredients and purée in a blender or food processor until smooth, but still slightly chunky. This is best done in two batches. Add salt to taste, add tabasco sauce, and more fresh dill if desired. Chill for several hours and serve ice-cold with a fresh dill sprig floating on top.

Olde Oatmeal Soup

Serves 4

With renewed interest in whole cereal grains, this is a great source of fiber.

4 tablespoons butter
$\frac{1}{2}$ cup rolled oats
2 medium tomatoes, peeled, seeded and chopped
$\frac{1}{4}$ cup chopped onion
2 cloves garlic, minced
3 cups chicken stock
salt and pepper to taste

1. In a medium saucepan over low heat, melt the butter. Add the oats and stir constantly for 2 to 3 minutes. Add the tomatoes, onion and garlic and sauté for 5 more minutes.
2. Add the stock and simmer for $\frac{1}{2}$ hour. Remove from heat and cool.
3. Purée slightly in a blender (just long enough to break up the vegetables). Season to taste with salt and pepper.

Ohm-Ma's Lentil Soup

Serves 6 to 8

My friend's Bavarian grandmother took our family into her own over the years and we remember her for this wonderful hearty meal.

1 meaty ham bone or 2 ham hocks
3 carrots, sliced
4 stalks celery, chopped
1 large onion, chopped
$\frac{1}{8}$ teaspoon nutmeg
2 cloves garlic, minced
1 pound lentils
1 pound kielbasa, sliced
salt and pepper to taste

1. Simmer ham bone or ham hocks in enough water to cover (3 to 4 quarts) for 3 hours. Add carrots, celery, onion, nutmeg, garlic, and lentils and cook for 1 hour until vegetables are soft.
2. Add sliced kielbasa and simmer over low heat for another 30 minutes. Season to taste with salt and pepper and serve with crusty bread or rolls. When reheating, you may need to add a bit more water.

Creamy Lentil Soup

Serves 4 to 6

$\frac{1}{2}$ cup lentils
$\frac{3}{4}$ cup sliced carrots
1 medium onion, chopped
2 stalks celery, chopped
2 cups stock (or 2 cups water and 2
  bouillon cubes)
2 tablespoons butter
2 tablespoons flour
2 cups milk
salt and pepper
4 slices bacon, cooked and crumbled

1. Soak the lentils in cold water to cover overnight. Drain and place with the carrots, onion, and celery in a medium saucepan. Add stock, cover and simmer for 45 minutes until lentils are soft and vegetables are tender. Cool.

2. Purée the mixture in a blender. Melt the butter, add the flour, whisking in the milk one-third at a time. Gradually add the puréed vegetables to the hot sauce and heat to a boil, stirring briskly. Adjust the seasoning and serve hot, garnished with bacon.

NOTE:
The butter may be replaced with bacon drippings if you prefer a smokier flavor.

Mushroom And Wild Rice Soup

Serves 6
A light and healthy indulgence.

1 pound fresh mushrooms, any variety,
  sliced
$\frac{1}{4}$ cup (4 tablespoons) butter
1 small onion, chopped
$\frac{1}{4}$ cup flour
1 cup chicken or vegetable broth
1 cup milk
salt to taste
1 cup cooked wild rice
$\frac{1}{8}$ teaspoon cayenne pepper
$\frac{1}{4}$ cup chopped scallions for garnish

1. Melt butter in a large saucepan over medium heat. Add mushrooms and onion; sauté for 8 to 10 minutes until vegetables are tender.

2. Sprinkle flour over mixture, stirring to blend well. Gradually add broth, stirring constantly. Add the milk. Cook, stirring constantly, until mixture is well blended, smooth, and slightly thickened.

3. Stir in the cooked wild rice, salt to taste, and cayenne pepper. Heat for 2 minutes and ladle into soup bowls, sprinkling each serving with chopped scallions.

Slow Roasted Tomato Fennel Soup

Serves 4 to 6

As the vegetables bake, they will caramelize, giving the soup a rich deep flavor from the natural sugars.

2 pounds plum tomatoes, halved
  lengthwise and seeded
1 fennel bulb, stalks removed,
  ferns reserved
6 cloves garlic, peeled and sliced
2 tablespoons olive oil
1 tablespoon sugar
salt and freshly ground pepper to taste
6 cups chicken broth
$\frac{1}{4}$ cup fresh basil leaves, chopped

1. Preheat the oven to 250°. Place the tomatoes, skin side down, on a large baking sheet. Core the fennel, slice into strips and scatter over the tomatoes along with the garlic. Brush the vegetables with the oil, sprinkle with the sugar, salt and pepper. Bake for 2 hours.

2. Remove vegetables to a saucepan and add the broth. Bring to a boil, reduce heat to low and simmer for 10 minutes. Coarsely chop the reserved fennel ferns and stir into soup. Remove from heat and cool.

3. Purée soup in a blender or food processor until smooth but still a little chunky. Return to saucepan, reheat, add basil and serve.

Plum Island Corn Chowder

Serves 6

We first had this chowder at the home of a college friend from Newburyport, Massachusetts, back in the late '60s. After spending a crisp fall afternoon walking the beach, we feasted on bowls of this delicious chowder. I asked for the recipe, and have enjoyed making it for my family ever since – often adding seafood for variety.

4 tablespoons finely chopped salt pork or
  bacon
1 onion, chopped
4 potatoes, peeled and diced
1 12-ounce can creamed corn
1 quart milk
a good chunk of butter (about 2
  tablespoons)
salt and pepper to taste

1. In a large saucepan, cook salt pork for 8 to 10 minutes until most of the fat has rendered out. Add the onions and sauté over low heat until golden. Add potatoes and enough water to cover and cook for 15 minutes until potatoes are tender.

2. Stir in corn (and any seafood if you so choose) and milk; simmer over low heat until heated through. Season to taste with salt and pepper and top with chunk of butter.

Spring Road Broccoli Soup

Serves 6

This is a family favorite, derived from various recipes, and years of soup making.

1 large bunch fresh broccoli
1 tablespoon butter
1 tablespoon olive oil
1 medium onion, chopped
1 clove garlic, finely chopped
4 cups water
1 bouillon cube, vegetable or chicken
1 medium potato, peeled and diced
salt and pepper to taste
$\frac{1}{2}$ cup half-and-half (or light cream)

1. Peel and chop the stems and broccoli. Sauté the chopped onion and garlic in a little oil and butter briefly before adding the chopped broccoli. Sauté about 10 minutes.

2. Add 4 cups water and bouillon cube. Add potato, salt and pepper. Simmer until the broccoli and potato are very tender. Cool to luke-warm and blend in blender. Return to the saucepan. Bring soup to a simmer; add the half-and-half. Be sure it is hot, but don't boil after the cream is added.

Fresh Pea Soup

Serves 8 to 10

My grandmother from New Hampshire used to serve this soup in her lovely teacups before Christmas dinner. Each saucer held a piece of buttery Christmas tree toast to dip in the soup. We always asked for seconds!

$2\frac{1}{2}$ cups fresh or frozen peas
$\frac{1}{4}$ teaspoon salt
$\frac{1}{2}$ teaspoon dried tarragon
6 cups chicken or vegetable stock
$\frac{3}{4}$ cup buttermilk
$\frac{1}{4}$ teaspoon freshly ground black pepper
salt to taste
pinch nutmeg

1. In a saucepan, barely cover the peas with lightly salted water, add tarragon and bring to a boil. Reduce heat and simmer 3 to 4 minutes until peas are tender. Remove 1 cup of peas with a slotted spoon and set aside. Continue cooking remaining peas until soft, about 5 minutes. Drain, reserving $\frac{1}{4}$ cup of the cooking water.

2. Purée peas in a blender or food processor with the reserved cooking water and return the mixture to the saucepan. Add the chicken stock and reserved peas. Stir in the buttermilk, pepper and salt; heat through. Serve hot or cold, sprinkled with nutmeg.

Winter Sweet And Sour Cabbage Soup

Serves 12

This recipe is not only delicious but a "fat-burning success" to help shed pounds when those icy walks might not be as long as you would wish.

2 pounds short ribs or beef chuck, fat removed
2 large onions, sliced
8 cups water
1 head red cabbage, shredded (about 2 pounds)
2 16-ounce cans stewed tomatoes
$\frac{1}{2}$ cup sugar
3 tablespoons lemon juice
2 slices lemon
1 teaspoon salt
$\frac{1}{2}$ teaspoon ground ginger
$\frac{1}{4}$ teaspoon freshly ground black pepper

1. In a large saucepan, combine beef, water and onions. Bring to a boil, reduce heat to low, cover and simmer for $1\frac{1}{2}$ hours. Skim fat.

2. Add cabbage, tomatoes, sugar, lemon juice, lemon slices and seasonings. Cover and cook for 30 to 45 minutes until meat is tender. Remove meat, cool, and cut into small pieces and return to saucepan. Serve hot with crusty pumpernickel or rye bread.

Curried Carrot Vichysoisse

Serves 6 to 8

$1\frac{1}{2}$ cups chopped leeks (including 1 inch of the green top, washed and well drained)
$\frac{1}{2}$ cup chopped onion
2 tablespoons butter
$1\frac{1}{2}$ tablespoons curry powder
$1\frac{1}{2}$ pounds carrots, sliced thin (about 4 cups)
1 pound potatoes, peeled and cut into $\frac{1}{2}$-inch pieces
1 teaspoon salt
$2\frac{1}{2}$ cups chicken broth
2 cups water
1 cup milk
1 cup sour cream
dash of white or cayenne pepper to taste
freshly grated carrot for garnish

1. In a heavy saucepan, cook the leeks and onion in the butter over moderately low heat, stirring, until the vegetables are tender.

2. Add the curry powder and cook, stirring, for 2 minutes. Stir in the sliced carrots, potatoes, salt, chicken broth, and 2 cups of water. Bring the mixture to a boil, reduce heat and simmer, covered, for 30 minutes, until carrots and potatoes are soft.

3. Cool slightly and purée in a blender or food processor until smooth. Add the milk, sour cream, and pepper; chill soup for at least 3 hours or overnight. Stir the soup before serving and garnish with grated carrot.

Lucille's Portuguese Kale Soup With Chick Peas

Serves 8

My family has always had an attachment to the sea. Lucille was the granddaughter of Captain Asa W. Fish. His wife, Frances E. Fish and her two children lived in New London on Huntington Street. Mrs. Fish did not want to stay in Hawaii with her husband, Asa, who whaled out of Hawaii, so stayed in Connecticut to raise her family.

2 tablespoons olive oil
1 large onion, chopped
2 cloves garlic, chopped
4 medium potatoes, peeled and diced
6 cups chicken broth
1 pound kale, trimmed
4 ounces chorizo sausage or pepperoni, sliced
1 cup cooked chickpeas
salt and pepper to taste
Tabasco sauce to taste

1. In medium saucepan, heat oil and sauté onion and garlic 3 minutes. Add potatoes and sauté 2 minutes, stirring constantly. Add chicken broth and cook potatoes until tender, about 20 minutes. Remove approximately half the potatoes and a cup of liquid and purée in food processor or food mill. Return puréed potatoes to saucepan. Wash kale and remove stems and thick leaf veins.

2. Layer several kale leaves, roll them up tightly and slice thin. Add to saucepan and cook 10 minutes. Add sausage and chickpeas, salt and pepper. Cook until kale is tender. Ladle soup into bowls. Add Tabasco sauce.

Soup does seven things: it appeases your hunger, slakes your thirst, fills your stomach, cleans your teeth, helps you digest, puts color in your cheeks, and helps you sleep.

Beans And Greens Soup

Serves 6 to 8

After enjoying this soup at Pilots' weekend at the Seaport, I decided to try my hand at it – serve with slices of the brushetta. Try adding chicken, sausage, other beans or other greens.

2 carrots, peeled and finely chopped
2 stalks celery, finely chopped
1 bunch leeks, greens removed, washed and chopped
2 tablespoons olive oil
2 48-ounce cans chicken broth
1 1-pound can chick peas, rinsed and drained
1 1-pound can red kidney beans, rinsed and drained
1 1-pound can white beans, rinsed and drained
1 1-pound can plum tomatoes, hand crushed
1 head escarole, rinsed and chopped
salt and freshly ground black pepper

In a large saucepan, sauté the carrots, celery, and leeks in the olive oil. Add all other ingredients except the escarole. Simmer 10 to 15 minutes. (Optional: "Zap" a few times with an immersion blender or run some solids through food processor for a rough chop and return to the pot. You want a bit of thickness but able to see the individual beans.) Add escarole and cook briefly to keep crisp. Season with salt and pepper to taste. Serve immediately with French bread, croutons, or Bruschetta:

CHEESY BRUSCHETTA
Makes 30 pieces

1 loaf day old French bread, sliced $\frac{1}{4}$-inch thick
$\frac{1}{2}$ cup olive oil
2 cloves garlic, peeled but whole
1 cup Parmesan cheese, grated or shredded

Place bread rounds on a cookie sheet. Toast in 300° to 350° oven for 10 minutes or until golden and dried. Lightly brush or mist with olive oil, rub with garlic, sprinkle with cheese. Return to oven for 2 to 5 minutes to set the cheese and lightly cook the garlic. Use immediately or store in airtight container.

Steve's Sweet And Sour Cabbage Soup

Serves 12

Experiment with other vegetables – great with parsnip, turnip, or green beans.

2 to 3 tablespoons olive oil
3 carrots, peeled and diced
3 stalks celery, diced
2 medium onions, peeled and diced
2 cloves garlic, minced
4 medium potatoes, diced
1 28-ounce can stewed tomatoes
1 tablespoon chopped parsley
$\frac{1}{2}$ teaspoon black pepper
$\frac{1}{4}$ teaspoon thyme
$\frac{1}{4}$ teaspoon ground cloves
$\frac{1}{2}$ cup brown sugar
$\frac{1}{2}$ cup vinegar
2 pounds cabbage, green, red or mixed, shredded

1. Add oil to a large (8-quart) saucepan and sauté carrots, celery, onions, and garlic until transparent. Add potatoes and 3 cups of water and simmer for 8 to 10 minutes until potatoes are tender.

2. Chop tomatoes into chunks and add to the soup along with parsley, pepper, thyme, and salt to taste. Return to a simmer and add cloves, brown sugar, and vinegar (adjusting amount according to your taste).

3. Add shredded cabbage and enough water to cover. Simmer for 45 minutes until cabbage is tender. Best served the following day with a loaf of French bread and cheese.

Aunt Nonni's Minestrone Soup

Serves 10 to 12

Sometimes we add tiny meatballs, sausage or ham.

2 tablespoon olive oil
1 cup diced celery
2 large carrots, diced
1 large onion, diced
1 22-ounce can plum style Italian tomatoes
1 cup cooked ceci (chick peas)
$1\frac{1}{2}$ cups peeled and diced potatoes
4 cups chicken stock
8 cups water
salt to taste
1 teaspoon oregano
hot red pepper flakes
$\frac{1}{3}$ cup grated Romano cheese
$\frac{1}{2}$ pound vermicelli, broken into 1-inch pieces
$1\frac{1}{2}$ cups diced, cooked chicken
chopped fresh parsley

1. In a large saucepan, sauté celery, carrots, and onion in olive oil for 12 to 14 minutes until slightly browned. Add tomatoes, ceci, potatoes, chicken stock, water, salt, oregano, and red pepper to taste. Bring to a boil and reduce heat and simmer for 20 minutes.

2. Stir in vermicelli and chicken, simmer for 30 minutes, stirring occasionally. Add grated cheese and serve hot, garnished with chopped parsley.

J & Js Pearl Street Minestrone Golden Soup

Serves 6 to 8

This soup is the centerpiece of the Holiday Bazaar Luncheon in Noank as well as a favorite with the seniors at Mystic River Homes.

$\frac{1}{2}$ cup dried cannellini beans
2 tablespoons olive oil
1 medium onion, chopped
1 clove garlic, minced
5 cups stock, beef or chicken
1 16-ounce can plum tomatoes with juice
1 large carrot, chopped
1 zucchini, chopped
$\frac{1}{4}$ head cabbage, shredded
   (outer leaves removed)
2 tablespoons fresh basil, chopped
$\frac{1}{2}$ tablespoon dry oregano
$\frac{1}{2}$ tablespoon sugar
1 bay leaf
$\frac{1}{3}$ cup elbow macaroni, uncooked
$\frac{1}{3}$ cup balsamic vinegar
salt and pepper
freshly chopped parsley
grated cheese, Pecorino Romano or
   Parmesan

1. Sort through beans, discarding any that are discolored. Add cold water to cover and soak 12 hours. Drain and add fresh water to cover by about 1 inch. Bring to boil slowly and simmer, partially covered, for $1\frac{1}{2}$ hours until beans are tender and most of the water is absorbed.

2. Heat oil in large saucepan and sauté onions and garlic until translucent. Add stock and tomatoes; coarsely break up with spoon. Bring to simmer. (Recipe may be stopped here and stockpot refrigerated until next day, refrigerate beans as well.)

3. Two hours before serving, reheat stock and beans to simmer, partially covered (watch beans in particular so they don't burn). One hour before serving, add carrots, zucchini, cabbage, basil, oregano, sugar and bay leaf. Bring back to simmer and cook partially covered 20 minutes until veggies are tender but still crisp (eat one or two to check). Add macaroni and cook another 10 minutes until al dente (soft/firm). Drain beans and add to saucepan along with balsamic vinegar (add a little at a time, sample for taste). Check seasoning; add salt and pepper, if necessary (remember that cheese is salty). Ladle into bowls and garnish with a pinch of chopped parsley and a teaspoon of grated cheese.

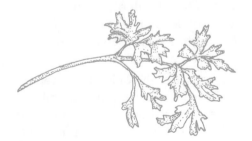

Harvest Squash Soup

Serves 8
This soup is served right in the squash shells.

4 acorn squash
3 carrots, sliced
1 onion, sliced
$\frac{1}{3}$ cup water
2 tablespoons butter
1 tablespoon all-purpose flour
1 teaspoon salt
$\frac{1}{2}$ to 1 teaspoon pepper
2 14$\frac{1}{4}$-ounce cans chicken broth
$\frac{1}{2}$ cup sherry
$\frac{1}{2}$ teaspoon ground nutmeg
$\frac{1}{8}$ teaspoon paprika
dash of ground allspice
dash of red pepper
1 cup half-and-half
1$\frac{1}{2}$ tablespoons sherry (optional)
kale leaves
paprika

1. Cut squash in half lengthwise and remove seeds. Place squash, cut side down, in broiler pan. Add hot water to pan to a depth of 1 inch. Bake at 350° for 30 minutes. Spoon pulp from squash to create a serving bowl, reserving pulp.

2. Place carrots and onion in saucepan; cover with water. Bring to a boil; cover, reduce heat and simmer for 15 minutes or until vegetables are tender. Drain; combine vegetables with reserved pulp and $\frac{1}{3}$ cup water in container of electric blender or food processor. Process 30 seconds, or until mixture is smooth. Set aside.

3. Melt butter in a large Dutch oven or heavy saucepan over low heat; add flour, salt and pepper, stirring until smooth. Cook 1 minute, stirring constantly. Gradually add vegetable mixture, chicken broth and next five ingredients; bring to a boil. Cover and reduce heat, simmer 1 hour, stirring occasionally. Stir in half-and-half and, if desired, 1$\frac{1}{2}$ tablespoons sherry. Cook until heated. If desired, serve in squash shells on a bed of kale. Sprinkle with paprika.

Three "P" Soup – Peanut, Pumpkin And Potato

Serves 10 to 12

1$\frac{1}{2}$ pounds yams or sweet potatoes
1 tablespoon butter
2 tablespoons minced shallot or onion
2 cups thick pumpkin purée, canned or homemade
8 cups chicken broth
1 cup natural or old-fashioned smooth peanut butter
2 teaspoons coarse-grained mustard
$\frac{1}{2}$ teaspoon nutmeg
salt to taste
freshly ground white or black pepper
snipped chives for garnish

1. Preheat oven to 350°. Bake yams on baking sheet for 1 hour, or until soft. Let cool and peel. Discard peels, and process pulp in food mill or processor. Measure 2 cups of potatoes and set aside. Refrigerate leftovers for another use.

2. In a large, heavy-bottomed saucepan, melt butter over medium heat. Add shallots or onion, and sauté for 2 minutes. Add 2 cups potatoes and pumpkin purée. Alternately add broth and peanut butter, stirring the mix after each addition until soup is smooth.

3. Over medium heat, bring soup almost to a boil, stirring often. Reduce heat and simmer for 25 minutes, stirring occasionally. Stir in mustard, nutmeg, salt and pepper. Before serving, garnish with chives.

Curried Apple Butternut Soup

Serves 8 to 10

I serve this soup as part of a mid-winter brunch – starting with Bloody Marys, soup, homemade quiche and calzones, a big tossed salad, to finish with cookies and chocolate peanut sin bars.

1$\frac{3}{4}$ to 2 pounds peeled butternut squash
1 teaspoon butter
2 large yellow onions
1 cup apple juice or cider
1 cup applesauce
3 cups chicken broth
$\frac{1}{4}$ teaspoon ginger
2 teaspoons curry powder
salt and pepper

Steam squash until soft, about 10 minutes, drain well. In a skillet, melt butter and sauté onions for 10 minutes until soft but not browned. Combine all ingredients in a blender or food processor (it will take 3 batches). Purée mixture, season to taste with salt and pepper. Pour into a warm soup tureen and serve hot.

Curried Roasted Squash and Pear Soup

Serves 8 to 10

1 butternut squash ($1\frac{1}{2}$ pounds), peeled and cut into $\frac{3}{4}$-inch cubes
6 ripe but firm Bartlett pears, peeled, cored, and cut into $\frac{3}{4}$-inch cubes
2 tablespoons olive oil
1 teaspoon granulated sugar
salt
freshly ground black pepper
$\frac{1}{2}$ cup water
$\frac{1}{3}$ cup finely chopped shallots
1 tablespoon dark brown sugar, firmly packed
1 $2\frac{1}{2}$-inch cinnamon stick
2 teaspoons curry powder
$\frac{1}{2}$ teaspoon ground cardamom
$\frac{1}{4}$ teaspoon ground coriander
6 cups chicken broth
2 tablespoons slivered fresh mint or cilantro leaves

Preheat oven to 400°.

1. On a large baking sheet with sides, toss squash and pears with 1 tablespoon olive oil and granulated sugar. Season with salt and pepper, drizzle with water.

2. Roast squash and pears for 30 to 40 minutes, or until both are tender. (Add a little more water if necessary to prevent burning.) Remove any pears that are cooked before squash. Measure 1 cup of pears and cut each cube in half; set aside.

3. In a food processor or blender, purée squash and remaining pears until smooth. (Add a little chicken broth if necessary.) Set aside.

4. In a Dutch oven or large saucepan, heat remaining 1 tablespoon of olive oil over medium heat. Add shallots and cook, stirring, until softened but not browned, 3 to 5 minutes. Add brown sugar, cinnamon stick, curry powder, cardamom, and coriander. Stir for 2 minutes more. Add reserved squash-pear purée and chicken broth. Bring to a simmer. Reduce heat to low and simmer, stirring occasionally, for 25 to 30 minutes. Season with salt and pepper. Discard cinnamon stick. Add reserved pears and simmer until heated through. Ladle into warmed soup bowls and garnish with mint (or cilantro). Serve immediately.

Turkey Pumpkin Soup With Stuffing Dumplings

Serves 10 to 12

$\frac{1}{4}$ cup, (4 tablespoons) butter
2 cups carrots, diced
2 cups onions, diced
2 cups celery, diced
2 cups leeks, diced
4 cups cooked scraps and bones from turkey
2 cups pumpkin or butternut squash, diced

1. In a large saucepan over medium heat, sauté carrots, onions, celery, and leeks in butter for 5 minutes until tender. Add turkey scraps and cover with water. Simmer uncovered for $1\frac{1}{2}$ hours.

2. Remove and discard any bones or skin. Add pumpkin or squash and simmer for 15 minutes.

STUFFING DUMPLINGS
4 cups leftover stuffing
6 eggs slightly beaten
$\frac{1}{4}$ cup fresh sage, chopped
$\frac{1}{4}$ cup fresh parsley, chopped
4 tablespoons butter, softened
4 cloves garlic, minced
$\frac{1}{3}$ cup grated Parmesan cheese

In a mixing bowl, combine stuffing, eggs, sage, parsley, butter, and garlic. Scoop heaping tablespoons of stuffing mixture into simmering soup and cook 10 minutes over low heat. Ladle soup and a few dumplings into deep bowls and sprinkle with Parmesan cheese.

Winter Ham And Bean Soup

Serves 10 to 12

a.k.a. What to do with the leftovers from that boiled dinner? This makes another hearty meal for a crowd.

2 pounds red kidney beans, soaked overnight
3 quarts broth (best to reserve ham cooking liquids)
3 medium turnips, peeled and diced
2 onions, coarsely chopped
1 pound carrots, peeled and sliced
8 cups peeled and cubed potatoes
2 to 4 cups leftover smoked shoulder ham pieces
salt and pepper
$\frac{3}{4}$ cup sugar
$\frac{1}{4}$ to $\frac{1}{2}$ cup cornmeal

1. Place drained beans in a large saucepan with broth, turnip and onion. Simmer over medium heat for 15 minutes until turnips are tender.

2. Add carrots, cook about 10 to 15 minutes, until tender. Add potatoes and more water if soup is becoming too thick at this point. When potatoes are tender, add ham, salt and pepper to taste, sugar and enough cornmeal to thicken. Cook for 10 minutes until heated through. This will make a very thick soup. Serve it with a green salad and crusty bread for a great meal.

Smokey Corn And Turkey Chowder

Serves 12-14

6 strips smoked bacon, chopped fine
3 medium onions, chopped
6 stalks celery, chopped
1 red pepper, chopped
8 medium potatoes, diced
4 tablespoons butter
4 cups chicken or turkey broth
2 cups water
5 cups chopped, cooked turkey
6 cups half-and-half
$\frac{1}{2}$ cup flour
2 14-ounce cans whole kernel corn, drained
salt and pepper to taste
$\frac{1}{4}$ cup chopped parsley
dash paprika

1. In a large saucepan, sauté bacon, onions, celery, red pepper, potatoes, and butter for 15 minutes until lightly browned. Add broth and water and bring to a boil. Add turkey and reduce heat to a simmer.

2. In a mixing bowl, combine half-and-half and flour. Whisk until smooth and slowly blend into soup. Add corn and simmer for 15 minutes, stirring occasionally. Season with salt and pepper; add parsley and serve piping hot, sprinkled with paprika.

Leek, Potato, And Sausage Soup

Serves 4

A quick, hearty, and satisfying soup for the chilly weather.

$\frac{1}{2}$ teaspoon cumin seeds
$\frac{1}{2}$ teaspoon caraway seeds
the white part of 2 medium leeks, halved lengthwise, sliced thin, washed well
2 tablespoons butter
4 cups chicken broth
2 small boiling potatoes (about $\frac{1}{2}$ pound), peeled and diced
$\frac{1}{2}$ pound kielbasa, cut crosswise into $\frac{1}{4}$-inch slices, quartered
2 tablespoons heavy cream
$\frac{1}{2}$ cup sliced spinach leaves (about 10)

1. In a dry, heavy saucepan, toast the cumin seeds and caraway seeds over moderate heat, stirring, for 2 to 3 minutes until they are very fragrant. Transfer them to a plate.

2. In the same pan, cook the leeks in the butter, stirring occasionally, for 5 minutes, or until very soft. Stir in the broth and potatoes. Bring the liquid to a boil and simmer for 10 minutes, or until potatoes are tender. Add the toasted seeds, kielbasa, cream, salt and pepper to taste. Simmer for 5 minutes to heat through, and stir in the spinach just before serving

Corn, Chicken, And Sausage Chowder

Makes 8 to 10 cups

1 tablespoon olive oil
1 pound kielbasa, cut diagonally into $\frac{1}{4}$-inch
  thick pieces
1 onion, chopped
1 bell pepper, red or green, chopped
2 cups chicken stock
3 cups water
2 russet (baking) potatoes, peeled and cut
  into $\frac{1}{2}$-inch pieces
2 whole, boneless chicken breasts (about
  $1\frac{3}{4}$ pounds), cooked and cut into bite-size
  pieces
1 pound frozen corn (about $2\frac{1}{2}$ cups)
2 bay leaves
1 5-ounce can evaporated milk or same
  amount of half-and-half
1 19-ounce can cannelli beans, drained
2 cups packed fresh spinach, washed and
  chopped coarsely
salt and pepper to taste
fresh parsley, chopped

1. In a heavy 6-quart saucepan, heat oil over
    medium heat and sauté kielbasa in batch-
    es until lightly browned, transferring to a
    plate as they are cooked. To the fat
    remaining in the pan, sauté the onion
    and bell pepper until softened and gold-
    en, add $\frac{1}{2}$ cup stock and simmer, scraping
    up brown bits, for 2 minutes. Add remain-
    ing $1\frac{1}{2}$ cups stock, water, and kielbasa and
    bring to a low simmer.

2. Add potatoes, chicken, half the corn and
    bay leaves and cook, covered, for 25 min-
    utes. Discard bay leaves. In a blender,
    purée remaining corn with milk and add
    to chowder along with beans. Add
    spinach and cook for 5 minutes, until
    soup is heated through and spinach is
    wilted. Season to taste with salt and pep-
    per and serve hot, sprinkled with chopped
    fresh parsley.

"The inhabitants of Cape Cod measure
their crops not only by bushels of corn,
but by barrels of clams. A thousand
barrels of clam bait are counted as equal
in value to six or eight thousand bushels
of Indian corn."
Cape Cod, Henry David Thoreau

Captain Franklin Hancox Clam Chowder

Serves 12

My great-great grandfather, Franklin Hancox, was the captain of the whaling ship, "Rebecca Groves," which sailed from Stonington, Connecticut to Patagonia in the mid 1800's. Said to be an adventurous and animated gentleman, it is told that on arriving home after a year at sea, while partaking of a bowl of his favorite chowder, he announced that he would then be off to seek his fortune in California during the Great Gold Rush of 1850. To this day, his chowder still brings complements whenever it is served.

CHOWDER BASE:
$\frac{1}{2}$ pound salt pork, finely chopped
1 to 2 onions, chopped
5 pounds potatoes (Maine or Eastern), peeled and diced
2 quarts shucked quahogs

NEW ENGLAND STYLE:
2 cups whole milk or light cream
freshly chopped parsley
salt and pepper to taste

MANHATTAN STYLE:
4 stewed tomatoes, chopped
1 tablespoon butter
2 diced carrots
1 diced green pepper
2 stalks celery, chopped
freshly chopped parsley
salt and pepper to taste

1. Try out (render) salt pork in a large saucepan until golden; remove and set aside. Sauté onion in pan until translucent, about 6 to 8 minutes. Add diced potatoes, barely cover with water and cook over medium heat until tender.

2. Strain clams, reserving juice, and chop fine. In a saucepan, bring clam juice to a boil, watching carefully as it foams up. Remove from heat and skim off the foam.

3. Add chopped clams and juice to potatoes, cook over low heat for 5 minutes. Do not let mixture boil. If you are serving New England style, add the milk, parsley, and seasonings and reheat gently. If you are serving Manhattan style, sauté the carrot, pepper and parsley in the butter for 6 to 8 minutes until soft. Add to chowder base with tomatoes, parsley and salt and pepper to taste. Serve with Pilot biscuits.

Brud's Best Clam Chowder

Serves 20

As a large family, we would always get together for picnics. The best one being the Fourth of July picnic. We would have a seafood and clambake. The food was cooked in a pit with a thick coating of seaweed just gathered from the beach, Pleasure Beach. The first course was the clam chowder. The chowder was a clear broth, to put tomatoes or cream into the mix would have been a crime!

$\frac{1}{4}$ pound salt pork, diced
12 small onions, sliced
16 large potatoes, peeled and diced
40 quahogs*
salt and pepper

In a large saucepan, render the salt pork over medium heat and remove any solids. (You should have 3 to 4 tablespoons of fat.) Add sliced onions and sauté until caramelized and golden brown. Add potatoes and chopped clams in layers, add reserved clam juice and enough water to cover. Gently boil, uncovered, until potatoes are done, about 20 minutes. Skim the chowder, add more water if necessary and season with salt and pepper.

*Best to open clams, don't steam the clams open or it will toughen the clam meat. Save and use all the juice. There is a very tough rim next to the belly. Remove it and finely mince that part of the clam; chop the rest of the clam.

Kennedy Fishhouse Chowder

Serves 6

A much-loved recipe for over 30 years for 5 reasons: it takes care of a large family, a full meal in a bowl, easily available ingredients, economical and lastly, a "no-brainer!"

1 large onion, finely chopped
4 tablespoons butter or margarine
3 large potatoes, peeled and sliced
2 teaspoons salt
$\frac{1}{2}$ teaspoon basil
$\frac{1}{4}$ teaspoon black pepper
2 cups water
1 1-pound package frozen cod or haddock fillets, defrosted or 1 pound fresh fish fillets
1 16-ounce can whole kernel corn
1 12-ounce can evaporated milk
fresh parsley, chopped

1. In a large saucepan, sauté onion in butter until tender. Add potatoes, salt, basil, pepper and water. Cover and simmer for 15 minutes. Place fish on top of potatoes, cover again and simmer for 15 minutes or until fish flakes.

2. Gently stir in corn and liquid with evaporated milk. Cover and heat just to boiling (do not let chowder boil). Ladle into a large heated soup tureen and sprinkle with chopped parsley. Serve with oyster crackers.

Cap'n Bob's Seafood Chowder

Makes 6 Downeast helpings or 12 normal helpings

After several summers feasting on Maine's best fresh seafood, we began to plan how we might open a "soup-only" café. This recipe is the result of many refinements, which we delight in serving to friends and family.

$\frac{1}{3}$ pound bacon, diced
2 medium onions, coarsely chopped
3 quarts water
4 pounds baking potatoes, peeled and diced
1 bay leaf
1 tablespoon ground thyme
1 pound shrimp, peeled and deveined
3 6-ounce cans chopped clams or 1 pound shucked clams, chopped, including juices
1 pound sea scallops, cut into small pieces
$\frac{1}{2}$ cup chopped fresh parsley
$\frac{1}{4}$ cup sherry
1 pint heavy cream or half-and-half
salt and pepper to taste

1. Using a heavy saucepan or Dutch oven, cook bacon for 5 minutes to render some of the fat. Add onions and sauté until soft and transparent. Add the water and potatoes, increase heat to a boil and then turn down to a simmer. Add bay leaf and thyme, cover and simmer slowly, stirring occasionally for 2 hours.

2. Uncover saucepan and simmer for another hour to reduce liquid. Add shrimp, clams, scallops and parsley, cook uncovered for $\frac{1}{2}$ hour. Add sherry, simmer for 15 minutes and remove from heat to cool for $\frac{1}{2}$ hour before adding cream. Heat slowly to serving temperature and serve with warm French bread and a light burgundy or white wine on the side.

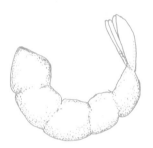

Grandma Auch's Clam Chowder Recipe

Serves 6

Written in her hand, and found in Mom's recipe box (in very well-used condition). As served at the Price family reunion June 22, 1996.

1 dozen large clams
3 potatoes cut in $\frac{3}{4}$-inch cubes
1 $\frac{1}{2}$-inch cube fat salt pork
1 onion, sliced
1 tablespoon salt
$\frac{1}{8}$ teaspoon pepper
$\frac{1}{2}$ cup flour plus 4 tablespoons
4 tablespoons butter
4 cups scalded milk
8 common crackers

I add a little thyme and marjoram, clean and pick over the clams, using one cup cold water; drain, reserve liquid, heat to boiling point and strain. Chop finely hard part of clams; (I put the clams and one potato through the meat chopper) cut pork in small pieces and try out; add onion, fry 5 minutes and strain into a stew pan. (I don't strain it.)

Parboil potatoes 5 minutes in boiling water to cover; drain and put a layer in bottom of stew pan, add chopped clams, sprinkle with salt and pepper and dredge generously with half of flour, and add 2$\frac{1}{2}$ cups boiling water.

Cook 10 minutes, add milk, soft part of clams and butter; boil 3 minutes and add crackers split and soaked in enough cold milk to moisten. Reheat clam water to boiling point, and thicken with butter and 4 tablespoons of flour, cooked together. Add to chowder just before serving. The clam water has a tendency to cause the milk to separate, hence is added at the last.

(I put a pinch of baking soda in the clam water to avoid separation and if necessary to have chowder standing before serving.) Keep hot *without* letting it boil.

Cy Loutrel's Clam Chowder

Serves 6

Daddy was a great cook. He always said the excellence of his chowder was due to the method, a bit tedious but with superb results. His favorite accompaniments were fresh cabbage slaw and pilot crackers, which by tradition (as with hard tack), sailors used to tap before breaking to expel the weevils.

$\frac{1}{4}$ pound salt pork, diced
4 large baking potatoes (Maine or Idaho), peeled and diced
1 quart shucked quahogs and juice
2 large yellow onions, diced
2 tablespoons flour
1 teaspoon salt
2 teaspoons freshly ground black pepper
$\frac{1}{2}$ cup milk

1. In a heavy saucepan, fry salt pork until fat is rendered out, about 20 minutes, remove cracklings and set aside.

2. Place potatoes in a medium saucepan, cover with water and boil for 20 minutes or until tender. Drain, reserving potato water.

3. Drain quahogs, reserving juice and grind clams in a meat grinder. Place the clam juice in a pan, bring to a low boil and "purify the juice" by skimming off any particles which rise to the top.

4. To the saucepan add the onions, ground clams, flour, salt, and pepper. Cook, whisking, for 5 minutes. Add the potatoes, clam juice, reserved potato water; bring to a boil and reduce heat to a simmer. Season to taste with more salt and pepper if needed and stir in milk. Turn off heat, add salt pork cracklings and let rest for 2 hours before serving.

New England Fish And Vegetable Chowder

Serves 6

One of the oldest recipes for fish chowder was printed in Boston in 1751. The recipe, in verse form, gave the basic elements of chowder; onions, salt pork, fish, salt, pepper and biscuits. Herbs and a dash of claret often provided additional flavors. This recipe also allows for unlimited variations. It has great color and flavor and works equally well with other types of fish – salmon, halibut or mahi-mahi.

6 strips bacon, cut into $\frac{1}{2}$-inch pieces
1 small onion, finely chopped
2 stalks celery, finely chopped
3 cloves garlic, minced
$\frac{1}{2}$ green pepper, finely chopped
3 tablespoons flour
3 8-ounce bottles clam juice
1 cup white wine
$\frac{1}{2}$ teaspoon salt
$\frac{1}{4}$ teaspoon black pepper
1 teaspoon thyme
3 bay leaves
3 medium potatoes, peeled and diced
2 carrots, sliced
$\frac{1}{2}$ pound fresh green beans, cut into
   $\frac{1}{2}$-inch pieces
1 pound cod, cut into 1-inch pieces
2 tablespoons sherry
1 cup whipping cream
1 cup milk

1. Cook bacon in a large saucepan until crisp; remove from pan. To the bacon fat in the pan, add onion, celery, garlic, and green pepper. Sauté for 5 minutes or until soft. Add flour and cook, stirring for 1 minute.

2. Add clam juice, white wine, salt, pepper, thyme, and bay leaves, whisking out any lumps as the mixture heats. Add potatoes, carrots, and green beans, and bring to a boil. Lower heat to a simmer, cover, and cook until vegetables are tender, about 5 minutes.

3. Stir in cod, sherry, cream, and milk. Cook for 8 to 10 minutes until fish just flakes; do not boil. Remove bay leaves, add reserved bacon and serve hot.

"For dressing a codfish: Put the fish first into cold water and wash it, then hang it over the fire and soak it six hours in scalding water. Shift it into clean water and let it scald for one hour; it will be much better than a boil."

American Cookery, Amelia Simmons, 1796

Ferguson Clam Chowder

Serves 8 to 10

A 100 year old family recipe – the important step is the "chipping" of the potatoes, it adds thickness and taste to the broth.

6 ounces salt pork, diced into $\frac{1}{4}$-inch pieces
3 medium onions, diced
12 small to medium potatoes, peeled
1 pint ground quahogs (round clams)
salt and pepper

1. In a heavy saucepan, sauté pork over medium heat until <u>light</u> brown. Remove from pan; sauté onion in pork drippings until <u>light</u> brown.

2. Chip the potatoes into small wedges and cook in 8 cups of boiling water until tender, about 10 minutes. Add clams, onions and salt pork and simmer for 15 minutes. Season to taste with salt and pepper and serve hot with Pilot crackers.

Hearty Haddock Chowder

Serves 8 to 10

6 tablespoons butter or margarine
1 medium onion, chopped
1 stalk celery, chopped
1 teaspoon black pepper
1 teaspoon garlic powder
$\frac{1}{2}$ teaspoon salt
3 pounds boiling potatoes, peeled and diced
$2\frac{1}{2}$ pounds haddock fillets, skinned
4 12-ounce cans evaporated milk
2 cups whole milk
salt and pepper
6 slices bacon, cooked until crisp and crumbled
fresh parsley, chopped

1. Melt butter in a 6-quart heavy saucepan, add onion and celery, sauté until softened. Add pepper, garlic powder, salt, potatoes, and enough water to just cover the potatoes (3 to 4 cups). Boil, covered, until potatoes are tender, about 10 minutes.

2. Lay fish fillets on top of potatoes and simmer, covered, until fish flakes apart, 6 to 8 minutes. Add both types of milk and heat, but do not boil. Season with salt and pepper to taste, and sprinkle with bacon and chopped parsley before serving.

Osgood Fish House Chowder

Serves 4

2 tablespoons butter
1 medium onion, chopped
2 carrots, chopped
2 stalks celery, chopped
2 teaspoons flour
1 teaspoon paprika
8 ounces bottled clam juice
2 cups chicken broth
1 cup heavy cream
3 medium potatoes, peeled and cut into $\frac{1}{2}$-inch pieces
1 pound firm white fish (cod, haddock, Halibut), cut into 1-inch pieces
salt and pepper to taste
fresh parsley, chopped

1. In a medium saucepan, melt butter and sauté onion, carrots and celery until softened, about 5 minutes. Sprinkle flour over vegetables and cook over medium heat for about 1 minute, stirring constantly. Add paprika and whisk in clam juice, broth and cream. Bring to a low boil.

2. Add potato to chowder and simmer until tender, 8 to 10 minutes. Add the fish and simmer until cooked through, about 5 minutes. Season to taste with salt and pepper, add parsley and serve hot.

Smith Court Shrimp And Cheddar Chowder

Makes 2 quarts

4 large onions, peeled and chopped or sliced
4 tablespoons butter
1 cup boiling water
6 medium potatoes, peeled and cubed
1 tablespoon salt
$\frac{1}{2}$ teaspoon seasoned pepper
6 cups milk
2 cups grated sharp cheddar cheese
2 pounds uncooked medium shrimp, peeled and deveined
3 tablespoons chopped fresh parsley

1. In a Dutch oven or heavy saucepan, sauté onion in butter until tender but not brown. Add boiling water, potatoes, salt, and pepper. Cover and simmer for 20 minutes or until potatoes are tender. Do not drain.

2. Meanwhile, in another pan, heat milk, add cheese and cook until cheese is melted and milk is hot. Add shrimp to potatoes and cook until shrimp just turns pink, about 3 minutes. Add hot milk and cheese, heat over low heat, being careful not to let chowder boil. Serve hot, sprinkled with chopped parsley.

Fish Chowder "In Under An Hour"

Serves 6

No time to cook? You can put this hearty soup together by the time the laundry is done.

8 slices bacon, chopped
2 tablespoons butter
1 medium onion, diced
2 carrots, finely chopped
2 celery stalks, finely chopped
1 tablespoon flour
2 cups water
1 teaspoon paprika
16 ounces bottled clam juice or fish stock
1 cup heavy cream
3 large baking potatoes (about 1 pound), peeled and diced
$1\frac{1}{2}$ pounds firm white fish, skinless and cut into 2-inch chunks – halibut, haddock, or cod are best
4 tablespoons minced parsley
salt and pepper to taste

1. In a heavy saucepan, cook bacon over moderate heat, stirring until crisp, transfer to paper towels to drain. Pour off bacon fat and discard.

2. Add butter to pan and cook onion, carrot and celery over medium heat, stirring occasionally, until softened. Sprinkle flour over mixture and cook, stirring, for 1 minute. Whisk in water and add paprika, clam juice and cream; bring to a boil.

3. Add diced potatoes to mixture and simmer chowder, uncovered, for 10 minutes. Stir in fish and simmer until just cooked through, about 5 to 8 minutes. Stir in parsley, bacon, and salt and pepper to taste. Serve with plenty of oyster crackers.

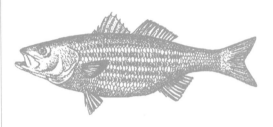

Captain John Smith in 1614 visited New England and recorded in his journal:

"What pleasure can be more than to recreate themselves before their owne doores, in their owne boats upon the Sea, where man, woman and childe, with a small hooke and line may take by angling such diverse sorts of excellent fish at their pleasure?"

Bread
Basket

Banana Stuffed French Toast

Serves 4

Thanks to Chef Cardillo, a real "wake up call" for breakfast.

1 loaf challah bread
2 large bananas diced
$\frac{1}{2}$ teaspoon cinnamon
$\frac{1}{2}$ teaspoon sugar
1 tablespoon butter
$\frac{1}{4}$ cup orange juice
1 teaspoon orange zest
mixture of cornstarch and water to form slurry to thicken filling if too loose
3 eggs
$\frac{1}{2}$ cup half-and-half or eggnog
2 cups maple syrup
$\frac{1}{2}$ cup chopped pecans, toasted
2 tablespoons melted butter
powdered sugar

1. Slice the bread into four thick slices, cut a pocket in the top of each slice. In a small pan, add the bananas, cinnamon, sugar, butter, orange juice and zest. Cook for about 5 to 10 minutes, add the cornstarch and water if it is too loose. Let the mixture cool.
2. Stuff the bread with the banana mixture. Whisk together the eggs and half-and-half. Dip the bread into the egg mixture and cook on griddle with vegetable spray until golden brown. Warm the maple syrup, butter and pecans, serve with the French toast, dusted with powdered sugar.

The Old Mystic Inn's Strawberry Stuffed French Toast

Serves 4

Our guests adore this.

1 loaf of raisin challah bread
4 ounces cream cheese
2 teaspoons cinnamon
1 teaspoon sugar
1 pint fresh strawberries
3 large eggs
$\frac{1}{2}$ cup half-and-half
2 cups maple syrup
$\frac{1}{2}$ cup chopped walnuts

1. Slice the challah bread into 4 thick slices, cut a pocket in the top of each slice. Whip the cream cheese, 1 teaspoon cinnamon and sugar. Spread the cream cheese into the center of the bread and place the strawberries inside.
2. Whisk the eggs, half-and-half and remaining teaspoon of cinnamon. Dip the bread slices into the egg mixture and cook on a hot griddle, sprayed with nonstick spray, until golden brown. Warm the maple syrup and the chopped walnuts and serve with the French toast, after dusting with powdered sugar.

Featherlight Yogurt Pancakes

Makes about 16 6-inch pancakes

Whenever my husband and our two boys used to travel to the farm in Maine to visit, my parents would request a batch of these oh-so-good pancakes. Besides serving them with lots of butter, their preference was molasses, where as ours was always warm maple syrup.

1 cup plain or vanilla yogurt
1 cup milk
2 eggs, slightly beaten
2 to 3 tablespoons sugar
  (depending on your sweet tooth)
2 tablespoons melted butter or margarine
2 cups flour
2 teaspoons baking powder
1 teaspoon baking soda

1. In a large bowl, combine yogurt, milk, eggs, sugar, and melted butter. In a sifter, combine the dry ingredients and sift over the yogurt mixture. Stir until well combined. Mixture will be bubbly. (If it seems too thick, thin with a little milk.)

2. In a lightly greased skillet (electric is best), spoon the batter into whatever size you prefer – the kids always want lots of silver dollar-size. Cook pancakes until they begin to bubble on top, flip and finish. Cook the whole batch at once as the batter loses its light quality the longer it sits. Top and enjoy.

NOTE:
These freeze very well and can be reheated in the toaster or microwave.

Ferry Point House Stuffed French Toast

Serves 6

8 ounces cream cheese, at room
  temperature
$\frac{1}{2}$ cup chopped walnuts
2 teaspoons vanilla
4 eggs, beaten
$\frac{3}{4}$ cup heavy cream
dash nutmeg
12 slices bread, homemade toasting loaf,
  Vienna, or any nut bread

1. Mix cream cheese, walnuts and 1 teaspoon vanilla. Spread mixture on 6 slices bread and top each with another slice.

2. Combine beaten eggs, heavy cream, remaining teaspoon of vanilla and nutmeg. Dip each sandwich into mixture, coating both sides and the edges. Grill in a buttered skillet or nonstick grill until golden on both sides. Top with a sauce made by heating 1 12-ounce jar of apricot jam with $\frac{1}{2}$ cup orange juice, or top with butter and maple syrup.

Schoolhouse Apple Pancakes

Serves 6-8

My mother taught first grade for 31 years. Each Mothers' Day she would serve a special lunch, inviting all the mothers into the classroom. For a present, the children made up a cookbook with all of their favorite recipes, this one from a favorite little boy in her class. Now, four generations of our family often get together and enjoy these pancakes for Sunday breakfast.

$2\frac{3}{4}$ cups flour
1 tablespoon baking powder
1 teaspoon salt
$\frac{1}{2}$ cup sugar
$\frac{1}{2}$ teaspoon cinnamon
2 eggs, beaten
2 cups milk
6 tablespoons butter or margarine, melted
2 cups grated apple (Macintosh is best)
$\frac{1}{2}$ teaspoon vanilla
1 teaspoon baking soda, dissolved in 2 tablespoons warm water

1. Mix flour, baking powder, salt, sugar and cinnamon in a large bowl. Add eggs, milk, butter, apples, vanilla and baking soda mixture. Stir until just mixed, mixture will be lumpy.

2. Spoon batter by $\frac{1}{4}$ cupfuls onto a hot, oiled griddle and fry on both sides until brown. Serve with plenty of butter and warm maple syrup.

Popover Sausage Bake

Serves 4

This will surely get the gang out of bed on Sunday morning – a true New England breakfast.

1 pound roll bulk breakfast sausage
2 eggs
1 cup milk
1 cup flour
$\frac{1}{2}$ teaspoon salt
1 tablespoon oil or melted butter

1. Cut sausage into 1-inch slices and place in an 8-inch ovenproof skillet. Brown sausage on both sides, drain fat, leaving about 1 tablespoon in the bottom of the pan.

2. Beat eggs until foamy and add milk, flour, salt and oil, mix with an electric mixer until well blended, about $1\frac{1}{2}$ to 2 minutes; do not over-beat. Pour batter over sausage and bake in a 400° oven for 15 minutes. Reduce oven temperature to 350° and bake for an additional 30 to 40 minutes until browned and puffy.

Baked Orange French Toast

Serves 6

8 slices French bread, cut into $\frac{3}{4}$-inch slices
6 eggs
grated rind of 1 large orange
$\frac{2}{3}$ cup orange juice
$\frac{1}{3}$ cup orange liqueur
1 cup half-and-half
3 tablespoons sugar
4 tablespoons butter
confectioners' sugar for dusting

1. Butter a 9-inch square baking pan. Lay bread slices evenly in pan. Combine eggs, orange rind, orange juice, liqueur, half-and-half, and sugar; pour over bread. Dot with butter cut into small pieces. Refrigerate for at least 2 hours or best, overnight.

2. In the morning, preheat oven to 350°. Bake for 30 to 35 minutes, or until puffed and set. Dust with confectioners' sugar before serving with melted butter.

Fall Apple Fritters

Serves 6

For some reason I forget about this recipe until the leaves start to turn. Then I make them weekly to go with cold apple cider – they disappear quickly.

2 cups chopped apple
2 tablespoons milk
2 eggs
1 tablespoon butter, melted
1 cup all purpose flour
3 tablespoons sugar
1 teaspoon baking powder
$\frac{1}{2}$ teaspoon salt
$\frac{1}{2}$ teaspoon cinnamon
$\frac{1}{2}$ teaspoon nutmeg
confectioners' sugar

1. In a medium bowl, combine apples, milk, eggs, and butter until well blended. Add remaining dry ingredients (except the confectioners' sugar) and mix well. If the batter seems a bit thin, sprinkle in a little more flour.

2. Drop by teaspoonfuls into hot oil (about 3 inches deep) in a large skillet or saucepan. Fry for 2 to 3 minutes, turning with a fork. Drain on paper towels and sprinkle with confectioners' sugar.

Rhode Island Johnny Cakes

Makes 20 cakes

So many ways to serve these – topped with butter, drizzled with maple syrup, or with your favorite creamed chipped beef.

1 cup flour
1 cup cornmeal (we like Kenyon's stone ground white meal from Usquepaug, Rhode Island)
1$\frac{1}{2}$ tablespoons baking powder
1$\frac{1}{2}$ teaspoons salt
2 eggs
1$\frac{1}{2}$ cups buttermilk
3 tablespoons butter, melted, plus extra to grease griddle

1. Mix all of the dry ingredients in a large bowl. In another small bowl, beat the eggs with the buttermilk until bubbly. Add to the dry ingredients and blend. Stir in the melted butter and let the batter rest for 20 minutes.
2. Preheat a griddle or heavy skillet that has been lightly greased. Drop by large spoonfuls into hot skillet and cook until pancakes bubble. Turn and cook for another minute until crispy and brown.

Overnight English Muffin Artichoke Strata

Serves 6

In the morning, just uncover the strata and bake it straight out of the refrigerator in a preheated oven.

3 English muffins, split and quartered
cooking spray
1 tablespoon butter or margarine, melted
1 cup chopped lean ham
$\frac{1}{2}$ cup grated fresh Parmesan cheese
2 tablespoons chopped fresh chives
1 14-ounce can artichoke hearts, drained and chopped
3 large garlic cloves, minced
$\frac{1}{8}$ teaspoon ground nutmeg
1 12-ounce can evaporated fat-free milk
3 large eggs

1. Arrange muffin pieces, crust sides down, in an 8-inch square baking pan coated with cooking spray; drizzle with butter. Arrange ham and next 4 ingredients (ham through garlic) over muffin pieces.
2. Combine nutmeg and remaining ingredients in a bowl; stir well with a whisk. Pour over muffin mixture. Cover; chill 8 hours or overnight. Bake in a preheated 375° oven for 50 minutes until browned and strata is set. Let stand 10 minutes before serving.

Top Of The Mountain French Toast

Serves 6 to 8

From the Tidewater Inn in Madison, Connecticut, this recipe was given its name by a frequent guest who always loved the breakfast fare. After the French toast breakfast she said, "Oh my, this must be the top of the mountain, breakfast couldn't be any better than this!"

1 cup brown sugar
$\frac{1}{2}$ cup ($\frac{1}{4}$ pound) butter
2 tablespoons dark corn syrup
2 tart apples (such as Granny Smith), peeled and sliced
5 eggs, beaten
$1\frac{1}{2}$ cups milk
1 teaspoon vanilla
1 loaf French bread sliced into $\frac{3}{4}$-inch pieces
confectioners' sugar

1. In a small saucepan cook brown sugar, butter, and corn syrup over low heat for 2 to 3 minutes until smooth. Pour into a 9-by-13-by-2-inch baking pan. Layer apple slices over syrup in pan and top with sliced French bread.

2. Combine beaten eggs with milk and vanilla, pour over the bread, cover and refrigerate overnight. Bake in a 350° oven for 40 minutes until golden and crusty. Spoon syrup over the hot French toast and sprinkle with "snow" – the confectioners' sugar. Cut into slices, serving 2 per person.

APPLE SYRUP

1 cup applesauce
1 10-ounce jar apple jelly
$\frac{1}{2}$ teaspoon cinnamon
$\frac{1}{8}$ teaspoon ground cloves
dash of salt

Combine all ingredients in a small saucepan and heat until the jelly is melted and the sauce is smooth.

Molasses Bran Bread

Makes 1 loaf

1 cup boiling water
$1\frac{1}{2}$ cups bran
1 tablespoon shortening
2 tablespoons molasses
1 yeast cake, dissolved in $\frac{1}{2}$ cup warm water
4 cups flour
$1\frac{1}{2}$ teaspoon salt

Pour boiling water over bran and let sit for 5 minutes. Add shortening and molasses, let mixture cool. Add yeast cake and gradually stir in flour and salt. Cover and let rise in a warm place for 30 to 45 minutes. Place dough in a lightly buttered loaf pan. Let rise again and bake in a 325° oven for 40 to 45 minutes.

Oxford House Oatmeal Scones

Makes 8 to 12 scones

From the charming inn in Freyburg, Maine – guests always ask for a second basket.

$\frac{2}{3}$ cup butter, melted
$\frac{1}{3}$ cup milk
1 egg, beaten
1$\frac{1}{2}$ cups flour
1$\frac{1}{4}$ cups Quick Oats (uncooked)
$\frac{1}{4}$ cup sugar
1 tablespoon baking powder
1 teaspoon cream of tartar
$\frac{1}{2}$ teaspoon salt
$\frac{1}{2}$ cup currants

1. Combine melted butter, milk and egg. Mix with dry ingredients until just moist, stir in the currants.

2. Shape the dough and pat out on a floured surface into an 8-inch circle. Cut the dough into 8 to 12 pie-shaped wedges. Bake on a greased cookie sheet in a 425° oven for 12 to 15 minutes until golden.

Gram's Hobo Bread

Makes 3 loaves

When my grandparents were first married, they bought an old house to restore and rented rooms on the third floor to boarders, most of whom were men who worked on the railroad. Her popular Hobo bread was made in coffee cans and would keep for days as it was so dense and moist. She would send people on their way with slices or whole loaves of it, and when they paid her a return visit they would always ask for more!

1$\frac{1}{2}$ cups raisins
2 cups hot water
3 teaspoons baking soda
1 cup brown sugar
1 cup white sugar
3 cups flour
4 teaspoons vegetable oil
2 teaspoons vanilla
$\frac{1}{2}$ teaspoon salt
1$\frac{1}{2}$ cups chopped walnuts

Soak raisins in hot water with baking soda at least 4 hours or overnight. Add remaining ingredients and mix well. Grease and flour 3 1-pound coffee cans or loaf pans. Divide the dough between the 3 cans and bake at 350° for 1 hour. Let stand 1 hour before removing from cans. Slice and serve plain or spread with cream cheese.

Papa's Bread

Makes 4 loaves

Papa, my grandfather, once decided to make homemade bread with not much success until my grandmother, Nanny, stepped in to teach him. He would proudly serve it buttered and toasted for breakfast to all of his grandchildren. Although duplicated over the years, his still remains the best.

8 to 10 cups flour
4 tablespoons salt
$\frac{1}{4}$ cup sugar
2 packages dry yeast
4 cups milk
2 tablespoons oil

1. In a large mixing bowl combine 2 cups flour, salt, sugar and yeast. In a saucepan combine milk and oil and cook over low heat until warm (not hot). Gradually add the milk to the flour mixture. Beat the mixture with an electric mixer on medium speed for 2 minutes. Mix in 2 more cups of flour, one at a time.

2. Turn out the dough onto a floured surface. Knead the dough for 10 to 15 minutes, adding flour gradually. The dough should be smooth, elastic and not sticky.

3. Grease a large mixing bowl, put the dough in the bowl, cover with a cloth and place in a warm place to rise. When the dough has doubled in size, punch it down. Cover and let rise again. Punch dough down. Divide and shape into four loaves and place in greased loaf pans. Let rise one more time. Bake in a preheated 400° oven for 40 minutes until golden brown. When tapped, loaf should sound hollow. Remove from pans and spread crust with butter for a nice shiny top.

Country Brown Bread

Makes 1 loaf

As a child, Mom's brown bread and baked beans was often Saturday night supper. The smell of the beans baking all day, the brown bread in the oven, are both wonderful memories of comfort food from a great cook.

1 cup white or graham flour
$\frac{1}{2}$ cup cornmeal
1 teaspoon baking soda
$\frac{1}{2}$ teaspoon salt
$\frac{1}{2}$ cup molasses
1 cup sweet milk
$\frac{1}{2}$ cup raisins

Mix flour, cornmeal, baking soda and salt. Add molasses, milk, and raisins, and stir until well mixed. Pour into a lightly greased coffee can or loaf pan and bake in a 350° oven for 45 minutes. Cool in pan for 20 minutes before removing. Slice and serve warm with lots of butter.

Mrs. Snider's Potato Bread

Makes 2 loaves

This hearty white bread was one that my mother learned to make as a child, from Moravian bakers at their old settlement in Salem, North Carolina. The ingredients are simple, and the overnight rising requires patience, reflecting perhaps on a simpler age.

1 heavy cup mashed potatoes
1 package dry yeast (1 tablespoon)
$\frac{1}{4}$ cup warm water
$\frac{1}{2}$ cup sugar
$\frac{1}{2}$ cup (8 tablespoons) butter
2 cups hot milk
2 eggs, beaten
$\frac{1}{2}$ cup sugar
pinch of salt
6 to 8 cups flour
1 heaping tablespoon baking powder

1. Mix potato, yeast, water and sugar in a large bowl and let sit for 3 hours. Melt butter in hot milk and add to potato mixture. Beat eggs, sugar, salt and baking powder; add to potato mixture.

2. Gradually blend in 6 to 8 cups flour, knead well. Place dough in a lightly greased bowl, cover, and allow to rise overnight. Punch down, divide in half and place in 2 9-by-5-inch loaf pans. Bake at 350° for 45 minutes.

Aunt Mary's Irish Soda Bread

Makes 1 loaf

Brought from Ireland at the beginning of the last century and passed along through four generations.

4 cups flour
1 teaspoon baking soda
2 teaspoons baking powder
1 teaspoon salt
$\frac{3}{4}$ cup sugar
$\frac{1}{2}$ cup (8 tablespoons) butter, at room temperature
$1\frac{1}{2}$ cups raisins
1 tablespoon caraway seeds
2 cups buttermilk
1 egg white, slightly beaten

1. Preheat oven to 350°. Grease an 8- or 9-inch cast iron pan. In a bowl, combine the flour, baking soda, baking powder, salt and sugar. Using a pastry blender, cut the butter into the flour mixture. Add the raisins, caraway seeds and buttermilk, mixing well.

2. With a wooden spoon, mix the butter into prepared pan, brush the top with beaten egg white and bake for 45 to 50 minutes until golden brown. Serve hot with lots of butter and a strong pot of tea.

Louise And Annabele's Irish Soda Bread

Makes 1 loaf

From two great aunts, this family favorite was always served with corned beef and cabbage. For some reason, this bread always comes out the best when the weather is cold and blustery.

3 cups unbleached flour
$\frac{1}{4}$ teaspoon salt
1 teaspoon baking soda
3 teaspoons baking powder
$\frac{1}{4}$ cup shortening or margarine
1 tablespoon honey
1 egg
$1\frac{1}{3}$ cups buttermilk
1 tablespoon caraway seeds
$\frac{1}{2}$ cup currants (or raisins)

1. Sift dry ingredients into a large bowl. Work in shortening with a pastry cutter until well blended. Combine honey, egg, and buttermilk; stir into flour mixture. Add caraway seeds and currants, mixing well.

2. Turn dough out onto a floured board and knead 10 times. Place in a greased 8-inch baking pan and flatten the loaf with your hand. Cut a cross in the top with a sharp knife. Bake at 350° for 40 to 45 minutes until toothpick inserted in center comes out clean. Remove from pan and cool before slicing.

Old Fashioned Brown Bread

Makes 1 loaf

A typical Saturday night dinner in New England often consists of hot dogs, baked beans, coleslaw and brown bread. As a part of this dinner, my mother baked this bread every Saturday night for years. Not the traditional dark bread, but light-colored as Dad liked it best, with raisins (which the kids hated!)

1 cup all-purpose flour
1 cup yellow cornmeal
1 teaspoon baking soda
1 teaspoon salt
$\frac{1}{2}$ cup light brown sugar (for darker bread, use dark brown sugar)
$1\frac{1}{2}$ cups unsweetened applesauce
$\frac{1}{2}$ to 1 cup raisins (optional)

1. Sift flour, cornmeal, baking soda and salt. Add brown sugar, applesauce and raisins, mixing well. Pour batter into a well-greased 2-quart mold or coffee can and cover with foil.

2. Place mold in a pan of hot water and place in a preheated 325° oven. Bake for 2 hours, unmold and cool bread on a rack before slicing. Serve with butter.

Nantucket Country Hearth Bread

Makes 2 loaves
From the fine kitchen of the Chestnut House Inn.

STARTER
$\frac{2}{3}$ cup whole milk, room temperature
$\frac{2}{3}$ cup warm water (105° to 115° F)
1 teaspoon dry yeast
1 teaspoon honey
1$\frac{3}{4}$ cups unbleached all-purpose flour

DOUGH
1 teaspoon dry yeast
1$\frac{1}{2}$ cups water, room temperature
5$\frac{1}{2}$ cups (about) unbleached all-purpose
    flour
$\frac{1}{4}$ cup olive oil
4 teaspoons salt

FOR STARTER:
Combine milk and warm water in large bowl. Sprinkle yeast over; stir to blend. Let stand until dissolved, about 10 minutes. Add honey and then flour, $\frac{1}{2}$ cup at a time, whisking until smooth (mixture will be thick and sticky). Cover loosely with plastic; let stand 4 hours (mixture will be thick and bubbly). (Can be made one day ahead. Chill overnight. Bring to room temperature before using.)

FOR DOUGH:
1. Using electric mixer with paddle attachment, beat yeast, then 1$\frac{1}{2}$ cups room-temperature water, 1 cup flour, oil and salt into starter. Continue beating on medium-low speed 2 minutes. Beat in enough flour, $\frac{1}{2}$ cup at a time, to form smooth yet sticky dough (dough will not pull away from sides of bowl). Scrape dough out onto floured work surface. Knead until smooth and elastic, adding more flour by tablespoonfuls if necessary to prevent sticking, about 5 minutes. Let dough rest uncovered 5 minutes. Form into ball. Place in large ungreased bowl. Cover with plastic. Let dough rise in warm draft-free area until doubled in volume, about 1 hour 15 minutes.

2. Flour large baking sheet. Punch down dough. Turn out onto floured work surface. Divide in half. Shape each piece into 6-inch round. Place on baking sheet. Let rise uncovered in warm draft-free area until doubled in volume, about 1 hour.

3. Position rack in center of oven and preheat to 400°. Using sharp knife, cut $\frac{1}{2}$-inch-deep, 3-inch-long diagonal slashes, forming X in top of each loaf. Dust tops lightly with flour. Bake until loaves are deep golden and sound hollow when tapped on bottom, about 35 minutes. Cool on rack. (Can be made ahead. Wrap in foil and store at room temperature 1 day or freeze up to 2 weeks.)

Garlic Bread Puddings

Serves 8

2 cups milk
8 garlic cloves, chopped
2 large whole eggs
2 large egg yolks
3 tablespoons minced fresh parsley
$\frac{3}{4}$ teaspoon salt
dash of Tabasco sauce
$2\frac{1}{2}$ cups $\frac{1}{2}$-inch cubes of Italian or French bread

1. In a saucepan, scald the milk with the garlic. Let the mixture stand off the heat for 20 minutes, and strain it through a sieve, discarding the garlic.

2. In a bowl, whisk together the eggs and yolks, add the milk, slowly, whisking and stir in the parsley, salt and Tabasco sauce to taste. Divide the bread cubes among 8 well-buttered $\frac{1}{3}$ cup muffin tins. Ladle the custard mixture over them, dividing it evenly and let the bread puddings stand for 10 minutes. (The puddings may be prepared in advance, for up to 8 hours, kept covered and chilled.)

3. Bake the puddings in a preheated 350° oven for 45 minutes until they are golden brown and puffed. Let the puddings cool for 10 minutes (they will sink as they cool), run a sharp knife around the edges and lift puddings out with a fork.

Sage, Bacon And Cheddar Biscuits

Makes 9 biscuits

2 cups flour
2 teaspoons baking powder
2 teaspoons sugar
$\frac{3}{4}$ teaspoon baking soda
$\frac{1}{2}$ teaspoon salt
2 tablespoons finely chopped fresh sage
5 tablespoons cold butter, cut into pieces
6 slices bacon, cooked crisp and crumbled
$\frac{3}{4}$ cup grated sharp cheddar
$\frac{3}{4}$ cup buttermilk

Preheat oven to 450° and lightly grease a large baking sheet.

1. In a large bowl, sift flour, baking powder, sugar, baking soda and salt. Stir in sage and blend in butter with fingertips or a fork until mixture resembles meal.

2. Add bacon, cheddar and buttermilk, stirring until mixture just forms a ball. Gather dough from bowl and knead gently on a lightly floured surface 10 times. Pat out dough into a 6-by-6-inch rectangle. Cut dough into 9 squares and arrange on prepared baking sheet. Bake in middle of oven for 15 minutes until golden brown.

Sweet Potato Biscuits

Makes 24 biscuits

1$\frac{1}{2}$ pounds sweet potatoes
4 cups unsifted all-purpose flour
$\frac{1}{2}$ cup sugar
2 tablespoons baking powder
2 teaspoons salt
1 teaspoon baking soda
1 cup ($\frac{1}{2}$ pound) unsalted butter, melted
1$\frac{1}{3}$ cups buttermilk

1. Preheat oven to 400°. Pierce sweet potatoes several times with small knife. Roast 1 hour or until very soft. Cool; remove skins. Mash until no lumps remain (you should have about 2 cups). Reduce oven temperature to 375°.

2. In large bowl, vigorously whisk flour, sugar, baking powder, salt and baking soda until no lumps remain (or sift, if desired). Make well in center of dry ingredients. In a 1-quart measure or bowl, combine sweet potatoes and melted butter; whisk until combined. Place in well along with buttermilk; combine until soft dough forms.

3. Turn out onto well-floured surface (dough will be sticky). Flour top of dough. Pat or roll into 1-inch thickness. Using a floured 2$\frac{1}{2}$-inch biscuit or cookie cutter, cut out biscuits, reflouring cutter between cuts. Transfer with spatula to ungreased baking sheet(s). Gather dough scraps, reroll and cut out biscuits as directed (you should get 24).

4. Bake 26 minutes or until lightly golden on bottom. Transfer biscuits to wire rack; let cool completely. Place in large, resealable freezer bag or container. Freeze up to 2 weeks. To serve; Preheat oven to 350°. Arrange frozen biscuits on baking sheet. Bake 16 minutes or until hot and crusty.

Rosemary Beer Bread

Makes 1 loaf
This recipe is quick, easy and impressive – nice to serve with any pork, sauerkraut and kielbasa dish.

3 cups self-rising flour
2 tablespoons sugar
$\frac{1}{2}$ cup freshly grated Parmesan cheese
1 tablespoon finely chopped rosemary
1 12-ounce can or bottle of beer
2 teaspoons melted butter

Preheat oven to 350°.

1. In a large bowl, mix flour, sugar, cheese and rosemary. Stir in the beer until the flour is just moistened. Pour the batter into a greased 9-by-5-inch loaf pan and let rest for 30 minutes.

2. Bake the loaf for 1 hour. Remove from the oven and brush top with melted butter. Allow to sit in pan for 5 minutes before removing from pan to cool on a wire rack before slicing.

Grindstone Hill Spinach Bread

Makes 2 loaves
A big hit with vegetarian friends, may be made ahead and frozen.

DOUGH:
2 tablespoons cornmeal
2 packages quick-rising yeast
$4\frac{1}{2}$ to 5 cups flour
1 tablespoon salt
1 tablespoon sugar
1 cup lowfat milk
$\frac{3}{4}$ cup water
1 tablespoon margarine

FILLING:
1 10-ounce package frozen spinach, cooked and thoroughly drained
1 15-ounce can black olives
4 ounces sundried tomatoes, packed in oil
$\frac{1}{4}$ cup feta cheese, crumbled
$\frac{1}{2}$ teaspoon salt
$\frac{1}{4}$ teaspoon freshly ground black pepper
1 egg white, beaten

1. Sprinkle cornmeal on baking sheet. In a food processor, mix yeast, $4\frac{1}{2}$ cups flour, salt and sugar. In the microwave, warm milk, water, and margarine to 110° F. With the food processor running, slowly add the liquid mixture. Mix until a ball is formed, adding a little more flour if needed. Place dough in a greased bowl, cover with waxed paper and place away from any drafts. Let rise until double in volume.

2. Preheat oven to 400°.

3. In a medium bowl, mix filling, all ingredients except egg white. Separate dough into 2 parts. Roll each piece into a 12-by-14-inch rectangle. Place $\frac{1}{2}$ of filling mixture in the center of each piece of dough. Roll up dough to make a loaf (the shape of a loaf of Italian bread). Place on baking sheet, and make 4 slits on top of each loaf. Let dough rise for 20 minutes. Brush loaves with egg white and bake for 30 minutes until brown and sounds hollow when knocked on. Remove loaves to a cooling rack and let rest for 10 minutes before slicing.

"The smell of good bread baking is like the sound of flowing water. It is indescribable in its evocation of innocence and *delight*." *M.F.K. Fisher*

Brown Nut Bread

Makes 3 loaves

This very old recipe was handed down from my grandmother, Ida Carlson (1865 - 1947). I still bake mine in her old baking powder cans, but mini-loaf pans may be used. It is wonderful sliced into rounds and spread with cream cheese.

1 cup chopped dates
$\frac{3}{4}$ cup boiling water
1 tablespoon soft butter
1 cup sugar
1 egg, beaten
2 cups flour
1 teaspoon baking powder
$\frac{1}{2}$ teaspoon baking soda
pinch of salt
2 tablespoons molasses
1 teaspoon vanilla
$\frac{1}{2}$ cup chopped nuts

1. Pour boiling water over dates and let cool. Mix butter, sugar and egg. Add dates, including the water. Sift dry ingredients and combine with date mix, stirring with a wooden spoon until well mixed.

2. Stir in molasses, vanilla, and nuts. Pour batter into lightly greased baking powder cans or mini loaf pans and bake at 375° for 35 to 40 minutes. Cool before slicing. Bread keeps well in the refrigerator tightly wrapped in foil.

Pumpkin Tea Bread

Makes 1 loaf

As with any tea bread, this one improves with age.

3 cups sugar
1 cup vegetable or canola oil
3 eggs
1 15-ounce can pumpkin
3 cups flour
$\frac{1}{2}$ teaspoon baking powder
1 teaspoon baking soda
$\frac{1}{2}$ teaspoon salt
1 teaspoon ground cloves
1 teaspoon cinnamon
1 teaspoon nutmeg

Preheat oven to 350°. Blend sugar and oil, add eggs and pumpkin and mix well. Stir in the remaining ingredients and pour into a greased Bundt or tube cake pan. Bake for 1 hour and 15 minutes; cool bread in pan. This bread freezes well.

"The history of man from the beginning has been the history of his struggle for his daily bread."
                    James Peale, 1798

Healthy Banana Bread

Makes 2 9-inch loaves and 1 4-inch mini loaf
Having hungry small children, I like to incorporate ingredients we always have on hand. This recipe was an instant hit. All their friends ask for a piece, as well as my now teenager, who devours it before school.

2 cups all-purpose flour
1 cup whole wheat flour
1 teaspoon baking soda
1 teaspoon baking powder
$\frac{1}{2}$ teaspoon salt
1 cup ($\frac{1}{2}$ pound) butter or margarine
2 cups sugar
4 eggs
$\frac{1}{4}$ cup wheat germ
2 teaspoons vanilla
grated rind of 1 lemon
2 mashed, overripe, large bananas
$\frac{1}{2}$ cup other variety of fruit; blueberry, pineapple, applesauce, raisins
1 cup plain yogurt
1 teaspoon EACH: cinnamon, ginger, mace, allspice

1. Sift flour, baking soda, baking powder and salt. In a large bowl, cream butter until soft. Add sugar and beat in eggs, one at a time. Add wheat germ, vanilla, grated lemon, fruit and spices.
2. Stir in flour mixture alternately with yogurt until well blended. Pour batter into greased loaf pans and bake in a preheated 350° oven for 50 minutes or until toothpick tested in center comes out dry. Remove from pan and cool bread on a rack before slicing. You may also bake this in muffin tins, reducing baking time to about 20 minutes.

Treasured Strawberry Bread

Makes 1 loaf
Mrs. Eva Butler (1898-1969), historian, teacher, anthropologist and an avid collector of Indian history and artifacts, founded The Indian and Colonial Research Center in Old Mystic, Connecticut. The historic Mystic bank, built in 1856, holds her collection. Mrs. Butler reconstructed and updated this recipe from Indian records left by Roger Williams.

$\frac{1}{4}$ cup shortening
1 cup yellow cornmeal
1 cup flour, sifted
4 teaspoons baking soda
$\frac{1}{2}$ teaspoon salt
1 pound frozen strawberries, defrosted or same amount of fresh, sliced

In a medium bowl, cream shortening with cornmeal, flour, soda and salt. Fold in strawberries and pour batter in a lightly greased 9-inch pie plate or loaf pan. Bake at 375° for 35 to 45 minutes until bread pulls away from the side of the pan.

Stonecroft Rhubarb Nut Bread

Makes 2 8-inch loaves
From the chef at a charming "Down East" Maine bed and breakfast.

$1\frac{1}{2}$ cups firmly packed brown sugar
$\frac{2}{3}$ cup vegetable oil
1 egg
1 cup buttermilk
1 teaspoon baking soda
1 teaspoon salt
1 teaspoon vanilla
$2\frac{1}{2}$ cups flour
$1\frac{1}{2}$ cups diced raw rhubarb
$\frac{1}{2}$ cup chopped pecans
$\frac{1}{3}$ cup sugar
1 tablespoon melted butter
$\frac{1}{2}$ teaspoon cinnamon

1. In one bowl, combine brown sugar, oil, and egg. In another bowl, combine buttermilk, baking soda, salt and vanilla. Add the milk mixture to the sugar mixture alternately with the flour, beating well after each addition.

2. Fold in the rhubarb and pecans and turn into 2 lightly buttered and floured loaf pans 8-by-4-by-3-inches. In a small bowl, mix the sugar, melted butter and cinnamon; sprinkle over the loaves. Bake in a preheated 325° oven for 45 minutes or until a cake tester inserted in the center comes out clean. Turn the loaves onto a wire rack to cool.

McIntire Doughnuts

Makes 10 to 14
My mother came from a long line of McIntires, a hearty breed of cattle dealers from Maine. This recipe was handed down from her great grandmother and has become a neighborhood favorite here in Norton, Massachusetts.

1 cup clabbered (sour) milk (leave fresh, whole milk at room temperature for 2 to 3 days or add 1 tablespoon vinegar to milk to use now)
$1\frac{1}{4}$ cups sugar
2 beaten eggs
$3\frac{1}{2}$ to 4 cups flour
1 teaspoon salt
1 teaspoon baking soda
bacon fat, lard, or a combination
cinnamon sugar (optional)

1. Mix milk, sugar and eggs in a large bowl. Add flour, salt and baking soda, mixing in more flour if needed; dough should be sticky.

2. Pat or roll dough out into a rectangle 8-inches wide-by-$\frac{1}{2}$-inch thick. Cut into $\frac{1}{2}$-inch strips and twist into cruller form. Heat bacon fat in a heavy skillet, at least enough to come halfway up sides of pan. Deep fry doughnuts, a few at a time, until browned on both sides. Drain on paper towels and sprinkle with cinnamon sugar.

Orange Rosemary Muffins

Makes 8 to 10 large or 24 mini muffins
These are wonderful served as small sandwiches on a brunch buffet. Split each muffin in half, spread with a generous amount of honey mustard and top with a slice of country ham.

$\frac{1}{2}$ cup (8 tablespoons) unsalted butter,
   at room temperature
1 cup sugar
2 large eggs
2 cups unbleached all-purpose flour
1 teaspoon baking soda
$\frac{1}{2}$ teaspoon salt
1 cup light sour cream
1 large orange
1 cup golden raisins
1 tablespoon dried rosemary

1. Preheat oven to 375°. Lightly grease miniature muffin cups. Using an electric mixer, beat the butter and sugar in a mixing bowl until smooth and creamy. Beat in the eggs, one at a time, then continue beating until light and fluffy.

2. Sift flour, baking soda and salt together. Add flour mixture to butter mixture alternately with the sour cream, blending thoroughly after each addition.

3. Grate the orange peel. Juice the orange, reserving the juice. Place raisins, orange peel and rosemary in a food processor fitted with the steel blade and process until finely minced. Stir raisin mixture into the batter.

4. Spoon the batter into muffin cups, filling each almost to the top. Bake until light golden brown, about 10 to 12 minutes for $1\frac{1}{2}$ -inch muffin cups, 11 minutes for 2-inch muffin cups. Remove muffins from oven and brush tops lightly with reserved orange juice. Turn out onto a wire rack and let cool completely. Store overnight in an air-tight container or zip-top plastic bags.

"The joys of the table are superior to all other pleasures, notably those of personal adornment of drinking and of love, and those procured by perfumes and music."
          Mohamed Bagdadi el Essan, 1226

Mardie's Cinnamon Buns

Ever since the late forties, our family has been summering on Block Island. Mardie, our dear mother and grandmother of our family, was a great cook. She was famous for her cinnamon buns done the old-fashioned way... from scratch with yeast cakes! One summer she promised to bake them for her two visiting grand-nephews, aged nine and ten, but she couldn't find yeast cakes in the Island Market. The next day she took the early ferry to the mainland, found her yeast cakes, and returned on the afternoon boat. Those cinnamon buns were a great success.

The following year those boys were on the Island before Mardie arrived. When she came on the ferry from Point Judith, the boys were on the dock to meet her. They waved to her up at the railing, and they shouted for all to hear, "Mardie! We've got the yeast cakes!!!"

This recipe is still being made by Mardie's children, and now her grandchildren, and the buns are being enjoyed by her great-grandchildren in their turn.

1 yeast cake (or 1 tablespoon dry yeast) dissolved in $\frac{1}{2}$ cup potato water
1 cup milk
$\frac{2}{3}$ cup shortening or a generous $\frac{1}{2}$ cup canola oil
$\frac{1}{2}$ cup sugar
$\frac{1}{2}$ teaspoon salt
1 cup mashed potato
2 eggs, beaten
6 cups flour

butter, brown sugar, cinnamon and raisins in generous amounts

1. Dissolve yeast cake in the potato water, lukewarm. In a large mixing bowl, heat the cup of milk and pour over the shortening, sugar, salt and mashed potato. When cool, add the dissolved yeast and 2 eggs. Then stir in flour – when it gets too stiff to stir, knead well with hands. Reserve a third of a cup of the flour for dusting board and hands. This dough can be kept in refrigerator for several days – let it get very cold (at least a few hours) – then roll thin and make buns in "usual manner" (as Mardie quotes).

2. "Usual manner": Grease shiny baking pans with butter and a scattering of brown sugar, then dust heavily with ground cinnamon. Set aside. Divide chilled dough into two pieces. Roll out a piece and spread with plenty of butter, brown sugar, cinnamon and raisins. Use all of these ingredients generously. Roll dough up into a log so that it can be cut into slices about $\frac{1}{2}$-inch thick. Place in pan so that each slice rests comfortably close to another. If necessary they can be squeezed in, but it makes the buns thick. Bake cinnamon buns at 350° on high rack for 20 to 30 minutes. Watch so brown sugar doesn't burn.

Plymouth House Hot Cross Buns

Makes 18 buns
What a shame to only make these at Easter!

1 cup milk, scalded
$\frac{1}{4}$ cup sugar
1 package active dry yeast
2 tablespoons water (at 105° to 115°)
1 large egg
2 tablespoons butter, softened
$\frac{1}{2}$ teaspoon cinnamon
$\frac{1}{8}$ teaspoon nutmeg
$\frac{1}{4}$ cup currants or raisins
$\frac{1}{4}$ cup finely chopped citron or
  dried apricots
$\frac{3}{4}$ teaspoon salt
$2\frac{2}{3}$ cups sifted flour
melted butter
apricot jam
icing (recipe follows)

1. Add sugar to milk and stir until sugar dissolves. Set aside to cool. Meanwhile, sprinkle yeast over water in a large mixing bowl. When milk has cooled to lukewarm, add it to the yeast mixture.

2. Beat in the egg and softened butter. Add cinnamon, nutmeg, currants or raisins, and citron or apricots. Stir in salt and part of the flour; use only enough to form a dough that can be handled easily. Knead in the remaining flour. (If using an electric mixer with a dough hook, knead in machine just until dough clears the sides of the bowl, then knead lightly by hand until smooth and elastic.) Dough will be sticky.

3. Place in a greased bowl. Brush top with melted butter. Cover and let dough rise in a warm place until doubled in bulk, about $1\frac{1}{2}$ hours. Shape dough into 18 balls and place in rows on a greased baking sheet. Brush with more butter, cover and let rise until almost double in bulk.

4. Preheat oven to 425°. Bake buns about 20 minutes, until golden brown. Remove at once from pan and, while hot, brush with apricot jam. When cooled, decorate each roll with an icing cross.

ICING:
Mix $\frac{3}{4}$ cup confectioners' sugar and 1 tablespoon water until smooth. Place in zip-top plastic bag with a small hole cut in one corner for piping to decorate.

Lemon Conserve

Makes 2$\frac{1}{2}$ cups

If you like the taste of lemon, what better than this spread on a slice of toasted bread? Also delicious as a spread between layers of sponge or angel cake with fresh berries.

6 egg yolks
1$\frac{1}{2}$ cups sugar
2 tablespoons freshly grated lemon rind
   (about 3 large lemons or a few more
   if small)
1 cup fresh lemon juice
$\frac{1}{2}$ cup ($\frac{1}{4}$ pound) butter

1. In the top of a double boiler, mix egg yolks with sugar, lemon rind and lemon juice and cook, stirring over boiling water until sugar dissolves. Add butter and continue cooking for 15 to 20 minutes, stirring constantly, until mixture is smooth and very thick. Cool and then chill; mixture will thicken a bit more as it cools.

Orange Honey Butter

Makes 1$\frac{1}{2}$ cups

For waffles, gingerbread or on toast for the elves.

$\frac{1}{3}$ cup honey
3 tablespoons frozen orange juice
   concentrate
$\frac{1}{4}$ pound soft butter
6 tablespoons confectioners' sugar

Mix all ingredients in blender until smooth and creamy. Serve at room temperature for best flavor.

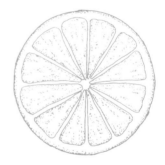

The Main
Event

On Board "Omega" – At Anchor Breakfast

Serves 4 to 6

Sitting in cozy harbors Downeast in Maine, waiting for the fog to clear, we always enjoy this hearty meal before casting off – its makes for a happy skipper and crew.

8 slices bacon, cut into $\frac{1}{2}$-inch pieces (or ham, kielbasa)
1 large, sweet onion, finely chopped
6 to 8 medium potatoes, cooked, peeled and sliced
butter
4 to 6 eggs (1 per person)
salt and pepper

1. Sauté bacon in a heavy skillet until golden; remove from pan and drain. Discard some of the fat, add onion, cook until transparent, about 5 minutes. Add the potatoes and butter as needed. Cook until potatoes are brown and crisp.

2. Beat the eggs, adding salt and pepper. Return bacon to pan, pour eggs over potatoes and cook over medium heat until eggs are set. Serve with catsup.

Scalloped Sour Cream Chicken Bake

Serves 4

1 frying chicken, cut up
$\frac{1}{2}$ cup flour
$1\frac{1}{2}$ teaspoons salt
$\frac{1}{2}$ teaspoon pepper
1 teaspoon paprika, plus some to sprinkle on top
1 teaspoon tarragon
1 tablespoon butter
1 tablespoon vegetable oil
2 cups thinly sliced potatoes
$\frac{3}{4}$ cup chopped scallions with tops
1 cup chicken broth
2 cups sour cream

1. Dredge chicken with flour and seasonings. Melt butter in a large skillet, add oil and brown chicken in batches until golden on both sides. Arrange in a 2-quart baking pan with a cover or use aluminum foil.

2. Arrange potatoes on top of chicken and sprinkle with chopped scallions. Add stock, cover and bake in a 325° oven for 40 minutes. Spread sour cream on top of potatoes, mixing some into the accumulated juices; stir lightly. Sprinkle with paprika and continue baking for 15 minutes.

Aunt Abby's Apricot Chicken

Serves 4

Every time I visit my sisters and nieces in Florida, I try to bring a bit of New England with me. I often prepare this easy dish for them as well as serving it to guests on our boat, "Heart O' Lee," after a long day sailing off the shores of Connecticut.

4 boneless skinless chicken breast halves
$\frac{1}{2}$ cup flour
salt and pepper to taste
5 tablespoons butter
4 tablespoons Apricot All Fruit Jelly
$\frac{1}{4}$ cup white wine
freshly chopped parsley

1. Mix flour and salt and pepper in a shallow bowl. Pound chicken breasts to flatten and dredge with flour. Melt 2 tablespoons of butter in a large skillet and sauté chicken breasts over medium heat, about 4 to 5 minutes per side until browned. Remove from pan and keep warm.

2. To the drippings in the pan, add white wine and apricot jelly, scraping the bottom to release any browned pieces. As mixture starts to bubble, whisk in the remaining 3 tablespoons of butter, 1 tablespoon at a time. Return chicken to the pan until heated through and serve with fluffy white rice, sprinkled with fresh parsley.

Summer Lemonade Chicken

Serves 4

Lots of zesty juices to spoon over your favorite pilaf.

$\frac{3}{4}$ cup lemonade concentrate
$\frac{1}{3}$ cup catsup
4 tablespoons brown sugar
3 tablespoons white wine vinegar
$\frac{1}{4}$ teaspoon ground ginger
1 tablespoon soy sauce
$\frac{1}{2}$ teaspoon EACH: paprika, chili powder, garlic powder, thyme, basil, salt and pepper
1 2$\frac{1}{4}$-pound chicken, cut into 8 pieces
$\frac{1}{2}$ cup flour
$\frac{1}{3}$ cup vegetable oil

1. In a mixing bowl, combine the lemonade, catsup, brown sugar, vinegar, ginger, soy sauce and seasonings.

2. Dredge the chicken in the flour. Heat the oil in a large skillet or Dutch oven and brown the chicken on both sides; drain off any excess oil. Pour the sauce over the chicken and bake, covered, at 350° for 35 to 45 minutes or until chicken is tender. Garnish with freshly grated lemon zest, if desired.

Latimer Point 1st Prize Chicken And Pears

Serves 6

Hop's favorite, taken from the _Boston Herald_ in 1977. Serve with white rice and a choice of condiments such as chutney, chopped almonds, chopped parsley, raisins or toasted coconut.

1½ pounds chicken breasts (4 large or 6 small)
salt, pepper, paprika
¼ cup butter
⅓ cup chopped onion
1 stalk celery, chopped
1½ tablespoons flour
1 teaspoon curry powder
1 tablespoon brown sugar
1 cup chicken broth
¼ cup white wine
juice of 1 lemon
3 Bartlett pears

1. Sprinkle chicken with salt, pepper and paprika. In a large skillet, melt butter; add chicken and brown on both sides, about 10 minutes. Remove to a baking pan.

2. Sauté onion and celery in remaining drippings in pan. Blend in flour, curry powder and brown sugar. Add chicken broth, wine and lemon juice. Cook until thickened, pour over chicken. Cover and bake at 350° for 25 minutes.

3. Cut pears into quarters; do not peel. Add to chicken and spoon sauce over. Bake an additional 25 minutes or until chicken is done and pears are tender.

Herbed Chicken And Shrimp Bake

Serves 8

**The Surf & Turf of chicken!!
(A 40-year old recipe.)**

2 cups sour cream
1 teaspoon dried tarragon
1 teaspoon dried thyme
1 teaspoon salt
1 teaspoon paprika
¼ teaspoon garlic powder
4 whole chicken breasts, halved
1 to 1½ cups cornflake crumbs
1 cup cooked small shrimp
½ cup pitted ripe olives, quartered

1. Combine sour cream with herbs and seasonings. Dip chicken into sour cream mixture, roll in cornflake crumbs. Place chicken pieces, skin side down, in a well-greased 13-by-9-by-2-inch baking pan. Bake uncovered in a 350° oven for 40 minutes; turn chicken and bake for 10 more minutes.

2. To the remaining sour cream mixture, add shrimp and olives; spoon over chicken. Bake for 10 minutes and serve, spooning the sauce around the chicken. Excellent with fluffy white rice.

Modern Grille Chicken Croquettes

Serves 4

From a Mystic eatery, established back in the '50s, a real comfort food dinner.

2 cups finely diced leftover cooked chicken
$\frac{1}{4}$ cup butter or margarine
$\frac{1}{3}$ cup flour
1 teaspoon salt
$\frac{1}{2}$ cup milk
1 tablespoon EACH: lemon juice and finely chopped onion
1 tablespoon chopped fresh parsley or tarragon, or $\frac{1}{2}$ teaspoon dried of either herb
1 egg, beaten
$\frac{1}{3}$ cup fresh white bread crumbs
$\frac{1}{3}$ cup vegetable oil

1. Melt the butter in a saucepan over low heat, and blend in the flour and the salt. Stir in the milk gradually and cook, stirring, until the sauce thickens. Cook over low heat for about 3 minutes. Take off the heat and set aside to cool.

2. Mix together the chicken, onion, lemon juice and parsley or tarragon. Spread the mixture on a plate and put in the refrigerator. Chill. Working on waxed paper, and with floured hands, shape the mixture into whatever you like, sausages or cones or patties, which are easiest of all. (Cones are really pretty tricky.) You should have enough mixture for 8 to 10 croquettes.

3. Dip each one in the beaten egg, and then in the bread crumbs. Heat the oil over medium-high heat until it's nice and hot but not smoking. Fry the croquettes in the hot oil until brown all over. Drain them on paper towels, and serve hot with additional white sauce, cheese sauce or whatever you fancy.

Chicken Breasts Baked In Cream

Serves 6

My great-great-grandfather, Gordon L. Allyn, was a whaling captain out of New London who made three trips around the world. In 1879, he published a journal of his adventures. It tells of his travels to the Navigator Islands in the South Pacific. He relates his observations while anchored in a nearby lagoon.

"Their method of cooking is somewhat peculiar. They dig a hole some two or three feet deep in the ground, into which they place a quantity of small-size stones. Having heated these stones very hot by building a fire on them, they wrap the pigs or fowls that they wish to cook in a kind of large leaves called 'tarra-leaves,' and place them on the heated stones. Closing the mouth of the excavation with earth to retain the heat. When sufficient time has elapsed, they produce the most nicely roasted and finely flavored meat that I ever tasted. The flavor is owing partly to the stuffing, which consists largely of bread-fruit and cocoa-nut milk."

The recipe doesn't require burying the chicken in tarra-leaves, however the slow simmering in cream creates a dish that melts in your mouth.

3 pounds chicken breasts, split
2 teaspoons salt
$\frac{1}{8}$ teaspoon black pepper
3 tablespoons shortening, butter or a combination
1 large onion, chopped
3 cloves garlic, minced
$\frac{1}{2}$ cup sherry
2 cups all-purpose cream
fresh chopped parsley

1. Sprinkle chicken breasts with salt and pepper and in a skillet brown on both sides in shortening. Remove to a large baking pan. Add onion and garlic to skillet, sauté for 3 to 4 minutes, scraping browned chicken bits from the bottom of the pan.

2. Combine onions and garlic with sherry and cream. Pour over chicken and cover tightly with foil. Bake for 2 hours at 300° or until chicken is tender. Sprinkle with fresh parsley. Serve with mashed potatoes or rice.

Vermont Chicken Pot Pie

Serves 4 to 6
I love meals like this with as little clean up as possible, a very pleasant one-dish meal.

$1\frac{1}{2}$ pounds boneless chicken breasts, cut into chunks
6 tablespoons butter
salt and pepper
3 tablespoons flour
$2\frac{1}{2}$ cups warm chicken broth
3 tablespoons white wine
1 10-ounce package mixed vegetables, corn, carrots or a combination, defrosted
2 to $2\frac{1}{2}$ cups Bisquik
$\frac{2}{3}$ cup milk
$\frac{1}{2}$ teaspoon dill

1. Melt 2 tablespoons butter in a heavy skillet and brown chicken on both sides, about 5 minutes. Season with salt and pepper and remove.

2. Melt remaining 4 tablespoons butter in pan, add flour and cook over medium heat for 3 minutes, scraping up any browned bits on bottom of the pan. Whisk in warm chicken broth and cook until thickened. Add wine, chicken and vegetables. Pour into a 2-quart casserole.

3. Beat Bisquik, milk and dill together, adding enough Bisquik to make a thick dough; turn onto a lightly floured board and knead for 30 seconds. Roll out to size of casserole, place on top and cut a few slits in dough. Bake at 375° for 20 to 25 minutes until top is golden brown.

Molded Herb Chicken Salad Veronique

Serves 6
This recipe has been scaled down from one which was served at our daughter's lovely summer wedding – a perfect warm weather addition to any buffet.

1 tablespoon gelatin
$\frac{1}{4}$ cup cold water
1 cup chicken broth
$1\frac{1}{2}$ cups diced, cooked chicken breasts
$\frac{1}{2}$ cup celery, finely diced
$1\frac{1}{2}$ cup seedless green grapes
$\frac{1}{2}$ pint sour cream
$\frac{1}{3}$ cup mayonnaise
1 tablespoon EACH: chopped chives, parsley, and tarragon
salt and pepper to taste
bunch of watercress

1. Soften gelatin in cold water and dissolve in hot chicken broth; cool.

2. Fold in remaining ingredients, mixing well and pour into a 2-quart ring mold that has been sprayed lightly with nonstick spray. Chill at least 6 hours or best overnight. Unmold onto a lettuce-lined platter and fill center with watercress leaves.

Grilled Chicken Burgers "BLT"

Serves 4

Our new Fourth of July favorite, let everyone build their own.

4 4-ounce boneless skinless chicken breasts
4 tablespoons olive oil
1 tablespoon sherry
1 clove garlic, minced
$\frac{1}{2}$ teaspoon EACH: salt, cracked black
   pepper, thyme, oregano, basil and
   paprika
$\frac{1}{2}$ teaspoon Worcestershire sauce
12 strips bacon, cooked and drained
2 large ripe tomatoes, sliced thick
4 lettuce leaves
4 tablespoons Ranch dressing
4 large Kaiser or sourdough rolls

1. Wash and pat dry the chicken breasts, place in a shallow pan.

2. In a mixing bowl, blend together the oil, sherry, garlic, seasonings and Worcestershire sauce. Pour over the chicken and marinate for 2 hours.

3. Cook the chicken on a preheated grill for 4 minutes per side, brushing frequently with marinade. Slice rolls in half, place 2 tomato slices and lettuce on one half. On the other half, place 1 tablespoon of dressing, chicken breast and 3 slices of bacon. Serve with lots of dill pickles.

Popover Tarragon Chicken

Serves 6

This popover creation is an herb flavored bread and main dish combined in an easy yet party special casserole.

1 2$\frac{1}{2}$- to 3-pound broiler-fryer chicken,
   cut up
3 tablespoons vegetable oil
salt and freshly ground black pepper
3 eggs
1$\frac{1}{2}$ cups milk
1$\frac{1}{2}$ cups all-purpose flour
1 teaspoon dried tarragon, crushed
$\frac{1}{2}$ teaspoon salt

1. In a large skillet, brown chicken in 2 tablespoons of oil over medium heat about 15 minutes, turning often to evenly brown. Season with salt and pepper. Place the chicken in a well-greased 13-by-9-by-2-inch baking pan.

2. In a medium mixing bowl, beat eggs; add milk and remaining 1 tablespoon of oil. Stir together flour, tarragon and $\frac{1}{2}$ teaspoon of salt. Add to egg mixture and beat with a mixer until smooth. Pour the egg mixture over the browned chicken and bake in a preheated 350° oven for 50 to 55 minutes until popover is puffed and golden.

Vermont Skillet Pot Pie

Serves 6

The original version of this recipe came from an impromptu get-together after skiing at Stratton Mountain. As you can see, everything came off the shelf or from the freezer.

6 boneless, skinless chicken breasts, about 1$\frac{1}{2}$ pounds
salt and pepper
2 teaspoons olive oil
1 large onion (1 cup chopped)
1 stalk celery, chopped
8 ounces mushrooms, sliced
2 cloves garlic, minced
2 teaspoons Worcestershire sauce
1 can (10$\frac{3}{4}$ ounces) cream of mushroom soup
1 can (10$\frac{3}{4}$ ounces) cream of chicken soup
$\frac{2}{3}$ cup milk (lowfat or regular)
1 cup frozen corn kernels
1 cup frozen peas and carrots mixture
$\frac{2}{3}$ cup grated cheddar cheese

1. Cut chicken into $\frac{1}{2}$-inch chunks or strips, sprinkle with salt and pepper. Heat oil in a large skillet and add chicken. Cook over medium heat until browned, about 5 minutes. Add onion, celery, mushrooms and garlic and continue cooking until vegetables are soft.

2. Add the Worcestershire sauce, cream of mushroom and cream of chicken soups and milk. You may need to add a bit more milk – the mixture should be loose but not too soupy. Stir to mix well. Add the corn, peas and carrots, and cheese. Cook until the vegetables are heated through and cheese is melted. Spoon into bowls and serve with warm French bread or biscuits.

Quick Brandied Chicken Livers

Serves 4

Serve this over split and toasted English muffins for an easy elegant supper.

5 tablespoons butter
$\frac{1}{4}$ cup chopped onion
$\frac{1}{2}$ pound sliced mushrooms
1 pound chicken livers, cut into bite-size pieces
$\frac{1}{4}$ cup flour
$\frac{1}{2}$ teaspoon salt
freshly ground black pepper
$\frac{1}{4}$ cup brandy
$1\frac{1}{2}$ cups half-and-half or light cream
2 tablespoons chopped parsley

1. Melt 2 tablespoons of the butter in a skillet. Add onions and mushrooms and cook until tender, about 4 to 5 minutes. Remove from the pan.

2. Pat livers dry, coat with flour, shaking off any excess. Add the remaining 3 tablespoons of butter to the pan, add livers, season with salt and pepper and cook over high heat until the pink color disappears.

3. Add the brandy and flame. Blend in the cream and cook over low heat until mixture thickens slightly. Serve sprinkled with chopped parsley.

Open Heart Saver

Serves 4

My wife was motivated to adapt many recipes after my heart surgery and this tasty, but healthy, dish is well worth preparing often.

3 chicken breasts, skinless and boneless, cut into $\frac{1}{2}$-inch pieces
1 tablespoon olive oil
$\frac{1}{2}$ medium onion, sliced
1 large green pepper, cut into strips
1 14-ounce can artichoke hearts
1 4-ounce jar pimentos, drained
6 ounces fresh green beans, cut in half
2 stalks celery, diced
10 to 12 bite-size broccoli crowns
6 mushrooms, sliced
garlic powder, oregano, basil, parsley, freshly ground black pepper
$\frac{1}{2}$ pound bow tie pasta
Parmesan cheese

1. Brown chicken in olive oil in a large skillet. Add onions and peppers and cook for 10 minutes. Add remaining vegetables and season to taste with spices.

2. Cover pan and simmer over medium-low heat for 30 minutes, stirring often. Cook pasta according to package directions, drain, and toss with chicken and vegetables. Serve hot sprinkled with Parmesan cheese or at room temperature as a salad.

Vineyard Haven Turkey Tettrazini

Serves 8

A great way to use up the last of the turkey dinner. This recipe came form the local postmaster's wife back in the 70's.

4 tablespoons butter
1 medium onion, finely chopped
2 cups sliced mushrooms
$\frac{1}{3}$ cup flour
1 cup light cream
2 cups chicken stock
salt and pepper
$\frac{1}{2}$ cup scallions, thinly sliced
2 cups cooked turkey, cut in bite-size pieces
8 ounces cooked fettuccine
2 cups bread crumbs
2 tablespoons melted butter
$\frac{1}{4}$ cup grated Parmesan cheese

1. Melt butter in a large saucepan, sauté onion and cook until translucent, about 5 minutes. Add mushrooms and sauté for another 5 minutes.

2. Mix in flour and cook for several minutes, stirring constantly. Whisk in cream and chicken stock; cook over medium heat until sauce has thickened. Season to taste with salt (seasoned salt is excellent), and pepper.

3. In a large bowl, mix sauce with scallions, turkey and cooked fettuccine. Pour into a buttered 2-quart shallow baking pan. Mix bread crumbs, butter and Parmesan cheese, sprinkle on top and bake at 350°

until lightly browned and bubbly, about 30 minutes.

Tipsy Roast Goose

Serves 8

The gin makes aromatic and unusual pan juices.

1 6- to 8-pound goose, cleaned, plucked, and dressed
8 apples, peeled and chopped
1 loaf stale bread, broken into small pieces
2 medium onions, diced
3 stalks celery and tops, diced
4 tablespoons butter, melted
1 tablespoon poultry seasoning
2 eggs, well beaten
$\frac{3}{4}$ cup gin
1 14-ounce can chicken broth
salt and pepper to taste

1. In a large bowl, toss the apples and bread together. Sauté the onion and celery in the melted butter and add to the bread-apple mixture along with the poultry seasoning and beaten eggs.

2. Stuff the goose, truss well and place breast-side up on a roasting rack. Pour the gin and chicken broth over the goose and season with salt and pepper. Roast in a 450° oven for 60 minutes, basting frequently. Reduce heat to 350° and roast for 30 minutes more. Remove goose to a platter; skim any grease from the pan, and reseason juices with salt and pepper.

Baked Ziti With Turkey Meatballs

Serves 8

This recipe evolved as a compromise to a family favorite when our daughter planned to bring some non-red meat eaters home for a long weekend from college – it turned out so well the girls even jotted down my recipe.

$1\frac{1}{2}$ pounds ground turkey
2 cloves garlic, minced
$\frac{3}{4}$ cup bread crumbs
$\frac{1}{2}$ onion, finely diced
1 teaspoon oregano
$\frac{1}{4}$ cup fresh chopped parsley
1 egg, beaten
1 teaspoon EACH: salt and freshly ground
  black pepper
$1\frac{1}{2}$ cups (about 6 ounces) grated
  Mozzarella cheese
1 cup grated Romano cheese
about 6 cups tomato or marinara sauce,
  your own or store-bought
1 1-pound container Ricotta cheese
1 pound ziti or penne, cooked (al dente,
  about 8 minutes) and drained

1. Preheat oven to 350°. In a large mixing bowl, combine turkey, garlic, bread crumbs, onion, oregano, parsley, egg, salt and pepper; mix well. Form into small meatballs, about 1 inch in diameter and brown in oil on both sides or bake for $\frac{1}{2}$ hour in a baking pan which has been sprayed with nonstick cooking spray.

2. In a small bowl, mix together the Mozzarella and Romano cheeses. Lightly oil a deep 4-quart baking dish. Spoon $1\frac{1}{2}$ cups of the tomato sauce and half the meatballs into the baking pan; spread half of the remaining sauce and half of the cheese mix over pasta. Top with remaining meatballs and drop dollops of the ricotta mixture on top.

3. Spread remaining pasta over Ricotta, top with remaining sauce and remaining cheese mixture. Bake for 30 to 35 minutes until golden brown. Let rest 10 minutes before serving.

Cider Glazed Turkey

Serves 10 to 12

A light, wonderful sauce unlike a gravy unfolds in this recipe

1 16-pound turkey, at room temperature
salt and freshly ground black pepper
3 apples, cored and sliced into $\frac{1}{2}$-inch
  thick rings
12 sage leaves
4 tablespoons butter, melted
1$\frac{1}{2}$ cups boiled cider
24 small boiling onions, peeled

1. Rinse turkey inside and out with cold water; pat dry with paper towels. Using your fingers, gently loosen the skin on breast and legs, being careful not to tear skin. Season the meat under the skin with salt and pepper.

2. Insert 4 apple rings and 3 sage leaves in between breast meat and skin; pat skin back in place. Place remaining apples and sage in turkey cavity and season with salt and pepper. Truss turkey with kitchen twine.

3. Place turkey breast-side up in a roasting pan that has a cover (preferably one of those old-fashioned blue and white speckled ones). Arrange onions around turkey and pour melted butter and boiled cider over turkey. Season with salt and pepper, cover and roast, basting every 20 minutes for 4 hours until a meat thermometer registers 180°. Let turkey rest 20 minutes before carving. Serve juices and onions alongside.

Walnut And Wild Rice Chicken Salad

Serves 6 to 8

A must for any summer buffet table.

1 cup white and wild rice blend
$\frac{1}{2}$ cup chopped scallions
$\frac{1}{2}$ cup chopped celery
$\frac{1}{4}$ teaspoon grated lemon peel
1$\frac{1}{2}$ tablespoons lemon juice
$\frac{1}{4}$ cup chopped fresh parsley
$\frac{2}{3}$ cup plain yogurt
3 tablespoons olive oil
$\frac{1}{2}$ teaspoon salt
$\frac{1}{4}$ teaspoon freshly ground black pepper
2 cups shredded cooked chicken
1 cup walnuts, coarsely chopped

Cook rice according to package directions. Cool. In a large bowl, combine scallions, celery, lemon peel, lemon juice, parsley, yogurt, oil, salt and pepper. Toss with rice, chicken and walnuts until well mixed. Refrigerate until serving.

Curried Turkey Salad With Grapes And Pecans

Serves 6

4 cups chopped cooked turkey
3 stalks celery, diced
$\frac{1}{2}$ cup diced scallions
2 tablespoons chopped parsley
1 cup sliced seedless grapes, red or green
$\frac{1}{2}$ cup toasted pecans, chopped
$\frac{3}{4}$ cup mayonnaise
1 teaspoon lemon juice
1 teaspoon Dijon mustard
1 teaspoon curry powder
salt and pepper to taste

1. In a large bowl, toss turkey, celery, scallions, parsley, grapes and pecans.

2. In a separate bowl whisk mayonnaise with lemon juice, mustard, curry powder and salt and pepper. Mix dressing with turkey and refrigerate for at least 2 hours before serving.

Rosemary Grilled Flank Steak

Serves 6

Everyone always asks for this quick and easy recipe; even children love this when it is served at our summer picnics here on Woodchuck Hill.

1 2$\frac{1}{4}$- to 2$\frac{1}{2}$ pound flank steak
6 cloves garlic, minced
3 tablespoons chopped fresh rosemary
   or 1 tablespoon dried
1$\frac{1}{2}$ tablespoons coarsely ground black
   pepper
$\frac{1}{2}$ cup soy sauce
$\frac{1}{2}$ cup olive oil
5 tablespoons honey

Mix all ingredients except steak in a 13-by-9-by-2-inch glass baking pan. Add steak, turning to coat meat well. Cover and refrigerate for at least 2 hours or best overnight.

Prepare a medium-hot barbecue or preheat broiler. Remove steak from marinade and discard marinade. Grill steak to desired doneness, about 4 minutes per side for medium-rare. Let stand for 5 minutes before slicing thinly, across the grain into strips.

Lighthouse Pot Pie

Serves 8

From a wonderful Noank hostess – Whose turn to cook?

5 cups chicken broth
3 carrots, cut into $\frac{1}{2}$-inch pieces
1 small onion, diced
$\frac{1}{4}$ pound sliced mushrooms
$\frac{2}{3}$ cup fresh peas
$\frac{1}{2}$ cup butter
$\frac{2}{3}$ cup flour
2 tablespoons chopped fresh parsley
salt and pepper
4 cups cooked chicken, turkey, or pork, cut
  into bite-size pieces

CRUST
1 cup flour
7 tablespoons shortening
$\frac{1}{2}$ teaspoon salt
3 tablespoons water

1. Bring chicken broth to a boil. Add carrots and onions, cook until tender-crisp, about 8 minutes. Add mushrooms and peas, cook for 5 more minutes. Drain and reserve liquid.

2. Melt butter in a saucepan, add flour and cook, stirring for 2 minutes. Whisk in reserved liquid and cook until sauce is thickened. Add cooked vegetables, meat, parsley and season to taste with salt and pepper. Pour into a greased 2-quart casserole.

3. For crust: Mix flour, shortening and salt. Add water 1 tablespoon at a time, mixing until dough forms a ball.

Knead dough on a lightly floured board, wrap and chill 1 hour. Roll dough to size slightly large than casserole, fit on top, crimp edge and cut a $1\frac{1}{2}$-inch hole in center. Bake pie at 400° for 40 minutes until crust is golden brown.

Bistro Beer Sirloin

Serves 6

12 ounces beer
$\frac{1}{2}$ cup sliced onion
$\frac{1}{4}$ cup olive oil
1 small green pepper, minced
3 tablespoons soy sauce
2 tablespoons honey
4 cloves garlic, minced
crushed red pepper to taste
$1\frac{1}{2}$ pounds sirloin steak, cut 1-inch thick

1. Combine beer, onion, olive oil, green pepper, soy sauce, honey, garlic and red pepper flakes in a glass pan. Place steak in pan, turn to coat, cover and refrigerate 6 hours to overnight.

2. Drain meat and reserve marinade. Grill meat over charcoal for 10 minutes per side or until done to your taste. Let stand for 10 minutes before cutting diagonally across the grain into thin slices. Boil reserved marinade 3 or 4 minutes and spoon over sliced meat.

Sherried Salisbury Steaks – Company Style

Serves 6

A far cry from cafeteria fare – real comfort food for the year 2000.

$1\frac{1}{2}$ pounds lean ground beef
$\frac{1}{2}$ cup seasoned bread crumbs
1 egg
1 tablespoon Worcestershire sauce
2 tablespoons minced onion
1 small carrot, minced
1 stalk celery, minced
4 tablespoons butter
1 large onion, sliced
2 teaspoons sugar
3 tablespoons flour
$\frac{1}{3}$ cup sherry
$1\frac{1}{2}$ cups beef broth
3 tablespoons tomato paste
$\frac{1}{2}$ teaspoon salt
$\frac{1}{4}$ teaspoon freshly ground black pepper

1. In a large mixing bowl, combine the beef, crumbs, egg, Worcestershire sauce, minced onion, carrot and celery. Shape into 6 oval patties and bake in a preheated 400° oven for 15 minutes.

2. While patties cook, heat the butter in a large skillet. Add the sliced onion and sugar. Sauté over low heat until onions caramelize. Sprinkle in the flour and continue to cook for 3 minutes. Add the sherry, broth, tomato paste and season-ings. Simmer until sauce thickens. Place patties on a serving platter with mashed potatoes or buttered noodles; smother with sauce and serve.

Fireside Roast Beef Hash

Serves 8 to 10

Great brunch fare. Serve with pastries and good strong coffee.

4 tablespoons butter
1 cup onion, finely chopped
2 cloves garlic, minced
$\frac{1}{2}$ cup green pepper, finely chopped
4 cups leftover roast beef, chopped
1 tablespoon Worcestershire sauce
2 teaspoons salt
$\frac{1}{2}$ teaspoon freshly ground black pepper
2 cups finely diced potatoes
1 cup beef broth

1. Heat the butter in a heavy skillet and sauté onion, garlic, and green pepper over high heat until onion is transparent. Add roast beef, Worcestershire sauce, salt, pepper, and potatoes. Pour in beef broth, cover and cook over low heat until potatoes are tender, about 20 to 25 minutes.

2. Turn heat to high to evaporate some of the liquid and reseason with salt and pepper. This is a soft hash, not a crispy one, and is best served with hot toasted bread on the side.

Yankee Red-Flannel Hash

Serves 4

In our family the traditional corned beef and cabbage is merely the means to the end – the favorite hash dinner.

$\frac{1}{2}$ cup finely chopped onion
$\frac{1}{4}$ cup (4 tablespoons) butter
3 cups diced cooked potatoes
1 16-ounce can beets, drained and diced
1$\frac{1}{2}$ cups cooked corned beef, diced (you can make this without cooking a whole corned beef – just ask at your deli counter for a 1$\frac{1}{2}$-pound piece of corned beef rather than sliced)
$\frac{1}{3}$ – $\frac{1}{2}$ cup beef broth
$\frac{1}{2}$ teaspoon salt
bottled hot pepper sauce to taste
fresh parsley sprigs

1. In a heavy skillet, cook onion in butter until tender. Toss with the potatoes, beets, corned beef, broth to moisten, salt and pepper sauce.

2. Cover and cook over medium heat, turning occasionally until brown and crusty. Serve hot with your choice of mustard or catsup. Great with poached eggs. Garnish with parsley.

So-Savory Beef Stew

Serve 6

Back in the '40s in Taunton, Massachusetts, a plate of Mom's stew tasted so wonderful after an afternoon of ice skating or sledding.

1$\frac{1}{2}$ pounds stew beef, trimmed of fat, cut into $\frac{1}{2}$-inch pieces
2 to 3 tablespoons olive oil
1 medium onion, chopped
$\frac{1}{2}$ cup red wine or sweet vermouth
3 cups water
1 envelope dry onion soup mix
1 tablespoon Worcestershire sauce
1 tablespoon soy sauce
pinch basil pinch thyme
3 medium potatoes, cut into bite-size pieces
3 carrots, sliced, or 1 10-ounce can, drained
salt and pepper to taste

1. In a large Dutch oven, brown meat on both sides in olive oil. Add chopped onion and cook 2 minutes. Add wine, water, onion soup mix and seasonings; simmer for 20 minutes.

2. Add potatoes and carrots, cover and cook for 30 minutes, stirring several times to prevent meat from sticking. Season to taste with salt and pepper and serve piping hot with crusty French bread.

Buffet Glazed Corned Beef

Serves 12 to 16

Such a nice change from a ham, served with crusty pumpernickel rolls and tangy mustard.

1 6 pound corned beef brisket
10 peppercorns
3 bay leaves
$\frac{1}{2}$ cup brown sugar, firmly packed

1. Simmer corned beef with peppercorns and bay leaves in water to cover (starting with cold water) for 3 to $3\frac{1}{2}$ hours until ready to glaze.
2. Place meat, fat side up, on a broiler rack or ovenproof platter. Sprinkle brown sugar evenly on top. Broil until sugar just begins to bubble, watching carefully so as not to burn. Place meat on a carving board; slice thin across grain, then into serving-size pieces. Serve with mustard sauce.

MUSTARD SAUCE
Makes $2\frac{1}{2}$ cups
4 tablespoons butter
4 tablespoons flour
3 tablespoons dry mustard
1 tablespoon sugar
2 teaspoons salt
dash of cayenne pepper
2 cups milk
2 eggs
$\frac{1}{4}$ cup vinegar

1. Melt butter over low heat in a medium saucepan. Stir in flour, mustard, sugar, salt and cayenne pepper; cook, stirring constantly until mixture bubbles. Slowly stir in milk, continue cooking and stirring until sauce thickens and boils, 1 minute.
2. Beat eggs slightly in a small bowl, whisk in a generous $\frac{1}{2}$ cup of hot mixture and add back to the saucepan. Cook over medium heat, stirring constantly, 1 more minute. Remove from heat, stir in vinegar. Serve warm or chilled (store any leftovers in refrigerator). This sauce is also excellent with a holiday ham.

Applesaucey Burgers

Serves 6

Just a bit of Yankee frugality.

1 pound ground beef, turkey or chicken
1 small onion, minced
$\frac{1}{2}$ cup applesauce
2 tablespoons brown sugar
$\frac{1}{4}$ cup catsup
$\frac{1}{2}$ cup bread crumbs

Mix all of the ingredients thoroughly and form into 6 patties. Place on a broiling pan (lined with foil for a quick clean-up) and bake for 15 minutes at 400°. Serve each patty on a roll and garnish as desired.

Rosbief "A La Joan"

Serves 6

A Belgian favorite and a crowd pleaser with our friends for over 20 years.

4 tablespoons butter
1 3-pound eye of the round roast
salt and coarsely ground black pepper
2 tablespoons water
1 onion, quartered
1 carrot, sliced
1 cup hot beef broth
1 tablespoon cornstarch, dissolved in $\frac{1}{4}$ cup water

1. Spread 2 tablespoons butter on bottom of roasting pan. Season roast on both sides with salt and pepper, place in pan and spread remaining 2 tablespoons butter on top. Roast in a preheated 400° oven for 15 minutes. Add water and vegetables to pan, reduce heat, roast for 30 more minutes (for medium-rare, longer for more well done). Remove roast from pan and keep warm.
2. Add beef broth to pan, scraping up drippings from the bottom. Whisk in cornstarch/water mixture and cook until thickened. Reseason with salt and pepper to taste. Let roast rest for 10 minutes before serving, slice thinly and serve with vegetable gravy on the side.

Pilots' Chilled Marinated Sirloin

Serves 6 to 8

My mother was a charter member of this Mystic Seaport volunteer "gang" and has had this dish in her repertoire for over 20 years – encore – encore!

1 $2\frac{1}{2}$- to 3-pound sirloin steak, trimmed of excess fat, cut 2 inches thick

MARINADE:
1 large clove garlic
1 teaspoon salt
$\frac{1}{2}$ teaspoon freshly cracked pepper
$\frac{1}{2}$ teaspoon dry mustard
2 tablespoons blue cheese
2 teaspoons instant coffee granules
2 tablespoons dry vermouth
$\frac{1}{2}$ cup olive oil

Combine marinade ingredients and blend with a whisk until you have a smooth paste. Rub marinade on both sides of the steak and marinate, covered, in the refrigerator for 8 hours or overnight. Turn several times during the marinating process. Brush with remaining marinade up to the final turn of the steak. Grill steak to rare or desired doneness turning at least once. Let cool 30 minutes or more. Wrap in heavy aluminum foil and refrigerate overnight for a more pronounced flavor. Slice thinly and serve chilled over summer greens.

All-American Meatloaf

Serves 6

With a little inspiration from Martha Stewart, first served onboard "Skye," anchored off the New York Yacht Club in Newport. Make it ahead, wrap tightly in foil to reheat or slice and serve on a firm, hearty bread for sandwiches.

3 slices white bread
1 large carrot, peeled and cut into $\frac{1}{4}$-inch-thick rounds
1 stalk celery, cut into $\frac{1}{2}$-inch pieces
$\frac{1}{2}$ medium yellow onion, peeled and roughly chopped
2 cloves garlic, peeled and smashed
$\frac{1}{2}$ cup flat-leaf parsley leaves, loosely packed
$\frac{1}{2}$ cup plus 3 tablespoons catsup
$4\frac{1}{2}$ teaspoons dry mustard
8 ounces ground pork
8 ounces ground veal
8 ounces ground beef
2 large eggs, beaten
2 teaspoons salt
1 teaspoon freshly ground pepper
1 teaspoon Tabasco sauce, or to taste
$\frac{1}{2}$ teaspoon chopped rosemary, plus more for sprinkling
2 tablespoons dark brown sugar
1 tablespoon olive oil
1 small red onion, cut into $\frac{1}{4}$-inch-thick rings

1. Heat oven to 400°. Remove crusts from bread, and place slices in the bowl of a food processor. Process until fine crumbs form, about 10 seconds. Transfer bread crumbs to a large mixing bowl.

2. Place carrot, celery, yellow onion, garlic, and parsley in the bowl of the food processor. Process until vegetables have been minced, about 30 seconds, stopping to scrape down the sides of the bowl once or twice. Transfer vegetables to bowl with the bread crumbs.

3. Add $\frac{1}{2}$ cup catsup, 2 teaspoons dry mustard, pork, veal, beef, eggs, salt, pepper, Tabasco sauce, and rosemary. Using your hands, knead the ingredients until thoroughly combined, about 1 minute. The texture should be wet, but tight enough to hold a free-form shape.

4. Set a wire baking rack into an 11-by-17-inch baking pan. Cut a 5-by-11-inch piece of aluminum foil, and place over center of rack to prevent meatloaf from falling through. Using your hands, form an elongated loaf covering the foil

5. Place the remaining 3 tablespoons catsup, remaining $2\frac{1}{2}$ teaspoons mustard, and brown sugar in a bowl. Mix until smooth. Using a pastry brush, generously brush the glaze over loaf. Place oil in a medium saucepan set over high heat. When oil is smoking, add red onion. Cook, stirring occasionally, until onion is soft and golden in places. Add 3 tablespoons water, and cook, stirring, until most of the water has evaporated. Transfer onion to a bowl to cool slightly, then sprinkle onion over the meatloaf. Bake 30 minutes, then sprinkle rosemary needles on top. Continue baking loaf for 25 more minutes until onions are crisp and brown. Let rest for 10 minutes before slicing.

Onion Smothered Short Ribs

Serves 6

Serve with lots of buttered noodles or mashed potatoes

2 medium-size Vidalia or other sweet onions, peeled and thinly sliced
3 pounds beef short ribs
salt, pepper, and flour
1 clove garlic, minced
1 bay leaf, crumbled
$\frac{1}{2}$ teaspoon dry rosemary
3 whole cloves
1 14-ounce can beef broth
2 tablespoons red wine vinegar
1 teaspoon prepared mustard
parsley for garnish

1. Separate onion slices into rings. This should make about 4 cups. Sprinkle short ribs with salt and pepper and dredge in flour. Place about $\frac{1}{2}$ of the onions in an oiled, 13-by-9-inch casserole or Dutch oven. Place ribs on top. Arrange remaining onions over ribs. Add garlic, bay leaf, rosemary and cloves. Pour beef broth over all. Cover and bake at 350° for 3 to $3\frac{1}{2}$ hours or until meat is very tender when pierced with a fork.

2. Remove meat and onions to a deep platter or shallow baking pan. Keep warm. Pour cooking liquid into saucepan and add wine vinegar and mustard. Bring to a boil and cook until slightly reduced. Pour sauce over ribs and onions. Garnish with parsley.

Boathouse Butterflied Leg Of Lamb

Serves 6

With a savory marinade, grilled at its best over a woodfire. A Wamphaussac Point specialty.

1 3- to $3\frac{1}{2}$-pound leg of lamb, boned and butterflied
$\frac{1}{2}$ cup (8 tablespoons) butter, melted
3 cloves garlic, crushed
$\frac{1}{2}$ cup olive oil
$\frac{1}{2}$ cup gin
$\frac{1}{3}$ cup lemon juice
1 tablespoon Worcestershire sauce
$1\frac{1}{2}$ tablespoons EACH: rosemary, sage, thyme
2 bay leaves
2 tablespoons chopped fresh parsley

1. Place lamb in a large, shallow pan (not aluminum). Combine remaining ingredients and pour over meat. Cover and refrigerate at least 6 hours or up to 24 hours, turning occasionally.

2. Prepare a hot fire, preferably wood, but charcoal or gas is also fine. Cook lamb for 10 minutes per side, basting with the marinade. The exterior will be crusty and the interior should be pink. Let rest for 5 minutes before slicing thinly, on an angle.

Quaker House Leg Of Lamb With Roasted Garlic Sauce

Serves 8

A truly fine dinner from a truly fine chef (who just happens to be my brother, Rick).

6 whole heads garlic, unpeeled
2 tablespoons plus $\frac{1}{2}$ cup olive oil
2 tablespoons chopped fresh sage
2 tablespoons chopped fresh rosemary
2 tablespoons chopped fresh thyme
4 garlic cloves, peeled
1 teaspoon ground black pepper
1 teaspoon salt
1 5- to $5\frac{1}{4}$-pound bone-in leg of lamb
$1\frac{1}{2}$ cups dry red wine
1 cup canned beef broth

1. Preheat oven to 375°. Place garlic heads in 9-inch pie pan. Toss with 2 tablespoons oil. Cover with foil. Roast until tender, about 1 hour. Cool. Squeeze softened garlic from skins into bowl and mash. (Can be prepared 1 day ahead. Cover and chill.)

2. Place sage, rosemary and thyme in blender. Add 4 garlic cloves, 1 teaspoon pepper and 1 teaspoon salt and blend until garlic is chopped. Gradually pour in $\frac{1}{2}$ cup oil and blend until purée forms. Place lamb on rack in large roasting pan. Rub herb purée all over lamb. Let stand at room temperature at least 1 hour and up to 2 hours.

3. Preheat oven to 375°. Roast lamb until thermometer inserted into thickest part registers 135°, about $1\frac{1}{2}$ hours. Transfer to platter; let rest 20 minutes.

4. Meanwhile, pour juices from roasting pan into saucepan. Spoon off fat; discard. Add wine to roasting pan. Set over medium-high heat; bring to boil, scrapping up any browned bits. Pour wine mixture into saucepan with roasting juices. Whisk in broth and $\frac{1}{2}$ cup mashed garlic (reserve any remaining garlic for another use). Add any accumulated juices from platter. Boil sauce until reduced to $1\frac{3}{4}$ cups, whisking occasionally, about 10 minutes. Season with salt and pepper. Slice lamb and serve with sauce.

Barbecued Leg Of Lamb

Serves 6 to 8

From my sister-in-law, a great Washington hostess.

1 leg of lamb, boned and butterflied
1 cup oil
$\frac{1}{4}$ cup wine vinegar
$\frac{1}{4}$ cup soy sauce
2 cloves garlic, crushed
1 tablespoon salt
freshly ground black pepper

HOT BARBECUE SAUCE
2 teaspoons Tabasco sauce
$2\frac{1}{2}$ cups chili sauce
1 teaspoon minced chili pepper
$\frac{3}{4}$ cup oil
$\frac{1}{2}$ cup lemon juice
2 tablespoons tarragon vinegar
2 cups chopped onions
1 tablespoon brown sugar
1 bay leaf, crumbled
1 teaspoon dry mustard
1 teaspoon salt
$\frac{1}{2}$ cup water

1. In a large pan, combine oil, vinegar, soy sauce, garlic, salt and pepper. Marinate lamb for at least 2 hours, turning several times.

2. In a saucepan combine all ingredients for barbeque sauce, bring to a boil, reduce heat and simmer for 15 minutes. Remove lamb from marinade, brush with barbeque sauce and cook on a hot grill for 20 to 30 minutes on each side, basting with sauce.

Pig In A Haystack

Serves 6

My husband attributes the creation of this easy-to-make dish to what he calls "the Old Mother Hubbard" predicament. The cupboards were bare except for what wound up in this recipe. The "pig" is the bacon, the "haystack" the pasta.

2 tablespoons olive oil
$\frac{3}{4}$ pound mushrooms, sliced
1 6-ounce package Canadian bacon or ham, cut into matchstick-size strips
1 bunch scallions, chopped
2 tablespoons capers
1 pint light cream
$\frac{1}{2}$ cup milk
1 cup grated Parmesan cheese
$\frac{1}{4}$ cup pine nuts, toasted
additional grated Parmesan cheese
1 pound cooked fettuccine or vermicelli

1. Heat oil in a heavy skillet over medium heat, add mushrooms, sauté until tender and beginning to brown, about 10 minutes. Add bacon, scallions, capers; toss to combine.

2. Add the cream, milk and Parmesan cheese; simmer, stirring until cheese is melted. Add the cooked pasta and cook until mixture is heated through. Transfer to a large warm bowl, sprinkle with pine nuts and serve, passing additional Parmesan cheese.

Grilled Pork Tenderloins With Maple And Mustard

Serves 4

This marinade is also great with chicken.

2¾- to 1-pound pork tenderloins, trimmed
 of fat
⅓ cup maple syrup
2 tablespoons plus 2 teaspoons Dijon
 mustard
2 tablespoons olive oil
2 tablespoons chopped fresh rosemary
4 cloves garlic, minced
1 teaspoon crushed black peppercorns
3 tablespoons port wine
2 tablespoons balsamic vinegar
1 shallot, minced
salt to taste
rosemary sprigs for garnish

1. In a small bowl, whisk together maple syrup, 2 tablespoons of the mustard, 1 tablespoon of the oil, rosemary, garlic and peppercorns. Measure out 3 tablespoons and reserve for basting. Place tenderloins in a shallow glass pan and pour remaining marinade over them, turning to coat. Cover and marinate in the refrigerator for at least 30 minutes or up to 2 hours, turning several times.

2. Meanwhile, prepare a charcoal fire or preheat a gas grill. In a small bowl or a jar with a tight-fitting lid, combine port, vinegar, shallot, salt and remaining 2 teaspoons mustard and 1 tablespoon olive oil. Whisk or shake until blended.

3. Grill the tenderloins, turning several times and basting the browned sides with the reserved marinade. Cook for 12 to 16 minutes until the outside is brown and crispy but the inside has a trace of pink (150° if you have an instant-read meat thermometer). Transfer the tenderloins to a carving board and let rest for about 5 minutes. Pour any juices that have accumulated on the cutting board into the port vinaigrette. Carve into ½-inch slices and drizzle with the vinaigrette. Garnish with rosemary sprigs.

Lemon-Glazed Pork Roast

Serves 6

This makes a superb gravy to ladle over mashed potatoes

1 4- to 5-pound pork loin roast
2 tablespoons minced onion plus 2 onions quartered
1 teaspoon marjoram
1 teaspoon salt
$\frac{1}{4}$ teaspoon black pepper
3 tablespoons fresh squeezed lemon juice, pulp included (2 to 3 lemons)
12 carrots, peeled and cut into 3-inch pieces
2 tablespoons flour
1 cup milk

1. Rub meat with 2 tablespoons minced onion, marjoram, salt and pepper. Place roast, fat side up, in a roasting pan and roast at 325° oven, allowing 35 to 40 minutes per pound (interior temperature of 185°). During last hour, baste roast and brush with lemon juice and pulp. Return to oven and finish cooking for last hour.

2. In a medium saucepan, simmer carrots and remaining quartered onions for 10 minutes. Drain, reserving 1 cup of liquid to use in the gravy. Add vegetables to roasting pan during last half-hour, turning once in pan juices. Remove roast and vegetables to a platter and keep warm.

3. Pour off all but 2 tablespoons fat in pan, leaving any brown pan drippings. Mix in flour and whisk in reserved vegetable water and milk, scraping pan and cooking until thickened, about 4 to 5 minutes. Season gravy with salt and pepper and pour into your best gravy boat.

Sausage Leek Potato Hotpot

Serves 4

A hearty one-dish meal – serve with a loaf of crusty pumpernickel bread

3 tablespoons butter
4 leeks, cut in half and sliced (white part only)
1 large onion, finely chopped
$2\frac{1}{2}$ pounds potatoes, peeled and cut into 1-inch cubes
$\frac{1}{2}$ teaspoon thyme
salt and freshly ground black pepper
3 cups chicken stock
8 sausages, any variety: knockwurst, bratwurst, or kielbasa
2 tablespoons fresh chopped parsley

1. Heat the butter in a large saucepan and sauté the leeks and onion for 5 minutes until soft.

2. Add the potatoes, thyme, salt and pepper. Pour in the stock. Cover and simmer gently for 30 minutes. Add the sausages and simmer for 15 more minutes. Serve in large bowls, sprinkled with parsley.

Pork Chops In Ruby Wine Sauce

Serves 6

6 1-inch thick pork chops
salt and pepper
1 tablespoon olive oil
3 cloves garlic, minced
$1\frac{1}{2}$ cups dry red wine
$\frac{1}{2}$ cup Marsala wine
$\frac{1}{3}$ cup slivered almonds
2 teaspoons flour
grated rind of 1 lemon
2 tablespoons minced fresh parsley

1. Season the chops on both sides with salt and pepper. Add the oil to a large skillet and brown chops on both sides, about 5 minutes. Pour off all but 1 tablespoon of oil from pan, add garlic and cook for 3 to 4 minutes, being careful not to brown.

2. Add the red wine and Marsala wine, bring liquid to a boil and braise chops for 30 to 40 minutes, covered, until tender. Transfer the chops to a platter and keep warm.

3. Mix the nuts with the flour and whisk into the sauce; simmer until sauce is thickened. Pour the sauce over the chops, sprinkle with lemon rind and parsley.

Company Stuffed Pork Chops

Serves 6

6 pork chops, $1\frac{1}{4}$ to $1\frac{1}{2}$ inches thick
$1\frac{1}{2}$ cups fresh bread crumbs, toasted
1 apple, seeded and chopped, skin on
2 ounces sharp cheddar cheese, shredded
2 tablespoons golden raisins
2 tablespoons butter, melted
2 tablespoons orange juice
1 tablespoon chopped fresh parsley
$\frac{1}{4}$ teaspoon thyme
$\frac{1}{4}$ teaspoon salt
$\frac{1}{8}$ teaspoon cinnamon

1. Preheat oven to 325°. With a sharp knife, cut a pocket in each of the chops. Season inside with salt and pepper.

2. Toss together bread crumbs, apple, cheese and raisins. Combine melted butter, orange juice, parsley, thyme, salt, and cinnamon. Pour over the bread and fruit mixture; gently mix. Lightly stuff each chop and place in a shallow baking pan. Cover pan with foil and bake chops for 45 minutes. Uncover, baste with pan juices, and continue cooking for 20 minutes until golden brown.

Mr. Greenman's Pork Roll

Serves 4 to 6

While visiting Mystic Seaport, we toured the fine home of this shipping business-man and were astonished to see an old collection of Czechoslovakian glass at the main entry to the house. With us was Anka Jurkova, a Slovakian, who then reminisced about a favorite pork roll dish from the old country that might once have graced the captain's table.

1 2- to 2½-pound loin of pork
¾ pound ground pork
1 medium onion, finely chopped
4 cloves garlic, minced
½ teaspoon freshly ground black pepper
1 teaspoon salt
½ teaspoon paprika
1 tablespoon caraway seeds

1. In a bowl, combine ground pork, onion, garlic, black pepper and ½ teaspoon salt. Mix and chill, covered for 1 to 2 hours.

2. With a sharp knife, butterfly the pork, lengthwise, making a flat piece. Spread the stuffing down the middle, roll up, and secure the roast with string or metal poultry pins.

3. Season outside with remaining ½ teaspoon salt, black pepper and rub with caraway seeds. Place in a lightly greased baking pan and bake at 350° for 1 hour 15 minutes until browned, basting occasionally. Let stand 15 minutes before serving with your favorite potato dish.

Porcupine Meatballs

Serves 4

An old favorite from Girl Scout camp, I love to leave this with the babysitter on Saturday night. The kids love it.

1 pound ground lamb or beef
½ cup uncooked rice
½ teaspoon salt
2 tablespoons grated Parmesan cheese
¼ teaspoon pepper
1 to 2 tablespoons oil
1 cup chicken broth
½ cup catsup
½ teaspoon basil

1. Mix lamb or beef with rice, salt, pepper and Parmesan cheese. Shape into 1-inch balls. Brown meatballs in oil in a heavy skillet and pour off any extra fat.

2. Add chicken broth, catsup and basil. Cover and cook over medium-low heat for 40 to 50 minutes until rice is tender and "sticks out" like porcupine spines. Serve with toothpicks or piled on a crusty roll.

"It's A Picnic" Hungarian Goulash

Serves 6

The above cookbook was a wedding present in 1971, now threadbare, dog-eared and stained. It not only is used at home but goes with us on camping trips and to our cabin in Maine. This recipe is under the chapter, "Picnics Afloat" with the following note:

"The Hungarians don't have an ocean, but they do have a great ocean-going stew. Goulash is rich, savory, a picnic in a pot, and more than just paprika."

3 pounds boneless pork
  (loin or tenderloin)
4 tablespoons flour
1 to 2 teaspoons salt
2 teaspoons paprika, hot or sweet
  Hungarian
$\frac{1}{4}$ teaspoon freshly ground black pepper
4 tablespoons butter
1 onion, chopped
2 cloves garlic, minced
1 4-ounce can sliced mushrooms, drained
1 green pepper, chopped
1 15-ounce can tomatoes, chopped
$1\frac{1}{2}$ cups water
6 red potatoes, cut into 1-inch chunks
1 pound sauerkraut, rinsed and drained
1 pint sour cream
1 tablespoon caraway seeds
freshly chopped parsley

1. Cut pork into 1-inch cubes. Combine flour, salt, paprika and pepper in a bowl and dredge meat in mixture.

2. Melt butter in a heavy Dutch oven and brown meat on both sides. Add the onion and garlic, sauté until transparent. Add mushrooms, green pepper, tomatoes and water. Cover and simmer 15 minutes, adding more water if necessary.

3. Add potatoes and simmer for 30 minutes or until pork is fork tender. Add the sauerkraut and sour cream. Sprinkle with caraway seeds, cover and bake at 350° for $\frac{1}{2}$ hour. Garnish with parsley sprigs and serve piping hot.

NOTE:
If you are preparing this on a boat and have no oven, finish by adding sauerkraut and caraway seeds and simmer, covered for $\frac{1}{2}$ hour. Stir in sour cream as soon as it is well heated through.

Joan's Pot Luck Jambalaya

Serves 8 to 10

After years of refining, this dish travels to many dinner get-togethers. Never any leftovers, everyone seems to love it.

3 tablespoons olive oil
$1\frac{1}{2}$ to 2 pounds boneless chicken breasts, cut into 1-inch pieces
1 to $1\frac{1}{2}$ pounds Andouille sausage, sliced (you may substitute kielbasa, smoked sausage or cooked hot Italian sausage)
1 cup diced smoked ham
1 large green pepper, chopped
1 large red pepper, chopped
1 large onion, chopped
1 14-ounce can tomatoes, chopped, with liquid
2 cups white rice
2 15-ounce cans chicken broth
2 bay leaves, crushed
3 tablespoons Cajun seasoning (Paul Prudholme or Kitchen Magic)
$1\frac{1}{2}$ pounds medium shrimp, cooked and peeled
freshly chopped parsley

1. Heat oil in a large pot or Dutch oven. Add chicken, sausage and ham, cook until browned, about 8 minutes. Add peppers and onion, sauté mixture for 5 minutes.

2. Add all of remaining ingredients, except shrimp and fresh parsley. Bring to a boil, cover, and simmer until rice is done, about 30 minutes. Add cooked shrimp just before serving and sprinkle with lots of chopped parsley.

Country Noodle Casserole

Serves 12 to 14

Great for a young crowd – we like to serve this with a big salad when we get together with other families after a day on the slopes.

$1\frac{1}{2}$ pounds lean sausage, browned, drained, and crumbled
1 1-pound package vermicelli or egg noodles, cooked and drained
3 cups cottage cheese
3 cups sour cream
3 cloves garlic, finely minced
2 medium onions, finely minced
2 tablespoons Worcestershire sauce
1 teaspoon salt
1 tablespoon horseradish
Tabasco sauce to taste
$\frac{1}{3}$ cup fresh parsley, chopped
1 cup grated Parmesan cheese

1. Combine all ingredients, except Parmesan cheese, in a large mixing bowl and toss together with 2 forks until mixed. Turn into a buttered, large, shallow casserole. Cover with foil and bake in a 350° oven for 40 minutes.

2. Remove cover, sprinkle with cheese, return to oven and bake until golden brown. Serve with additional grated cheese on the side.

Favorite Macaroni And Cheese Bake

Serves 6

1 8-ounce package elbow macaroni
1 small onion, finely chopped
2 tablespoons butter
2 tablespoons flour
$1\frac{1}{2}$ teaspoons dry mustard
1 teaspoon salt
$\frac{1}{4}$ teaspoon pepper
2 teaspoons Worcestershire sauce
$1\frac{3}{4}$ cups milk
8 ounces grated cheddar cheese
  (or any combination, Swiss, Parmesan)
1 4-ounce can sliced mushrooms, not drained
2 pimentos, diced
2 ripe tomatoes, cut into wedges

1. Cook macaroni in boiling, salted water, drain. While macaroni cooks, sauté onion lightly in butter in medium-size skillet. Stir in flour, mustard, salt, pepper and Worcestershire sauce; cook, stirring until mixture bubbles. Whisk in the milk and continue cooking until sauce thickens. Stir in the cheese (reserving $\frac{1}{2}$ cup for the top).

2. Combine drained macaroni, mushrooms, and pimentos. Mix with cheese sauce and pour into a buttered 8-cup baking pan. Arrange tomato wedges around the edges, poking them gently into the macaroni. Sprinkle with remaining grated cheese and bake in a 350° oven for 30 minutes until bubbly.

Harvest Stuffed Sugar Pumpkins

Serves 6 to 8
An old recipe from my father's family, a real fall treat drizzled with maple syrup.

2 tablespoons butter
$1\frac{1}{2}$ pounds ground pork
$1\frac{1}{2}$ pounds ground beef
2 medium onions, diced
5 medium potatoes, cooked and coarsely mashed
poultry seasoning (Bell's)
salt and pepper
1 sugar pumpkin, 5 to 6 pounds
3 strips bacon

1. Melt butter in a large skillet, and brown pork, beef and onions until meat is no longer pink, about 10 minutes. Mix in mashed potatoes and liberally season with poultry seasoning (about half a box or 3 to 4 tablespoons), salt and pepper.

2. Cut top off pumpkin and scoop out the seeds. Stuff pumpkin with meat mixture and put the lid back on. Drape bacon over the top and bake at 375° for 1 hour to 1 hour and 15 minutes, depending on the size of the pumpkin. You can test for doneness with a metal skewer or fork, inserted in the thickest part. The pumpkin should be soft. When you serve, scoop some of the pumpkin and the meat onto each plate.

Double Cheese Zucchini Lasagne

Serves 8

Do you have an over-productive zucchini patch? This recipe can help.

2 to 3 medium-size zucchini (2 quarts), grated
salt
3 chopped onions
2 tablespoons olive oil
1 18-ounce can tomatoes, or about 1 quart
  fresh tomato purée
1 tablespoon fresh oregano
$\frac{1}{2}$ teaspoon thyme
$\frac{1}{2}$ teaspoon rosemary, crushed
2 bay leaves
$\frac{1}{4}$ cup chopped parsley
black pepper
4 cloves garlic, minced
$2\frac{1}{2}$ cups grated Swiss cheese
6 ounces Feta cheese, crumbled
lasagne noodles, cooked and drained

1. Place the grated zucchini in a colander in the sink, salt it lightly and let it sit. In a large skillet, sauté the onions in the olive oil until transparent. Add the tomatoes, herbs, salt, pepper, and garlic. Simmer for 20 minutes, stirring occasionally. Remove bay leaves.

2. With a paper towel, press any excess moisture out of the zucchini. Butter a 9-by-13-inch baking pan. Layer as follows: a third of the sauce, a quarter of the noodles, half the zucchini, half the Feta, a quarter of the noodles, and then repeat, finishing with the remaining sauce. Sprinkle Swiss cheese on top and bake for 45 minutes. Let stand 5 minutes before cutting.

Baked Pasta Florentine

Serves 8 to 10

Developed for some vegetarian friends – a great way to use up fresh garden vegetables.

1 pound penne, cooked and drained
3 tablespoons olive oil
4 cloves garlic, minced
1 small onion, chopped
1 pound mushrooms, sliced
1 pound spinach, coarsely chopped
3 large tomatoes, cubed
1 pound Ricotta cheese, skim or whole milk
8 ounces shredded Mozzarella cheese
$\frac{1}{2}$ cup grated Parmesan cheese,
  plus additional cheese to sprinkle on top

1. Add oil to a large skillet and sauté garlic and onion for 6 to 8 minutes until soft. Add mushrooms, spinach and tomatoes and cook for about 20 minutes. Remove from heat and lightly mix in the Ricotta, Parmesan and Mozzarella cheeses.

2. In a well-greased 9-by-13-inch baking pan, layer pasta with vegetables. Sprinkle with additional Parmesan and bake in a 350° oven for 25 to 30 minutes until heated through.

Confetti Pepper And Cheese Strata

Serves 6

1 medium onion, thinly sliced
2 cloves garlic, minced
$1\frac{1}{2}$ teaspoons olive oil
1 large green bell pepper, sliced thin
1 large yellow bell pepper, sliced thin
12 slices thin, white sandwich bread, cut
    into $\frac{3}{4}$-inch cubes (about 5 cups)
$\frac{1}{2}$ cup freshly grated Parmesan cheese
4 large eggs
4 egg whites
$2\frac{1}{2}$ cups milk
$\frac{1}{2}$ cup fresh parsley leaves, chopped
$\frac{1}{2}$ teaspoon salt
Tabasco sauce to taste

1. In a large nonstick skillet, cook onion
    and garlic in oil over medium heat,
    stirring, until onion is golden. Add bell
    peppers and cook for 5 minutes until
    peppers are tender and any liquid in
    pan is evaporated.

2. Spread half of mixture and half of
    bread evenly in a $2\frac{1}{2}$-quart baking pan
    (13-by-9-by-2 inches) that has been
    sprayed with nonstick cooking spray.
    Sprinkle with half of Parmesan ($\frac{1}{4}$ cup)
    cheese, and top with remaining bread
    and vegetables.

3. In a bowl, whisk together whole eggs,
    whites, milk, parsley, salt, and Tabasco
    sauce to taste. Pour evenly over bread
    and chill strata, covered at least 3
    hours or up to 12. Preheat oven to
    375° and let strata sit at room
    temperature for 20 minutes. Sprinkle
    remaining $\frac{1}{4}$ cup Parmesan cheese on
    top and bake 45 to 55 minutes, or
    until puffed and golden brown around
    the edges. Serve topped with your
    favorite salsa or chopped fresh
    tomato.

Lobster Fettuccini With Chives

Serves 6 to 8 as an entrée or first course

$1\frac{1}{2}$ pounds cooked lobster meat,
    cut into bite-size pieces
1 pound fettuccini or similar pasta,
    cooked and drained
4 tablespoons olive oil
4 tablespoons butter
4 cloves garlic, minced
crushed red pepper flakes to taste
2 tablespoons fresh chopped chives
2 tablespoons fresh chopped parsley
salt and pepper to taste

1. Heat oil in a large skillet and sauté but-
    ter, garlic and hot pepper flakes until
    garlic is light brown. Lower heat and
    add the lobster meat, chives, and parsley.
    Season with salt and pepper.

2. Toss the drained pasta with the lobster,
    mix well and serve immediately on hot
    plates. Garnish each serving with a fresh
    chive blossom if they are available.

Mushroom, Leek, And Sausage Pie

Serves 4 to 6

I make this ahead and take it along when we are out on our boat – with a salad, it is a nice dinner on a hot summer night. No clean up!

1 9-inch pie crust
2 large leeks
4 tablespoons butter
$\frac{3}{4}$ pound mushrooms, sliced
3 eggs, lightly beaten
$\frac{3}{4}$ cup half-and-half
1 teaspoon salt
$\frac{1}{2}$ teaspoon dill
freshly ground black pepper to taste
$\frac{1}{2}$ pound kielbasa, thinly sliced

1. Preheat oven to 350°. Bake pie crust for 8 minutes (prick with a fork in several places) and remove from oven.

2. Cut roots and tops off the leeks, leaving 2 inches of the green leaves. Wash thoroughly and cut into $\frac{1}{2}$-inch rings. Drain well.

3. Melt butter in a medium skillet, add leeks and mushrooms and cook for 5 minutes until soft. Combine eggs, half-and-half, salt and pepper, mixing well.

4. Arrange leeks, mushrooms and kielbasa in partially baked pie shell and pour egg mixture over all. Bake for 30 minutes until top is browned and center is set. Cool for 15 minutes before slicing or serve at room temperature.

Yankee Lobster Thermidor

Serves 4

A real special occasion dinner.

3 $1\frac{1}{4}$-pound lobsters, boiled
2 tablespoons butter
2 tablespoons flour
$\frac{1}{2}$ teaspoon salt
$1\frac{1}{2}$ teaspoons dry mustard
1 teaspoon freshly chopped parsley
dash cayenne pepper
1 cup cream or half-and-half
1 4-ounce can mushrooms, stems and
   pieces, drained
$\frac{1}{3}$ cup Parmesan cheese
paprika

1. Remove meat from lobsters, cut into $\frac{1}{2}$-inch chunks. Melt butter in a medium saucepan, add flour, salt, mustard, parsley, and cayenne pepper. Gradually whisk in flour and cook until sauce is thick and smooth, stirring constantly.

2. Add lobster and mushrooms to sauce and pour into a lightly buttered $1\frac{1}{2}$-quart casserole. Top with cheese, sprinkle with paprika and bake at 400° for 12 to 15 minutes or until golden brown.

Sautéed Lobster And Tagliatelle

Serves 2

With thanks to a pair of great chefs from One South Café.

2 $1\frac{1}{2}$-pound lobsters
$\frac{1}{4}$ cup white wine for steaming
$\frac{1}{4}$ cup water for steaming
1 tablespoon olive oil
1 clove garlic, chopped
2 tablespoons shallots, chopped
2 ripe plum tomatoes, seeded and julienne
3 scallions, chopped
3 tablespoons butter
fresh parsley and basil, chopped
salt and pepper to taste
$\frac{1}{2}$ pound tagliatelle, cooked al dente

1. Steam the lobsters in the wine and water until fully cooked. Cool and remove the meat from the shells. Save the shells for garnish. Reserve cooking liquid. Cut meat into bite-size pieces.

2. Heat 1 tablespoon olive oil in skillet. Add lobster meat and shallots, sauté for 1 minute. Add garlic and sauté 30 seconds more. Add reserved cooking liquid, plum tomatoes and scallions. Toss with tagliatelle.

3. Add butter and toss again, season with salt and pepper to taste. Garnish with fresh chopped parsley and basil for garnish.

Grilled Lobster Sandwich

Serves 2

A special occasion alternative to a hot lobster roll; a specialty at Skipper's Dock Restaurant in Stonington.

6 to 8 ounces lobster meat, cooked and cut into $\frac{1}{2}$-inch pieces (one $1\frac{1}{2}$ to $1\frac{3}{4}$ pound lobster or 2 small culls)
4 slices white bread, buttered
4 slices American or Swiss cheese
1 tablespoon butter
1 tablespoon sherry
salt and pepper
parsley sprigs

1. Place 2 slices of bread, buttered side down, in a skillet. Top with cheese and other 2 bread slices, as with a grilled cheese sandwich.

2. In a small skillet, melt the butter with the sherry and warm gently for 1 minute. Add the lobster meat and toss.

3. Grill sandwiches on one side until nicely browned and turn. Gently open sandwich and divide sherried lobster meat evenly. Recover sandwich and cook until bottom is browned. Remove to warm plates; cut in half diagonally and garnish with parsley sprigs.

Lobster Royale, Toll House

Serves 10

The once famous Toll House had stood for over 240 years and originally served as a stopping spot for stagecoach travelers. It was here, halfway between Boston and New Bedford, that tolls were paid and horses changed. My in-laws, Ernest and Frances Philbrick, met there while working, as a chef and waitress, back in the 1930s. Unfortunately, the Toll House is no longer, fallen victim to a long ago fire and condominium development.

10 whole 1-pound boiled lobsters
sauce for lobster (below)

Split each lobster from head to tail and lay open. Remove claw meat, keeping it whole. Discard contents of body cavity except liver tomalley. Leave tail meat intact, but remove intestinal tract. Place claw meat in body cavity to fill well. Cover with following sauce. Be sure that both body and tail meat are sufficiently covered for sauce to run down under meat and fill cavity so as to moisten throughout. Place lobsters close together in baking pan, so as to stand upright. Brown quickly in 450° oven and serve immediately. (If prepared ahead and sauce is cold, reheat in 375° oven. Do not cook long enough for sauce to boil out.)

SAUCE FOR LOBSTER
8 tablespoons ($\frac{1}{2}$ cup) butter, melted
$\frac{2}{3}$ cups flour
1 teaspoon prepared mustard
$\frac{1}{4}$ cup vinegar
$\frac{1}{4}$ teaspoon Worcestershire sauce
juice of $\frac{1}{4}$ lemon
1 cup grated cheese
3 cups hot milk
1 cup white wine
1 cup sliced mushrooms, sautéed in butter
1 cup soft bread crumbs

Blend together butter, flour, mustard, vinegar, Worcestershire sauce, lemon juice and grated cheese. Slowly stir in hot milk. Continue stirring until thickened. Add wine, mushrooms and bread crumbs.

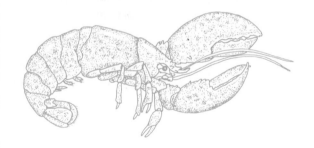

Maple-Glazed Roasted Salmon

Serves 6

1 $2\frac{1}{2}$-pound salmon fillet
$\frac{1}{4}$ cup grated peeled fresh ginger
$\frac{1}{4}$ cup rice vinegar or white wine vinegar
$\frac{1}{4}$ cup maple syrup
6 shallots, halved lengthwise
$\frac{1}{2}$ teaspoon salt
$\frac{1}{4}$ teaspoon black pepper
2 tablespoons maple syrup, divided
chopped parsley

1. Preheat oven to 450°. Combine ginger, vinegar and $\frac{1}{4}$ cup maple syrup in bottom of a large platter. Add fish, skin side up, to ginger mixture. Cover and marinate in refrigerator 20 minutes. Remove fish from marinade; pat dry with paper towel to remove excess marinade.

2. Place a baking sheet in oven for 5 minutes. Place shallots and fish, skin side down, on baking sheet; sprinkle with salt and pepper. Brush fish with 1 tablespoon syrup. Bake at 450° for 10 minutes. Brush again with remaining tablespoon of syrup; bake an additional 7 minutes or until fish flakes easily when tested with a fork. Sprinkle with parsley.

Linguini With Smoked Salmon Cream

Serves 4

Every Christmas our family orders a fine, smoked salmon from Sullivan's Harbor in Maine. I developed this recipe to use the "leftover" pieces.

1 pound linguini
2 tablespoons butter, unsalted
1 small onion, chopped
8 medium mushrooms, sliced
$\frac{1}{4}$ cup white wine (optional)
$\frac{3}{4}$ cup light cream
$\frac{1}{3}$ to $\frac{1}{2}$ pound smoked salmon,
  cut into strips
freshly ground black pepper
2 tablespoons freshly chopped parsley
  or dill

1. Cook linguini according to directions, al dente. While pasta is cooking, melt butter in a large sauté pan. Cook onion over medium heat until soft but not brown, about 5 minutes. Add mushrooms and sauté until soft.

2. Add white wine to pan and stir. Add cream and heat over low heat; do not let mixture boil. Gently mix in salmon; drain pasta and add to pan. Mix in parsley, season with black pepper before serving.

Balsamic-Glazed Scallops

Serves 4

2 cups water
1 tablespoon balsamic vinegar
$\frac{1}{4}$ teaspoon salt
1 cup uncooked long-grain rice
1 tablespoon olive oil
$1\frac{1}{2}$ pounds sea scallops
$\frac{1}{4}$ cup balsamic vinegar
2 tablespoons honey
1 teaspoon dried marjoram
chopped fresh chives with blossom
  if possible

1. Combine first 3 ingredients in a medium saucepan; bring to a boil. Add rice, cover, reduce heat, and simmer 20 minutes or until rice is tender and liquid is absorbed. Remove from heat; set aside (do not uncover rice).

2. Heat oil in a large nonstick skillet over medium-high heat until hot. Add scallops; sauté 5 minutes. Remove scallops from skillet; set aside.

3. Add $\frac{1}{4}$ cup vinegar, honey, and marjoram to skillet; bring to a boil. Reduce heat to medium; cook 3 minutes. Return scallops to skillet; cook 2 minutes or until thoroughly heated. Serve scallops and sauce over rice. Garnish with chives.

Champagne Poached Salmon

Serves 12

1 5 to 6 pound salmon, head removed
1 bottle champagne
1 onion, sliced
1 lemon, sliced
butter, about 4 tablespoons
parsley sprigs

1. Using a large, shallow baker or jellyroll pan, line with enough heavy-duty foil, overlapping the edges, to make a tent. Generously butter the foil.

2. Place half of sliced onion and lemon on bottom of pan. Fill cavity of fish with remaining onion and lemon. Butter top of fish and place in pan.

3. Pour whole bottle of champagne over salmon and make a tight tent with the foil, insert a meat thermometer in the thickest part of the fish and crimp shut (make sure foil is secure so there won't be any leaks).

4. Bake in a 350° oven for 20 minutes per pound or until fish reaches an internal temperature of 165°. Remove pan from oven and pull back foil. After the salmon has cooled, scrape the skin from the top of fish and carefully remove to a lettuce-lined platter and garnish with parsley sprigs. Serve with dill sauce made by combining sour cream or mayonnaise with fresh chopped dill and lemon juice. This may be served warm or chilled with toast points or party rye bread slices.

Simple Salmon

Serves 4

When a friend from Norway was visiting, she showed me the easiest possible way to prepare and enjoy salmon fillets.

Fill a large frying pan about $\frac{3}{4}$ full of water. Add some dill (fresh or dried) and some salt. Bring to a boil. Add a 1-$\frac{1}{2}$ pound salmon fillet (water should cover the fish). Cover the pan, and <u>turn off the heat</u>. Set the timer for 10 minutes. At the end of that time, the fish should be cooked perfectly, and still be moist. If it is a particularly thick piece, it may need more time, with low heat. Serve immediately. You may serve with a sauce, but it doesn't need it. The traditional Norwegian way is to serve it with boiled potatoes, pickles, and cucumbers. (Recipe follows.)

SCANDINAVIAN CUCUMBERS
This is my mother's recipe, and it was part of the Christmas Eve smorgasbord every year.

1 or 2 cucumbers
salt
water, divided use
$\frac{1}{3}$ cup vinegar
2 tablespoons sugar

1. Peel cucumbers, then run a fork down the length, on all sides, for decoration. Slice very thin. Put in salted water for a few hours, or even overnight.

2. Combine 1 cup water with vinegar and sugar. (If too vinegary, add a little [very little] more water.)

3. Drain and rinse cucumbers. Combine with the sugar, vinegar and water syrup. Keep them in the syrup for 2 to 3 hours before serving.

**"Thank you, good selectman,
For your salmon.
A finer fish or fatter
Never swam a river
Nor smoked on any platter"**
A New England traveller

Maple Glazed Grilled Salmon

Serves 4

4 1-inch thick salmon steaks, about
  6 ounces each
$\frac{1}{3}$ cup maple syrup
3 tablespoons cider vinegar
1 tablespoon Dijon mustard
1 tablespoon soy sauce
1 tablespoon vegetable oil
2 cloves garlic, finely chopped
$\frac{1}{4}$ teaspoon freshly ground black pepper

1. In a small bowl, whisk together syrup, vinegar, mustard, soy sauce, vegetable oil, garlic and pepper. Put salmon steaks in a shallow baking pan in a single layer and add the maple marinade, turning to coat. Cover with plastic wrap and refrigerate for about 1 hour, turning once.

2. Prepare grill. Remove the salmon steaks to a plate, shaking off excess marinade. Transfer the marinade to a medium-size saucepan and bring to a boil; reduce heat to low and simmer, stirring occasionally, until the marinade is thick and has reduced to $\frac{1}{4}$ cup, about 5 minutes. (If the glaze gets too thick, thin it with a little water.)

3. Oil the grill rack. Brush one side of the salmon with the maple glaze and grill, with the glazed side towards the heat, for about 5 minutes. Brush the unglazed side and turn the fish over.

Grill for about 5 minutes more, or until the fish is cooked in the center.

Special Request Scalloped Oysters

Serves 4

1 cup milk cracker crumbs
1 pint oysters, drained, reserve juice
6 tablespoons cream
$\frac{1}{2}$ cup ($\frac{1}{4}$ pound) melted butter

Optional:
$\frac{1}{2}$ cup chopped celery
$\frac{1}{2}$ cup chopped green pepper
salt and pepper

1. Plan to use 2 layers of oysters and 3 layers of crumbs. In a buttered 2-quart baking pan, start with a layer of cracker crumbs. Alternate layers with oysters and crumbs seasoning each layer with salt and pepper; sprinkling with celery and green pepper if desired.

2. Pour cream and oyster juice on top of oysters before the final layer of crumbs. The top layer should be dry. Drizzle melted butter on top and bake at 400° for 20 minutes until browned.

Baked Scallops Supreme

Serves 4

From the kitchen of a gracious Noank hostess.

1 pound scallops, cut in half if large
4 tablespoons butter
1 medium onion, finely diced
2 stalks celery, chopped
1 clove garlic, minced
1 tablespoon parsley
$\frac{1}{4}$ cup cracker crumbs
1 tablespoon flour
$\frac{1}{4}$ cup milk
$\frac{1}{4}$ cup vodka
pinch of paprika
salt and pepper to taste
$\frac{1}{3}$ cup shredded Monterey Jack cheese

Preheat oven to 425°.

1. Melt 3 tablespoons butter in a medium pan, add onion, celery and garlic. Sauté for 4 to 5 minutes until vegetables are tender. Lightly mix in parsley, cracker crumbs, and scallops. Turn into a lightly buttered 2-quart baking pan.

2. Melt remaining tablespoon of butter, blend in flour and paprika. Whisk in milk, cook until thickened and remove from heat. Stir in vodka and season with paprika and salt and pepper. Pour over scallop mixture, sprinkle cheese on top and bake for 12 to 15 minutes until nicely browned.

Scallops In Creamy Herb Sauce

Serves 2

Dress this up spooned into patty shells or serve over your favorite pasta or rice.

1 pound scallops, sea or bay,
   rinsed and drained
$\frac{2}{3}$ cup white wine
$\frac{1}{3}$ cup water
pinch of salt
$\frac{1}{4}$ teaspoon freshly ground black pepper
2 tablespoons butter
1 tablespoon flour
$\frac{1}{2}$ teaspoon EACH: fresh snipped
   tarragon, chives, parsley and dill
$\frac{2}{3}$ cup half-and-half
paprika

1. If using large scallops, cut in half. Bring wine, water, salt and pepper to a medium-high simmer. Add scallops and cook for 4 to 6 minutes until tender. Remove with a slotted spoon and reserve liquid.

2. Melt butter in saucepan, blend in flour to make a smooth paste and slowly whisk in reserved liquid, cooking until sauce is smooth. Add herbs, blend in cream and simmer, stirring for 2 to 3 minutes. Add scallops, heat through, and serve hot, sprinkled with a little paprika.

Skewered Shrimp With Apricot-Curry Glaze

Serves 6

A quick and easy dinner or party appetizer.

1½ pounds large shrimp, uncooked, peeled, deveined, tails on
3 tablespoons olive oil
3 tablespoons apricot preserves
1½ tablespoons white wine vinegar
1 tablespoon Dijon mustard
3 teaspoons curry powder
4 cloves garlic, minced
salt and hot red pepper flakes to taste
shredded iceberg lettuce
lemon wedges
12 10-inch bamboo skewers

1. Whisk together oil, preserves, vinegar, mustard, curry powder, garlic, salt and pepper to taste. Add shrimp, toss to coat and refrigerate at least 2 hours. Meanwhile, soak bamboo skewers in water for 30 minutes.

2. Preheat broiler or prepare a grill. Thread shrimp on skewers, dividing equally. Broil shrimp about 6 inches from heat or cook on a hot fire until cooked through, about 3 minutes per side. Place shredded lettuce on platter; arrange shrimp skewers on top and garnish with lemon wedges.

1-2-3 Garlicky Baked Shrimp

Serves 4

1½ pounds medium shrimp, peeled and deveined
½ cup dry fresh bread crumbs
3 tablespoons finely chopped fresh parsley
1 teaspoon grated lemon rind
¼ teaspoon salt
3 cloves garlic, minced
2 tablespoons fresh lemon juice
4 teaspoons olive oil
Tabasco sauce

1. Combine the bread crumbs, parsley, lemon rind, salt, garlic, and lemon juice. Add the olive oil and a few dashes of Tabasco sauce to taste; mix lightly.

2. Spray 4 individual gratin dishes with nonstick cooking spray. Divide shrimp evenly among dishes. Sprinkle bread crumbs over the shrimp and bake in a 400° oven for 12 to 14 minutes or until shrimp are done and bread crumbs are lightly browned.

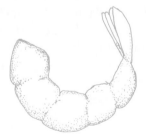

Kennebunk Crab Cakes

Makes 6 to 8 2-inch crab cakes

4 tablespoons butter
$\frac{1}{2}$ medium red pepper, diced
$\frac{1}{2}$ medium onion, diced
$\frac{3}{4}$ cup mayonnaise
3 eggs, lightly beaten
4 slices white bread, torn into small
   crumbs
2 tablespoons Old Bay Seasoning
1 tablespoon dry mustard
1 teaspoon dry basil
1 teaspoon dry oregano
2 tablespoons chopped fresh parsley
1 tablespoon chopped fresh chives
1 pound lump crabmeat
salt and pepper to taste

1. In a small saucepan, sauté pepper and onion in 2 tablespoons butter until soft. In a mixing bowl, mix mayonnaise, eggs, bread crumbs, and seasonings; add sautéed vegetables.

2. Gently fold in the crabmeat being careful to keep the lumps intact as much as possible; season with salt and pepper. Shape into 2-inch patties and refrigerate for at least one hour. Sauté in remaining 2 tablespoons butter over medium-high heat until brown on both sides. Serve with lemon wedges.

Crabmeat Quiche Tasi

Serves 6

An always requested weekend meal after spending the day with friends at favorite spots along the Connecticut shore.

1 9-inch prepared frozen piecrust
8 ounces crabmeat
1 cup finely chopped celery
2 tablespoons chopped onion
2 tablespoons chopped green pepper
2 eggs, beaten
1 cup mayonnaise
$\frac{1}{2}$ cup bread crumbs
   (reserve 2 tablespoons)
$\frac{1}{2}$ cup cheddar cheese, shredded
   (reserve 2 tablespoons)
$\frac{1}{4}$ teaspoon salt
black pepper
1 tablespoon lemon juice

1. Combine crabmeat, celery, onion, green pepper, eggs, mayonnaise, bread crumbs, cheddar cheese, salt, pepper, and lemon juice. Pour into prepared frozen piecrust.

2. Sprinkle top with reserved 2 tablespoons bread crumbs and cheese. Bake at 400° for 25 minutes until center is set and top is golden brown. Serve hot with a green salad.

Crispy Camden Crab Cakes

Serves 4

1 pound lump crabmeat
1 egg, beaten
$\frac{3}{4}$ cup dry bread crumbs
$\frac{1}{4}$ cup mayonnaise
$\frac{1}{4}$ cup chopped scallions
1 teaspoon grated lemon zest
$\frac{1}{4}$ teaspoon dried tarragon
$\frac{1}{4}$ teaspoon salt
black pepper
2 tablespoons fresh chopped parsley
1 to 2 tablespoons vegetable oil

1. Carefully pick over crabmeat, removing any shell. In a mixing bowl, combine egg, $\frac{1}{4}$ cup bread crumbs, mayonnaise, scallions, lemon zest, tarragon, salt, black pepper to taste and parsley. Add crabmeat and gently mix until well blended.

2. Form mixture into 8 $2\frac{1}{2}$-inch patties. Place remaining $\frac{1}{2}$ cup bread crumbs on a plate and dredge patties in crumbs. If not using right away, cover and refrigerate.

3. In a skillet over medium-high heat, heat oil until hot. Add crab cakes and cook until crisp and golden, turning once and adding a bit more oil as needed. Drain crab cakes and serve with Caper Sauce Tartar.

CAPER SAUCE TARTAR
Makes $1\frac{1}{2}$ cups

1 cup mayonnaise
1 tablespoon lemon juice
2 tablespoons chopped fresh parsley
2 tablespoons finely chopped gherkins
1 tablespoon chopped red onion
2 tablespoons capers
salt and black pepper

Combine all ingredients, seasoning with salt and pepper to taste. Chill for several hours or best overnight. This is also great with Fish & Chips or any other fried seafood.

Mom's Famous Crab Cakes

Makes 6 to 8 cakes

This recipe is submitted by Mom's oldest son in her honor. It is always a special treat when the four brothers and two sisters get together, and Mom makes a mound of crab cakes. On one occasion, Mom must have been very tired, and, in her mind, she mixed the recipe for crab cakes with the recipe for barbecue and accidentally added Liquid Smoke to the mixture. (Not recommended!) No one said a word for fear that she would not make our special crab cakes ever again! Now it has become a family memory, "Remember the time Mom put Liquid Smoke in the crab cakes?"

1 pound crabmeat (Blackfin or regular)
2 slices bread, crumbled
1 egg
4 ounces (4 tablespoons) butter or
   margarine, melted
2 to 3 dashes Worcestershire sauce
1 tablespoon cream-style mustard
2 tablespoons Miracle Whip salad dressing
$\frac{1}{2}$ teaspoon salt
Tabasco sauce
$\frac{1}{2}$ cup chopped fresh parsley
bacon fat (the best) or oil for frying the patties

1. In a large bowl, flake the crabmeat, discarding any shell pieces.
2. Add all the ingredients, and mix gently, leaving lumps of crabmeat.
3. Shape the mixture into round patties.
4. Melt bacon fat for frying patties in large skillet. (Cast iron if available.)
5. Place patties in skillet; brown on both sides being careful not to overcook.

Braised Cod With Golden Onions

Serves 4

4 6-ounce cod fillets
3 tablespoons butter
2 large onions, thinly sliced
$\frac{1}{2}$ teaspoon dried thyme
2 bay leaves
$\frac{2}{3}$ cup whipping cream
$\frac{1}{4}$ cup dry white wine
2 tablespoons chopped fresh chives

1. Melt butter in heavy, medium skillet, add onion and sauté until golden and soft, about 12 minutes. Add thyme and bay leaf and cook for 1 minute until mixture is fragrant.
2. Season cod fillets with salt and pepper and place on top of onions. Add cream and white wine and swirl skillet to blend liquids. Bring to a simmer, reduce heat and cover. Cook cod fillets until just cooked through, about 7 minutes.
3. Using a spatula, remove cod to a warm platter. Boil sauce until slightly thickened, about 3 minutes. Season to taste with salt and pepper, discard bay leaves and spoon sauce over fish. Garnish with chopped chives.

"Unfishy" Sweet Bluefish

Serves 6 to 8
1 large bluefish fillet, 3 to 4 pounds
1 lemon
1 orange
1 peach, sliced
1 12-ounce jar peach or apricot preserve

1. Rinse fillet and pat dry. Place fillet, skin side down, on a large sheet of heavy duty aluminum foil or double sheet of regular foil. Cut lemon in half and squeeze over fish. Cut orange in half, squeeze 1 piece over the fish and slice the other half.

2. Spread preserves over fillet and top with orange slices and peach wedges. Wrap tightly in foil, sealing edges securely. Bake fish at 400° for 30 to 40 minutes or cook on a hot grill for 10 minutes on each side. Open package, skin side down, and slide fish onto a warm serving platter (or serve directly from foil). A summer feast with fresh corn on the cob, grilled onions, and a cucumber salad.

The first time I went fishing for bluefish, I was 13. A fella by the name of Gil Kelman took me, and my sweetheart, Cindy, out on his boat. We cruised from Stony Creek up the coast, then halfway across the "Sound." Gil was constantly watching the horizon and sniffing the breeze. He explained that he watched for birds "working the surface," or diving and rising again quickly. That would indicate bait or chum on the surface. (The remains of a bluefish feeding frenzy!) This same "chum" gave off a smell likened to watermelon! "When you smell watermelon," explained Gil, "head into the wind. You'll find the blues."

Sure enough, it worked! We found bluefish feeding on the surface! We tried every lure in our arsenal, but to no avail. Then Gil opened a cabinet and brought forth what he called, "My secret weapon." He held a six-pack of orange soda, and a bag of nacho cheese tortilla chips! "Take one sip of soda, then eat one chip, and try casting again," he instructed us. We obeyed without hesitation.

My first cast, a "blue," took my lure, and proceeded to give me the best "fish-fight" I'd yet experienced! All of us began to "hook up" and we shortly caught a cooler full of blues.

To this day, Cindy (now my wife) and I use Gil's "secret weapon" with our kids. Amazingly, it still occasionally works, mystifying young and old alike! "The secret is undoubtedly in the brands that you buy," explains Gil, with a wink!

Swordfish With Carol's Tomato-Orange Sauce

Serves 4

This recipe can be prepared on one burner in a small boat galley – I have often prepared it onboard our boat "Sweet P" after a long day offshore.

2 pounds swordfish
   (cut into 4 8-ounce steaks)
$\frac{1}{4}$ cup olive oil
1 small red onion, finely chopped
1 clove garlic, minced
1 teaspoon dried basil
$\frac{1}{2}$ to 1 teaspoon red pepper flakes to taste
$\frac{1}{2}$ cup orange juice
3 tablespoons lemon juice
$\frac{1}{2}$ cup dry white wine
1 cup coarsely chopped tomatoes
2 tablespoons fresh parsley, chopped
$\frac{1}{2}$ teaspoon salt
pepper to taste

1. In a large skillet over medium heat, cook the onion, garlic, basil, and red pepper flakes in olive oil for about 5 minutes until vegetables are soft but not brown. Add orange juice, lemon juice, and wine; increase heat to high and cook until mixture is reduced to a syrup, 4 to 6 minutes.

2. Stir in tomatoes, parsley, salt and pepper, reduce heat to low and arrange the swordfish on top of mixture. Cover and cook until swordfish is cooked through and slightly firm to the touch. Serve swordfish hot with sauce poured on top. This sauce may also be served with grilled swordfish steaks.

Quick-And-Leeky Baked Fish

Serves 4

Only 5 minutes from refrigerator to oven. You will love the pan juices.

$1\frac{1}{2}$ pounds leeks, trimmed, washed, and chopped
$1\frac{1}{2}$ pounds fish fillets, salmon, cod, or haddock
$\frac{1}{2}$ cup dry white wine, chicken or fish stock
salt and freshly ground pepper
1 tablespoon Dijon mustard
1 to 2 tablespoons butter
fresh chopped parsley

1. Preheat oven to 400°. Scatter leeks over the bottom of a shallow baking pan. Top with the fish, pour the wine or stock on top and season fish with salt and pepper.

2. Spread mustard on top of fish, dot with butter and cover with foil. Bake at 350° for 15 minutes or until fish flakes with a fork. Serve with white rice or pilaf, the pan juices and leeks spooned over the top. Sprinkle with fresh parsley.

Paul's Pasta Seafood Risotto

Serves 4

A take-off on a couple of recipes, a favorite dish at this great Groton restaurant on the Thames.

1 pound mussels, scrubbed and debearded
8 cherrystone clams
$\frac{1}{2}$ cup dry white wine for steaming shellfish
3 tablespoons olive oil
$\frac{1}{2}$ cup chopped onion
2 tablespoons minced shallots
1 clove garlic, minced
2 cups Arborio rice
3 cups clam juice
3 cups V-8 juice
8 ounces sea scallops
8 ounces large shrimp, peeled and deveined
$\frac{1}{4}$ teaspoon saffron threads
1 teaspoon freshly ground black pepper
1 cup frozen peas, thawed but not cooked
2 ounces freshly grated Parmesan cheese

1. Steam mussels and clams in white wine, just until they open. Drain off liquid and add to the clam juice. Set shellfish aside and keep warm.

2. Heat oil in large skillet and sauté the onion, shallots and garlic over low heat until soft. Add the rice and stir about 2 minutes.

3. In another saucepan, bring the V-8 juice, clam juice and reserved shellfish liquid to a boil. Add the saffron to this mixture, reduce heat and simmer.

4. Slowly add 1 cup of the hot liquid to the rice mixture and allow it to come to a simmer. When the liquid has been absorbed, add another $\frac{1}{2}$ cup and simmer. Continue adding the liquid $\frac{1}{2}$-cup at a time until almost all the liquid has been added.

5. Add the shrimp and scallops and continue stirring in $\frac{1}{4}$ cupfuls of the liquid until the seafood is just cooked through and the rice is tender. This takes about 25 minutes.

6. Stir in the Parmesan cheese, black pepper and peas. Arrange risotto in a large serving bowl and garnish with the clams and mussels. Serve immediately with a green salad and crusty bread.

"Methinks our children are as cheerful, fat, and lusty with feeding upon these mussels, clambanks and other fish as they are in England with their fill of bread."
Savior in New England, 1654

Quaker Hill Seafood Spinach Supreme

Serves 8
For the past 30 years this has always been a big hit with guests.

1 pound fresh shrimp, cooked, shelled, and deveined
$\frac{1}{2}$ pound Bay scallops, poached in milk to cover for 5 minutes, drained, and liquid reserved
$\frac{1}{2}$ pound fresh or frozen lobster, cooked and cut into $\frac{1}{2}$-inch pieces
$\frac{3}{4}$ cup (12 tablespoons) butter
$\frac{1}{2}$ pound spinach, chopped
$\frac{1}{2}$ head Boston lettuce, shredded
6 scallions, finely chopped
$\frac{1}{2}$ cup parsley, chopped
2 medium stalks celery, finely chopped
$\frac{1}{4}$ cup buttered bread crumbs
1 teaspoon salt
$\frac{1}{8}$ teaspoon freshly ground black pepper
$\frac{1}{4}$ teaspoon mace
4 tablespoons flour
2 cups light cream
$\frac{1}{2}$ to $\frac{3}{4}$ cup milk
$\frac{1}{4}$ cup grated Parmesan cheese
salt and pepper

1. Melt $\frac{1}{2}$ cup butter in large skillet; add spinach, lettuce, scallions, parsley, and celery. Cover and simmer about 10 minutes. Add bread crumbs, seasoning, and mace. Spread mixture in the bottom of a 3-quart shallow greased baking pan. Cover spinach mixture with cooked seafood.

2. Melt remaining butter; blend in flour. Gradually stir in cream and the reserved liquid from the scallops, making up to 4 cups with milk. Bring to a boil, stir constantly, and simmer for 2 minutes until thick.

3. Stir in cheese and season to taste. Pour over seafood, sprinkle with buttered bread crumbs. Bake 350° for 20 to 25 minutes or until bubbly hot. This casserole may be made ahead of time, refrigerated, then baked for 35 to 40 minutes.

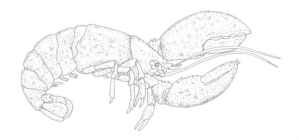

Legal Seafood's Famous Fishcakes

Serves 4

From the restaurant of the same name, "If it isn't fresh, it isn't right!"

6 tablespoons butter
$\frac{1}{3}$ cup chopped scallions, white part only
$1\frac{2}{3}$ cup freshly mashed potatoes
1 tablespoon sour cream
6 ounces flaked, cooked white-fleshed
    fish, such as cod, haddock, pollock,
    halibut, or flounder
1 egg
$\frac{1}{4}$ teaspoon dry mustard
salt
freshly ground black pepper
3 tablespoons minced parsley
1 cup dried bread crumbs
1 tablespoon vegetable oil

1. Heat 2 tablespoons of butter and
    sauté scallions for about 5 minutes,
    don't brown. Cook potatoes and mash
    them with 1 tablespoon butter and
    the sour cream; combine them with
    fish.

2. Beat the egg; add mustard, salt and
    pepper. Stir in scallions and parsley.
    Combine this mixture with potatoes
    and fish. Form the mixture into 8
    cakes $2\frac{1}{2}$ inches in diameter and dip
    each cake into the crumbs.

3. Heat the remaining butter and oil and
    sauté cakes slowly over medium heat
    for about 3 minutes on each side, or
    until lightly browned and hot
    throughout. Serve with catsup or tar-
    tar sauce.

Tuna Potato Patties

Serves 2

These golden cakes go well with a dollop of sour cream and a sprinkle of chives.

$1\frac{1}{2}$ cups frozen hash brown potatoes,
    thawed to room temperature
1 6-ounce can solid white tuna in water,
    drained and flaked
1 large egg, lightly beaten
1 tablespoon chopped red or green
    pepper
$\frac{1}{4}$ teaspoon salt
$\frac{1}{8}$ teaspoon freshly ground black pepper
3 teaspoons olive oil

1. Partially mash potatoes in a bowl
    with a fork until they begin to hold
    together. Add tuna, egg, pepper,
    seasonings and 1 teaspoon of the
    olive oil. Shape into four $\frac{1}{2}$-inch thick
    patties.

2. Heat the remaining 2 teaspoons of
    oil in a nonstick skillet over medium
    heat. Add the patties and cook until
    browned, about 5 minutes. Carefully
    turn the patties and cook until they
    are golden on the other side, about 5
    more minutes.

East End Clam Pie

Serves 8

FOR THE PIECRUST:
2 cups flour
$\frac{1}{2}$ teaspoon salt
$\frac{1}{4}$ teaspoon baking powder
8 tablespoons chilled butter,
   cut into small pieces
2 tablespoons chilled vegetable
   shortening, cut into small pieces

FOR THE FILLING:
3 medium russet potatoes, peeled and
   quartered
2 cups clam juice
5 strips bacon, cut into $\frac{1}{2}$-inch pieces
1 medium onion, finely chopped
$\frac{1}{4}$ cup chopped fresh parsley
1 tablespoon fresh thyme leaves, minced
3 cups chopped clams, cherrystones,
   quahogs, or steamers
2 tablespoons flour
salt and freshly ground black pepper
2 tablespoons chilled butter, cut into
   small pieces

1. For the piecrust: Mix together the flour, salt, and baking powder in a medium bowl. Quickly work butter and shortening into flour mixture with the tips of your fingers until mixture resembles coarse meal. Sprinkle with 8 tablespoons ice water and stir with a fork until just combined. Form into a ball, flatten, and divide in half. Cover with plastic wrap and refrigerate for at least an hour.

2. For the filling: Boil potatoes in clam juice in a covered saucepan over medium heat until soft, about 30 minutes. Drain, lightly mash with a fork and set aside.

3. Meanwhile, sauté bacon in a skillet over medium heat until crisp. Transfer bacon to a paper towel to drain. Add onion to bacon fat and sauté until golden, about 10 minutes. Mix together bacon, onions, parsley, thyme, clams, flour and potatoes in a small bowl. Season with salt and pepper to taste.

4. Preheat oven to 400°. Roll out dough on a lightly floured surface into two 12-inch circles. Place one crust into a 9-inch deep pie pan. Add the clam filling, mounding it up in the center. Dot with butter and cover with remaining crust. Trim dough, leaving about 1 inch around edge; fold under and crimp layers together with a fork. Prick a small hole in the center for steam to escape. Bake until golden, 50 to 60 minutes.

"Fishbone" Seafood Linguini

Serves 4

With a little experimenting from the garden, I came up with this interesting dish.

1 pound scallops
1 pound mussels, rinsed, steamed and shucked
1 pound shrimp, peeled
1 tablespoon extra virgin olive oil
1 tablespoon butter
3 medium carrots, julienned
2 medium zucchini, julienned
2 small yellow squash, julienned
2 cloves garlic, minced
1 cup dry white wine
2 tablespoons fresh dill, chopped
$\frac{2}{3}$ pound linguini, cooked, al dente, according to package directions
1 tomato, seeded and diced
1 cucumber, seeded and diced
$\frac{1}{4}$ cup pine nuts
$\frac{1}{4}$ cup freshly grated Parmesan cheese

1. Heat olive oil and butter in a large skillet, add carrots, zucchini, squash, and garlic and cook until tender crisp (about 5 minutes). Add white wine. Cook for 2 to 3 minutes and remove vegetables.

2. Sauté scallops in remaining pan juices until just opaque. Add mussels, shrimp, and dill, and heat until bubbly. Pour sauce over cooked linguini, toss with diced tomato and cucumber. Serve hot, sprinkled with pine nuts and Parmesan cheese.

"See those clouds; how they hang! That's the greatest thing I have seen today. I thought I might go a-fishing. That's the true industry for poets. It's the only trade I have learned. Come, lets go along."

Henry David Thoreau – Walden

Hot And Spicy Seafood Stew

Serves 8

My mother grew up on a farm in New Jersey, and my father hails from Alabama. After marriage, they settled in Greenwich, Connecticut. As children we were always told to finish everything on our plates. From these frugal roots comes the recipe for the stew; some leftovers, some fish that my husband has caught, and other tidbits found "socked away" in the freezer.

1 tablespoon olive oil
3 cloves garlic, minced
1 onion, diced
3 carrots, sliced
1 green pepper (hot or bell), diced
1 red pepper (hot or bell), diced
2 large thin skin potatoes, not peeled, diced
2 35-ounce cans plum tomatoes
1$\frac{1}{2}$ pounds seafood, any variety of fish, scallops, shrimp, squid
1 10-ounce can baby clams with liquid
1 10-ounce box chopped okra
1 to 2 sliced zucchini or yellow squash
$\frac{1}{2}$ cup chili paste or any hot barbecue sauce
2 pounds fresh mussels, washed and debearded
fresh ground black pepper

1. Heat Dutch oven for 5 minutes over medium heat, add oil to coat bottom. Brown garlic, onion, carrots, peppers, and potatoes, 5 to 7 minutes. Purée tomatoes until chunky in blender (or you may substitute equal amounts of tomato sauce and water).

2. Add tomatoes along with seafood, clams, okra, and squash, adding water or stock to cover if needed. Cover, reduce heat and simmer for 45 minutes to 1 hour, checking for doneness of fish and vegetables. Add chili paste, more if you enjoy more heat, and season with black pepper. The stew may be prepared ahead to this point.

3. Add mussels, bring to a boil, cover and cook for 15 minutes or until mussels are opened. Serve stew with rice or cornbread, and pass the Tabasco sauce.

VARIATIONS:
My children love broccoli so I often add it, also diced extra firm tofu or a 16-ounce can of drained kidney or white Northern beans.

The Farmers
Market

Hearts Of Romaine With Creamy Lime Vinaigrette

Serves 6

1 large garlic clove, minced
$\frac{1}{2}$ teaspoon Dijon mustard
2 tablespoons fresh lime juice
2 tablespoons mayonnaise
$\frac{1}{4}$ teaspoon salt
pepper to taste
$\frac{1}{4}$ cup plus 2 tablespoons olive oil
1 to 2 tablespoons water
2 heads of romaine, the pale-green inner leaves washed, spun dry, and torn into bite-size pieces

In a blender or small food processor, blend the garlic, mustard, lime juice, mayonnaise, salt and pepper to taste until the mixture is smooth. With the motor running, add the oil in a stream. Blend the mixture until it is emulsified, add enough of the water to thin the vinaigrette to the desired consistency, and blend the vinaigrette until it is combined well. In a large bowl, toss the romaine with the vinaigrette.

Crisp Radish Salad

Makes 4$\frac{1}{2}$ cups

4 cups radishes, thinly sliced
  (these may be done in a food processor)
1 medium red onion, finely diced
$\frac{1}{4}$ cup fresh cilantro, chopped
$\frac{1}{4}$ cup fresh parsley, chopped
$\frac{1}{2}$ cup thinly sliced celery
3 tablespoons fresh lemon juice
3 tablespoons extra virgin olive oil
$\frac{3}{4}$ teaspoon salt
freshly ground black pepper

In a large bowl (clear glass looks best), combine all ingredients, toss to coat and refrigerate at least 2 hours. Serve with your favorite picnic fare.

Oven Roasted September Vegetables

Serves 10 to 12

A little from the end of the summer garden mixed with a preview of fall.

8 cups mixed vegetables, including, but no limited to:
zucchini and yellow squash, cut into chunks
eggplant, peeled and cubed
onions, halved and cut into wedges
whole garlic cloves, peeled
carrots, peeled and cut into small chunks
purple turnip, peeled and cut into small chunks
fennel, tops removed and sliced
corn on the cob, cut into 1-inch chunks
2 to 3 tablespoons olive oil
1 teaspoon thyme
2 tablespoons balsamic vinegar
salt and pepper to taste

Preheat oven to 400°.

1. Cut vegetables into uniform slices and toss with olive oil, thyme, vinegar, salt and pepper. Place in a roasting pan large enough to allow you to turn them in one layer halfway through cooking.

2. Roast for 30 minutes; turn vegetables with a wide spatula and continue cooking for another half hour, or until vegetables are tender and lightly browned. Reseason with salt and pepper and toss before serving warm or at room temperature.

Black Bean Salad

Serves 4 to 6

1 16-ounce can black beans, rinsed
1 box frozen corn, thawed
1 stalk celery, diced
1 small onion, diced
$\frac{1}{2}$ bunch cilantro to taste, washed and chopped
1 red bell pepper, diced
1 lime, zested then juiced
$\frac{1}{4}$ to $\frac{1}{3}$ cup olive oil
1 teaspoon Dijon mustard
salt and pepper to taste

Mix first 6 ingredients in a medium bowl. Mix the rest of the ingredients in a small bowl. Toss together and refrigerate for at least 1 hour.

In New England, corn is sometimes planted in hills in the Indian manner. Seven kernels went into each hill, following a jingle that may have come down from Pilgrim times:
> **One for the cutworm**
> **One for the crow**
> **Two to perish**
> **And three to grow**

Margie's Eggplant Casserole

Serves 6 to 8
A hearty one dish-meal with a spicy twist.

1 medium eggplant, unpeeled and cubed
4 tablespoons olive oil
3 medium onions, chopped
1 small green pepper, chopped
$\frac{1}{2}$ pound mushrooms, sliced
1 pound ground beef, lamb, or chicken
2 cloves garlic, minced
$\frac{1}{4}$ teaspoon ground cloves
$\frac{1}{4}$ teaspoon ground allspice
$\frac{1}{2}$ teaspoon dill
salt and pepper
2 cups cooked rice
$\frac{1}{2}$ pound sliced Mozzarella cheese
1 22-ounce can crushed tomatoes
$\frac{1}{2}$ to $\frac{3}{4}$ cup Parmesan cheese

1. In a large skillet, sauté eggplant in 3 tablespoons olive oil for 5 minutes until tender. Remove from pan. Add remaining 1 tablespoon olive oil to pan and sauté onion, mushrooms, green pepper, meat and garlic. Season to taste with salt and pepper, add cloves, allspice and dill.

2. Combine eggplant and rice. In a 2-quart baking dish, layer meat/vegetables with eggplant/rice and Mozzarella cheese. Pour tomatoes on top and sprinkle with Parmesan cheese. Bake at 350° for 45 minutes until browned.

Butternut Squash Purée

Serves 4

1 2- to 3-pound butternut squash, peeled and cubed
1 2-inch piece of fresh ginger, minced
2 tablespoons butter
1 teaspoon salt
freshly ground black pepper to taste
1 tablespoon brown sugar
2 tablespoons chopped fresh parsley
2 tablespoons sliced almonds, toasted

Put squash and ginger in a pot, cover with water, bring to a boil over medium heat and cook until soft, 30 to 35 minutes. Drain squash and mash to a coarse purée. Stir in butter, salt, pepper, brown sugar, and parsley; keep warm. Before serving, sprinkle squash with toasted almonds.

Roasted Winter Vegetables With Balsamic Vinegar And Thyme

Serves 8

A fantastic change from the usual offerings to accompany your holiday roast or turkey.

4 large beets, peeled,
  cut into $\frac{1}{2}$- to $\frac{3}{4}$-inch-thick wedges
2 pounds turnips, peeled,
  cut into $\frac{1}{2}$- to $\frac{3}{4}$-inch-thick wedges
2 pounds large red-skinned potatoes,
  peeled, cut into $\frac{1}{2}$- to $\frac{3}{4}$-inch-thick
  wedges
2 pounds red onions, peeled,
  cut into $\frac{3}{4}$-inch-thick wedges with some
  core still attached
$1\frac{1}{2}$ pounds carrots, peeled,
  cut into $\frac{1}{2}$- to $\frac{3}{4}$-inch-thick pieces
$1\frac{1}{4}$ pounds rutabagas, peeled,
  cut into $\frac{1}{2}$- to $\frac{3}{4}$-inch-thick wedges
10 tablespoons olive oil
5 tablespoons balsamic vinegar
3 tablespoons chopped fresh thyme

1. Place vegetables in very large bowl. Add oil, 3 tablespoons vinegar and thyme; toss to coat. Sprinkle with salt and pepper. (Can be made 2 hours ahead.)

2. Place oven racks in top third and bottom third of oven; preheat to 400°. Brush 2 large baking sheets with oil. Divide vegetables between sheets. Roast until tender, stirring occasionally, 1 hour. Drizzle 2 tablespoons vinegar over. Season with salt and pepper. (Can be made 2 hours ahead. Let stand at room temperature. Rewarm in 400° oven 20 minutes.)

Ratatouille Torte "Chez Breed"

Serves 8

From a favorite uncle, who also happens to be a superb cook – a perfect accompaniment to grilled lamb.

2 large onions, sliced
1 clove garlic, crushed
$\frac{2}{3}$ cup olive oil
1$\frac{1}{2}$ pounds tomatoes, peeled, seeded and diced
1 tablespoon chopped fresh sage leaves
1$\frac{1}{2}$ teaspoon chopped thyme
2 1-pound eggplants, sprinkled with salt and rinsed, sliced lengthwise
4 medium zucchini, sliced
4 medium red peppers, roasted, peeled and cut into $\frac{1}{2}$-inch strips
2 tablespoons unsalted butter
3 tablespoons flour
2 cups half-and-half
3 large eggs, beaten
6 ounces freshly grated Parmesan Reggiano cheese

1. Sauté onion in 2 tablespoons olive oil until soft, add garlic and cook until most of the liquid has evaporated. Add tomatoes, sage, and thyme; cook until thick, about 8 to 10 minutes. Season to taste with salt and pepper.

2. Brush eggplant and zucchini with remaining oil and grill over a medium-hot fire or in the oven, until tender. In a medium saucepan, melt butter, add flour, and cook, stirring for 2 minutes. Gradually whisk in half-and-half and cook until thickened. Add Parmesan cheese and when mixture has cooled (about 10 minutes), beat in the eggs.

3. Preheat oven to 400°. Layer half of the eggplant slices in lightly greased 10-by-14-inch baking pan. Top with half of the tomato mixture. Spread $\frac{1}{3}$ cheese sauce over tomatoes. Add layers with half the zucchini and peppers, repeat with eggplant, tomato and sauce, finishing with a layer of sauce. Sprinkle with remaining Parmesan cheese and bake for 35 minutes until custard is set. Cut into squares and serve hot or at room temperature.

"Vegetables should be brought in from the garden in the early morning, they will then have a fragrant freshness, which they lose by keeping too long. As this is their chief value, I should as soon think of roasting an animal alive, as of boiling a vegetable too long after it is dead."
  A Cooks's Own Book – 1908 (Farmer's Market)

Sweet Potato Casserole With Apples And Marshmallows

Serves 16

6 pounds red-skinned sweet potatoes (yams), peeled and cut into $\frac{1}{3}$-inch thick rounds
1 cup chopped pecans
1 cup raisins
1 cup brown sugar, packed
1$\frac{1}{2}$ teaspoons ground cinnamon
8 medium Granny Smith apples, peeled and cut into $\frac{1}{3}$-inch slices
10 tablespoons butter, melted
1$\frac{1}{2}$ cups miniature marshmallows

1. Preheat oven to 400°. Butter a 15-by-10-by-2-inch glass baking pan. Toss together potatoes, pecans, raisins, brown sugar and cinnamon in a large bowl. Place half of apples in prepared pan. Arrange half of sweet potato mixture on top and drizzle with half of melted butter. Repeat layering with remaining apples, then remaining sweet potato mixture. Drizzle with remaining butter and cover with foil.

2. Bake casserole, covered, until potatoes are tender when pierced with a fork, about 1 hour 45 minutes. (Can be made ahead, cooled and refrigerated. Rewarm, covered, at 350° about 45 minutes.)

3. Preheat broiler. Sprinkle marshmallows over casserole and broil until marshmallows are lightly browned, watching closely to avoid burning, about 1 minute.

Sweet Potatoes Baked With Rum, Cider, And Raisins

Serves 6 to 8

An easy-to-assemble dish, on the sweet side, that goes well with roasted pork or turkey.

3 pounds sweet potatoes
   (about 6 medium-size potatoes)
$\frac{1}{4}$ cup (4 tablespoons) butter
$1\frac{1}{4}$ cups apple cider
$\frac{1}{3}$ cup dark rum
$\frac{1}{4}$ cup packed brown sugar
1 teaspoon salt
$\frac{1}{2}$ teaspoon allspice
$\frac{1}{4}$ teaspoon cinnamon
1 teaspoon ginger
$\frac{1}{2}$ cup raisins

1. Preheat the oven to 375°. Peel the potatoes and cut into 1-inch cubes. Arrange potatoes in a buttered 2-quart casserole.

2. Heat the butter, cider, rum, brown sugar, salt, allspice, cinnamon, and ginger in a small saucepan, stirring, until the butter and sugar have melted. Pour mixture over the potatoes, sprinkle with raisins, and cover casserole tightly with foil.

3. Bake the potatoes for 1 hour or until the potatoes are tender, stirring gently several times. Uncover the casserole and continue baking at 425° for 20 minutes until the juices are thickened.

Summer's End Succotash

Serves 8

Passed down through three generations, this recipe has probably never even been written down. Every year we would eagerly await harvesting the shell bean crop to make the succotash, putting away a few batches in the freezer to enjoy at Thanksgiving.

12 cups water
1 pound lean salt pork
3 pounds fresh shell beans (sometimes called cranberry beans because their color is cranberry and white)
1 dozen ears of corn
salt and pepper

1. Fill a large saucepan with water. Remove skin from salt pork and discard. Cut salt pork into small cubes and add to the saucepan. Bring water to a boil. Reduce heat to low and simmer for $\frac{1}{2}$ hour.

2. While salt pork is simmering, remove the beans from the pods and rinse with water. Cut corn off of the cobs and set aside. After the pork has been simmering $\frac{1}{2}$ hour, add the beans and simmer another $\frac{1}{2}$ hour, then add the corn. Continue to simmer the mixture for an additional $\frac{1}{2}$ hour until the corn is cooked. Season to taste with salt and pepper and serve with butter.

Caramel Sweet Potato Flan

Serves 6 to 8

2 to 3 sweet potatoes or yams
  (1$\frac{1}{4}$ pounds)
1$\frac{1}{2}$ cups sugar
$\frac{1}{4}$ cup water
8 eggs
2 egg yolks
1 14-ounce can sweetened condensed milk
1 cup heavy cream
1 cup half-and-half
1$\frac{1}{2}$ teaspoons vanilla
$\frac{1}{2}$ teaspoon EACH: ground cinnamon, allspice, and nutmeg

1. Preheat oven to 325°. Scrub the sweet potatoes or yams and bake for 1 to 1$\frac{1}{2}$ hours, depending on size, until soft. Cool slightly, cut in half and scoop out the flesh. Purée until smooth in a blender or food processor fitted with a steel blade. You should have 1$\frac{1}{2}$ cups.
2. Prepare the caramel (this may be done while the potatoes are baking). In a small heavy-bottomed saucepan, bring the sugar and water to a boil over high heat. Swirling the pan, but not stirring, cook until the syrup turns a golden brown. This will take about 5 minutes. Immediately pour into a 9-inch glass flan or soufflé dish, tipping the dish from side to side to cover the bottom and partially up the sides.
3. Beat the eggs and egg yolks in a large bowl until light and fluffy. Add the cooled sweet potato purée and remaining ingredients and beat well.
4. Pour the mixture into the prepared dish and place in a baking pan. Pour boiling water in pan halfway up the sides of the flan. Bake for 1 hour and remove from the water. Cool to room temperature and chill at least 6 hours. To unmold, run a knife around the edge of the flan, place a serving plate on top and invert. Pour any caramel remaining in pan over the top.

Buttery Shredded Beets

Serves 4
An explosion of deep red on your plate.

6 medium beets
$\frac{1}{2}$ teaspoon salt
$\frac{1}{2}$ teaspoon garlic salt
$\frac{1}{4}$ teaspoon pepper
3 tablespoons butter
$\frac{1}{2}$ teaspoon tarragon
4 lemon slices

Peel and grate beets with a medium grater or in a food processor. Place in a skillet, sprinkle with salt, garlic salt and pepper. Dot with butter, cover and simmer 30 minutes until tender, stirring several times. Add tarragon during last 10 minutes of cooking and serve with lemon slices.

Baked Sweet Onions Steward

Serves 4

4 medium sweet onions, such as Vidalia
  or Bermuda
salt and pepper
4 tablespoons butter
4 teaspoons Worcestershire sauce
2 teaspoons cumin
4 teaspoons brown sugar
$\frac{1}{2}$ cup chicken broth
$\frac{1}{2}$ cup dry white wine
1 tablespoon fresh parsley, chopped

1. Peel and trim onions. With a sharp knife, cut out a 1-inch diameter-by-1-inch deep cavity in the top of each onion, reserving the scraps. Sprinkle each onion with salt and pepper to taste.

2. Divide among the cavities, the butter, Worcestershire sauce, cumin and brown sugar. Arrange the onions in a baking pan, add the broth, wine and the reserved onion scraps to the pan. Bake at 425° for 45 minutes to one hour, basting occasionally, until tender and golden. Garnish with parsley.

Wild Rice And Corn Custard

Serves 4

A perfect side dish for poultry, game or pork.

1 tablespoon butter plus extra to grease
  casserole
1 small onion, finely chopped
$\frac{1}{2}$ medium green pepper, seeded and
  chopped
2 eggs
2 cups milk
$\frac{1}{2}$ teaspoon salt
1 teaspoon sugar
1 cup cooked wild rice
1 cup corn (fresh or frozen and defrosted)

1. Lightly butter a $1\frac{1}{2}$-quart casserole. Sauté the onion and pepper in butter in a small skillet until the onion is golden, about 5 minutes.

2. In a small bowl, beat the eggs until foamy. Blend in the milk, sautéed onion and pepper, salt, sugar, wild rice, and corn; pour into buttered casserole. Bake for 35 to 40 minutes or until center seems firm when the casserole is jiggled. You may also cook the custard in individual dishes, reducing time to 30 minutes.

Charcoal Roasted Beets And Red Onions

Serves 4

6 medium beets, trimmed of all but 1-inch of
  greens
2 medium red onions, unpeeled
2 tablespoons olive oil
$\frac{1}{3}$ cup chicken stock
3 tablespoons balsamic vinegar
$1\frac{1}{2}$ teaspoons fresh thyme
salt and pepper to taste

Prepare a moderately hot fire on a grill that
has a cover (such as a Weber). You may also
roast the beets in a 400° oven.

1. Place the beets and red onions in a
   10-inch cast iron skillet and drizzle with
   olive oil. Put the skillet on the grill and
   roast the vegetables for 1 to $1\frac{1}{2}$ hours
   depending on the size of the vegetables.
   The onions should be soft to the touch
   and a fork should pierce the beets easily.

2. Remove the vegetables from the skillet to
   cool. Add the stock, balsamic vinegar and
   thyme to the pan and place over high
   heat. Bring the liquid to a boil, scraping
   the bottom of the pan and cook for 4 to
   5 minutes until brown and syrupy.

3. Peel the beets and slice into julienne
   strips. Cut the onions into thin rings and
   toss both with the juices in the pan.
   Season to taste with salt and pepper
   before serving.

Quince Purée

Serves 6

**Delicious served as an accompaniment to
a holiday roast – at our house, a crown
roast of pork.**

2 pounds quince, peeled and cored
2 tablespoons brown sugar
salt to taste
1 leek, white part only, finely chopped
2 tablespoons butter
black pepper to taste
$\frac{1}{2}$ cup heavy cream, at room temperature

1. In a saucepan place the quince, 1
   tablespoon of the sugar and a pinch
   of salt with water to cover. Cook over
   medium heat for 45 minutes or until
   the quince is soft; drain. Process in a
   food processor until smooth.

2. Sauté the leek in the butter until
   translucent. Add the quince, the
   remaining sugar, salt and pepper.
   Simmer for 2 to 3 minutes until hot.
   To serve, drizzle a little cream over
   each portion.

Old World Kale

Serves 4

1 bunch kale (about 8 cups)
2 teaspoons olive oil
1 cup sliced mushrooms
2 cloves garlic, minced
1 large tomato, diced
2 cups chicken stock
1 tablespoon raisins
$\frac{1}{2}$ teaspoon thyme
$\frac{1}{2}$ teaspoon oregano
salt and freshly ground black pepper
2 teaspoons balsamic vinegar

1. Strip the curly leaves away from the tough center stems. Discard the stem and tear leaves into bite-size pieces.

2. In a large nonstick skillet, heat the olive oil over medium heat. Add the mushrooms and cook, stirring frequently for 2 minutes until the mushrooms are lightly golden. Add the garlic and diced tomato and cook 1 minute longer.

3. Stir in the kale and chicken stock, bring to a boil, reduce heat and simmer. Add the raisins, thyme, oregano, black pepper and salt. Cover loosely and cook for 15 minutes, stirring occasionally, being sure not to boil away all of the liquid. Stir in the balsamic vinegar, toss and serve either hot or at room temperature.

Parmesan Leek Gratin

Serves 4 to 6

This dish is quick to make with a delicious, crunchy Parmesan topping – serve with roast lamb or beef.

4 large leeks, thoroughly washed so all the grit is removed
$\frac{1}{2}$ cup chopped scallions
salt and freshly ground pepper to taste
1 cup freshly grated Parmesan cheese

1. Cut washed leeks into rounds, including some of the greens. Place in a saucepan with 1 cup water, bring to a boil and simmer for 5 minutes until tender. Drain well.

2. Butter a flat ovenproof casserole and add the drained leeks. Sprinkle the scallions on top, and top with salt and ground pepper. Spread the Parmesan cheese evenly on top of the leeks. Preheat the oven to broil. Just before serving, slide the leeks under the broiler and cook until the cheese is bubbly and golden brown.

Old Style Delmonico Potatoes

Serves 10 to 12

A classic from Dot's mom, Irene; makes any day a holiday.

5 pounds Idaho or russet potatoes, peeled and diced
1 cup cream
4 cups milk
1½ cups Parmesan cheese
salt and pepper
2 tablespoons butter
paprika

Cook potatoes in boiling water for 6 to 8 minutes until just fork tender. Cool. Mix cream, milk and 1 cup of Parmesan cheese and refrigerate for 1 hour to thicken. Gently break up potatoes with a fork, mix in cheese/milk and season to taste with salt and pepper. Spoon potatoes into a lightly greased 3-quart casserole, sprinkle with remaining ½ cup cheese and dot with butter and paprika. Bake at 375° for 1 hour until browned and bubbly.

Potato Pancakes With Corn And Peppers

Makes 12 patties

4 large russet or Idaho potatoes (approximately 2 pounds), peeled and diced
1 cup fresh corn kernels
1 small green pepper, seeded and diced
3 tablespoons butter
3 egg yolks
½ teaspoon salt
black pepper to taste
1½ cups milk
3 tablespoons chopped fresh parsley
1½ cups milk
4 tablespoons vegetable oil

1. In a medium skillet, sauté corn and green pepper in butter for 3 to 4 minutes until nicely browned. Remove from heat.

2. Boil potatoes until tender, drain well. Place in a food processor and blend with yolks, salt, pepper and milk until mixed. Fold in the sautéed corn, peppers and parsley. Chill.

3. Shape potato mixture into patties and fry in batches in the oil, starting with 2 tablespoons of oil and adding more as you need it. Drain well on paper towels and serve hot.

Garlicky Potato And Onion Pie

Serves 6

This goes well with just about anything – grilled steaks, ribs, or any roast turkey or pork.

6 russet potatoes (about 2 pounds)
4 cloves garlic, sliced
1 cup half-and-half
2 teaspoons butter
pinch nutmeg
salt and black pepper
1 medium yellow onion, peeled and
   thinly sliced
2 tablespoons freshly grated Parmesan
   cheese
$\frac{1}{3}$ cup cracker crumbs
1 tablespoon chopped chives

1. Preheat the oven to 400°. Peel the potatoes. Set 3 aside and cut the other 3 into 1-inch cubes. Put the cut potatoes in a saucepan with a pinch of salt and the garlic cloves. Cover with water, bring to a boil over high heat, lower heat to a simmer and cook potatoes until tender, about 15 minutes. Drain potatoes, leaving $\frac{1}{4}$ cup of the cooking liquid in the pan. Add 2 tablespoons half-and-half, the butter, nutmeg and salt and pepper. Mash with a fork or masher until potatoes are fluffy.

2. Butter a 9-inch pie pan. Thinly slice the remaining 3 potatoes with the slicing disk of a food processor or by hand.

Lay the potato slices on the bottom of the pie pan, overlapping the edges and spread the onions over the top. Sprinkle with salt and pepper and drizzle with remaining half-and-half.

3. Spread the mashed potatoes over the onions and sprinkle with Parmesan cheese and cracker crumbs. Bake until browned and bubbly about 45 minutes. Sprinkle with chives and let rest for 10 minutes before slicing into wedges.

Grandma Js Potato Pancakes

Makes approximately 24

6 large potatoes, grated
$\frac{1}{2}$ cup flour (enough so mixture
   doesn't stick)
2 eggs, beaten
1 medium onion, finely chopped
salt and pepper to taste
shortening for frying (about $\frac{1}{2}$ cup)

Combine all ingredients, except shortening, in a large bowl. Melt shortening in a large skillet and when hot, spoon batter, about $\frac{1}{4}$ cup for each pancake, into skillet. Cook over medium-high heat for 8 to 10 minutes until brown. Turn and cook on other side. Drain well and serve with sour cream or applesauce.

Blue Cheese Double-Baked Potatoes

Serves 4

4 large Idaho potatoes
$\frac{1}{2}$ cup heavy cream
3 tablespoons blue cheese at room
  temperature
2 tablespoons butter
1 tablespoon chopped fresh chives
2 tablespoons freshly grated Parmesan
  cheese
$\frac{1}{4}$ teaspoon freshly ground black pepper

1. Preheat oven to 425°. Bake potatoes
    until tender all the way through,
    about 1 hour. Let cool 15 minutes.
    Cut an X in the top of each potato
    and squeeze gently to loosen the
    flesh. Scoop centers out, leaving
    about $1\frac{1}{4}$-inch wall all the way around.
    Lower oven temperature to 400°.

2. In a saucepan, combine the cream and
    blue cheese over medium heat, stirring
    to blend. When heated through, mix
    in the potato pulp. Add butter, chives,
    Parmesan cheese and pepper. Use the
    mixture to restuff potatoes, place on a
    baking sheet and bake for 15 to 20
    minutes, until heated through and
    browned.

Crispy Oregano Potatoes

Serves 6

1 pound potatoes, unpeeled
  (Yukon Gold, Idaho, or Russet)
4 tablespoons vegetable oil
4 cloves garlic, finely chopped
1 tablespoon dried oregano
$\frac{1}{2}$ teaspoon coarse salt

1. Put the potatoes in a medium
    saucepan and cover with water.
    Simmer over medium heat until
    cooked but firm. Let cool and cut
    into $\frac{1}{2}$-inch slices.

2. Heat the oil and garlic in a large skillet
    over medium heat. Add the potatoes
    and salt before the garlic begins to
    brown. Fry the potatoes on both sides
    until golden. Sprinkle with oregano
    and continue to fry for another
    minute to combine flavors.

Mary L's Famous Herb Sauce

Makes 6 8-ounce jars

A decades-old Herb Society recipe, often sold at plant sales, always the first item to sell out. It goes well with cold chicken, seafood, salad greens and summer vegetables.

1 quart mayonnaise
1 pint sour cream
2 teaspoons lemon juice
2 teaspoons salt
4 teaspoons paprika
4 tablespoons fresh chives, chopped
4 tablespoons onion, chopped
2 teaspoons curry powder
6 teaspoons Worcestershire sauce
2 teaspoons fresh rosemary, chopped
2 teaspoons fresh basil, chopped
2 teaspoons fresh tarragon, chopped
2 teaspoons fresh marjoram, chopped

Combine ingredients well in a large bowl. This can be kept refrigerated up to 3 months.

Buttermilk Balsamic Dressing

Makes 1$\frac{1}{2}$ cups

This tangy dressing is great on salad greens, fresh fruit salad or drizzled over vegetables.

1 cup buttermilk
4 tablespoons balsamic vinegar
2 tablespoons Dijon or whole grain
  mustard
1 tablespoon honey
1 tablespoon light mayonnaise
$\frac{1}{2}$ teaspoon dried basil, crushed
$\frac{1}{2}$ teaspoon dried tarragon, crushed
$\frac{1}{4}$ teaspoon freshly ground black pepper
$\frac{1}{8}$ teaspoon salt
2 tablespoons chopped fresh parsley

In a jar with a tight-fitting lid, combine all of the ingredients and shake well. Taste for seasonings and adjust if necessary. If you prefer a slightly sweeter dressing, add an additional tablespoon of mayonnaise. Refrigerate for at least 1 hour or overnight. Dressing will thicken as it stands and may be kept in the refrigerator for up to 2 weeks.

Latitude 38° Salad Dressing

Makes 2 cups

Courtesy of one of our favorite food writers and critics, Lee claims this to be her all time favorite salad dressing – it hails from a restaurant in Oxford, Maryland.

$\frac{1}{2}$ cup rice wine vinegar
4 tablespoons white vinegar
4 tablespoons Dijon mustard
2 teaspoons minced garlic
$\frac{1}{3}$ cup sugar
$\frac{1}{2}$ cup olive oil
$\frac{1}{2}$ cup salad oil

In a large blender or food processor, combine vinegars, mustard, garlic and sugar. Combine oils and with blender running, slowly pour in a steady stream until blended. This tastes best if made in advance and refrigerated.

Easy Escarole Sauce

Makes 1$\frac{1}{2}$ cups

This uncooked bright green sauce adds a pungent flavor when ladled over hot or cold grilled chicken.

10 large escarole leaves, stems removed
   (enough to make 2 cups, chopped)
4 large cloves garlic
1 cup olive oil
2 tablespoons mixed Italian seasoning
$\frac{1}{2}$ cup chopped fresh basil leaves

Refrigerate overnight or up to 4 weeks, being careful when serving that someone doesn't get the whole garlic clove in their salad.

Watermelon Vinaigrette

Makes 1 cup

4 tablespoons currant jelly
$\frac{1}{2}$ cup puréed watermelon
3 tablespoons white wine vinegar
$\frac{1}{2}$ teaspoon garlic pepper
2 tablespoons vegetable oil
salt

In a small saucepan, heat jelly until melted; cool. Whisk in remaining ingredients and season with a pinch of salt. Store in refrigerator until ready to use.

Bean Town Baked Beans

Serves 12

32 ounces dry navy beans
4 teaspoons salt
8 cups boiling water
$\frac{1}{2}$ cup dark molasses
$\frac{1}{2}$ cup dark brown sugar
1 teaspoon black pepper
1 tablespoon dry mustard
8 ounces salt pork, chopped, browned and drained
1 large onion, diced

1. Rinse beans in cold water. Place in a large saucepan; add salt and boiling water. Bring back up to a boil, turn heat to low and simmer for 1 hour.

2. Add molasses, brown sugar, pepper and dry mustard, mixing well. Layer beans and salt pork in a Dutch oven or covered bean pot, adding onion to the middle layer. Bake covered for 6 to 7 hours until tender, adding more water to keep beans moist if needed.

**"But since he stood for England
And knows what England means,
Unless you give them bacon
You must not give him beans."**
G.K. Chesterson

Baked White Bean Purée With Garlic

Serves 6 to 8
**A new twist on reliable old baked beans.
Serve with grilled sausages or burgers.**

1 pound small navy or cannelli beans
$\frac{3}{4}$ cup olive oil
1 cup stock, beef, chicken, or vegetable, and enough water to cover beans
3 bay leaves
1 teaspoon dried sage
8 cloves garlic, peeled
salt and freshly ground black pepper

1. Place beans in a heavy ovenproof casserole with a good lid. Add remaining ingredients and mix well. Cover and bake at 325° for 3 to 4 hours or until the beans are soft and the liquid is absorbed.

2. Remove bay leaves and cool for 20 minutes. Place beans in the food processor and purée until smooth. Add a bit of extra olive oil or stock if mixture is too thick. Adjust seasonings and serve warm or at room temperature.

**"On Saturday morning the baking beans
With dark brown pork and onion means,
That brown bread in the pot still steams
The perfect touch to all it seems!"**
Karen Morgan

Frances Garrison's Baked Beans

Serves 6 to 8

While visiting my dear friend from Peggy's Cove, Nova Scotia, she served me her famous baked beans; you will never have the pleasure of tasting any better.

1 pound yellow eye beans
$\frac{1}{2}$ cup molasses
$\frac{1}{2}$ cup brown sugar
$\frac{1}{2}$ cup catsup
$\frac{1}{2}$ teaspoon ginger
1 teaspoon dry mustard
salt and pepper
$\frac{1}{2}$ pound bacon

1. Place beans in a pot, cover with water and cook until soft but not mushy, making sure water is always covering beans. Strain the beans, reserving the water (this is called "suddle") and place them in a bowl.

2. Add molasses, brown sugar, catsup, ginger, dry mustard and salt and pepper to taste, fold gently. Line a 3-quart casserole or bean pot with half the bacon. Pour the beans in and cover with remaining bacon.

3. Pour your suddle (reserved bean water) over the beans, cover and bake at 325° for 2 hours. Check the beans several times, making sure they don't dry out, adding more bean water as necessary.

Nauyang Corn Fritters

Serves 6

This may be made from either cooked or uncooked corn, scraped fresh from the cob. A great way to use the leftover ears.

2 eggs
2 cups corn
2 teaspoons flour
2 tablespoons milk or cream
2 teaspoons melted butter
1 teaspoon salt

Beat eggs until light. Add corn and remaining ingredients. Lightly grease a griddle or heavy skillet and drop by tablespoonfuls. Fry medium-hot for 4 to 5 minutes on each side until crisp and golden brown.

Colonial Corn Puffs

Makes 2 dozen puffs
Drizzle some maple syrup over these savory bites.

2 eggs, separated
$\frac{2}{3}$ cup milk
2 tablespoons butter, melted
1 cup creamed corn
2 tablespoons chopped fresh parsley, chives, or scallions
2 cups flour
3 teaspoons baking powder
2 teaspoons salt

1. Beat the egg yolks and add milk, butter, corn, parsley, flour, baking powder, and salt.

2. Beat the egg whites until stiff peaks form and fold into the corn mixture. Drop by tablespoonfuls into hot oil and fry until brown, turning once, about 3 minutes. Drain on paper towels and serve hot.

Cliff Street Corn Pie

Serves 6
My mother, Dorothy Brooks, was a wonderful cook whose memorable holiday meals were true productions. Christmas dinner was built around a standing rib roast with all the trimmings. Our family has continued the tradition, and this side dish often appears on both the Thanksgiving and Christmas tables.

2 eggs
$\frac{1}{2}$ cup sugar
2 tablespoons melted butter
1 teaspoon vanilla
$\frac{1}{3}$ cup half-and-half
1 15-ounce can creamed corn
1 15-ounce can kernel corn, drained

Beat eggs in a large bowl. Add sugar, butter, vanilla, half-and-half, and corn, mixing well. Pour into a lightly buttered 2-quart casserole and bake at 375° for 30 to 45 minutes until puffed and golden brown. This dish can be prepared in advance and reheated in the microwave.

Pondhouse Corn Cakes

Makes 12 to 14 cakes

1 cup stone-ground yellow cornmeal
$\frac{1}{2}$ cup all-purpose flour
1 teaspoon salt
$\frac{1}{4}$ teaspoon baking soda
$\frac{1}{2}$ teaspoon freshly ground pepper
2 teaspoons sugar
4 tablespoons unsalted butter, melted
  and cooled
1 large egg
1 cup buttermilk
1 cup thawed frozen corn, coarsely chopped
$\frac{1}{4}$ cup finely chopped onion
$\frac{1}{3}$ red pepper, chopped
1 fresh jalapeño pepper, seeded and
  minced (wear gloves)
1 cup coarsely grated Monterey Jack cheese

1. In a bowl, whisk together the cornmeal,
    flour, salt, baking soda, pepper and sugar.
    In another bowl, whisk together 2
    tablespoons butter, egg and buttermilk;
    stir in the corn, onion, red pepper, chili
    pepper and Monterey Jack; stir in the
    cornmeal mixture, stirring until the batter
    is just combined.

2. Heat a griddle over moderately high heat
    until it is hot, brush it lightly with the
    reserved butter, and working in batches,
    drop the batter by a $\frac{1}{4}$ cup measure onto
    the griddle. Spread the batter slightly to
    form 3- to 4-inch cakes. Cook the cakes
    for 2 to 3 minutes on each side, or until
    they are golden, transferring them as
    they are cooked to a platter; keep warm.

Taffy's Tomato Chutney / Marmelade

Makes 8 pints
**Mother's recipe... welcomed with joy by
family and friends each fall.**

3 quarts tomatoes (12 cups after cutting) –
  red, yellow, or green
2 oranges, not peeled
2 lemons, not peeled
2 tablespoons whole cloves
6 tablespoons broken cinnamon sticks
10 cups of sugar

1. Dip tomatoes briefly in boiling water.
    Peel and cut into chunks. Discard most
    of the seeds. Cut oranges and lemons
    into see-through thin slices, remove
    seeds. Tie the cloves and cinnamon
    sticks loosely in a cheesecloth bag.

2. Cook tomatoes, oranges, lemons,
    cloves, and cinnamon sticks in a non-
    aluminum saucepan until tender. Add
    sugar and cook, stirring, until thick.
    Test for thickness on a chilled plate.

3. Pour into clean hot jars and seal. The
    inner seal should pull down flat. If you
    can push it down, plink-plunk, then
    that seal is not tight. Unsealed jars go
    in the refrigerator for immediate use.
    Sealed jars will not need to be refrig-
    erated until after they are opened.

Alvonia's Hot Slaw

Serves 6

I remember as a child, after a day of sledding, going home with pink cheeks, very cold, most times wet, and always hungry. Mama would have cooked a big dinner and most times the dishes contained vinegar. When the heat and the vinegar met your nostrils, tears formed and washed your cold cheeks. The meal would be roast pork and sauerkraut, sauerbraten, hot German potato salad or my favorite, hot slaw.

1 small head of cabbage
1 tablespoon cornstarch
2 tablespoons sugar
1 egg, beaten
vinegar to taste
cream

1. Wash cabbage, slice thinly and cook in salted water until tender, about 15 minutes. Drain, reserving $\frac{1}{2}$ cup water.

2. Combine cornstarch, sugar and beaten egg in saucepan, adding a little cream to make a light paste. Stir cabbage and cooking water into the sauce, simmer over low heat, adding vinegar in small amounts (to taste) until thickened.

Refrigerator Pickles

Yield: 8 pints

An easy way to make pickles on a hot summer day.

4 quarts small pickling cucumbers, sliced thin
4 cups cider vinegar
4 cups sugar
1 teaspoon turmeric
1 tablespoon mustard seed
$\frac{1}{4}$ cup pickling salt
3 medium onions, peeled and sliced

Mix all ingredients together in a large bowl and let stand for 2 hours, tossing occasionally. Pour into sterilized jars; cover tightly with lids and refrigerate. These crunchy uncooked pickles will keep until Thanksgiving or up to six months.

Continental Bean Relish

Makes 2 cups
A tradition on the table at this Saugus, Massachusetts restaurant for over 30 years.

1 12-ounce can kidney beans, rinsed and drained
$\frac{1}{4}$ cup minced scallions
1 clove garlic, minced
$\frac{1}{4}$ cup mayonnaise
1 tablespoon horseradish
$\frac{1}{4}$ cup sweet pickle relish
dash Worcestershire sauce
salt and pepper

Combine all ingredients, seasoning to taste with salt and pepper. Cover and refrigerate for at least 2 hours or up to 2 days. Serve with Melba toast (as they do there) or crackers.

Herb Society Mint Jelly

Makes 3 pints
Always a big seller at our yearly fall plant sale.

2 cups firmly packed fresh mint, or 1 ounce dried
4 cups water
(for dried herbs use $4\frac{1}{3}$ to $4\frac{1}{2}$ cups water)
$2\frac{2}{3}$ cups sugar
1 package Sure-Jell Light Fruit Pectin

1. If using fresh herbs, wash the leaves and stems. Finely chop or crush and place in saucepan. Add the water and bring quickly to a boil. Remove from heat, cover, and let stand 10 minutes. Strain.

2. Measure $3\frac{3}{4}$ to 4 cups of this mint tea. Mix $\frac{1}{4}$ cup sugar and the fruit pectin in a small bowl, then stir the mixture into the tea. Bring to a full rolling boil over high heat, stirring constantly. Quickly stir in the remaining sugar. Bring back to a full boil and boil 1 minute longer, stirring constantly. Remove the pan from the heat. Skim off any foam.

3. Fill clean canning jars (prepared according to package directions) immediately to within $\frac{1}{8}$ inch of the top. Wipe jar rims and threads. Cover quickly with lids, and screw the bands on tight. Process in a boiling water bath with 2 inches of water over the tops of the jars. Process 10 minutes for half-pints and 15 minutes for pint.

Primrose Peach Pickles

Makes 12 pints

This family recipe comes from a page of my great-grandmother's cookbook, from which many recipes are dated as far back as 1850.

MRS. WHEATON'S RECIPE TO PICKLE PLUMS, TOMATOES OR PEACHES

Take 7 pounds of fruit. Dissolve 4 pounds of sugar in 1 quart of vinegar; 3 ounces of cloves, 2 ounces of cinnamon. Make a little bag of the fruit in a large stone jar, throw the sugar and vinegar, heated to a boil, over it; let them stand a day. Turn all the vinegar off and scald it again, and throw it again over the fruit. Do this three mornings. Then on the fourth day throw all into a kettle and let them boil slowly for $\frac{1}{2}$ hour.

An updated version; pickling peaches is a traditional event at the end of the season – a fabulous accompaniment to any roast or other meat dishes.

7 to 8 pounds large peaches (about 30 large peaches), peeled and quartered
1 quart cider vinegar
4 pounds sugar
1 3-ounce box cloves
1 2-ounce box cinnamon sticks

1. Place vinegar and sugar in a large saucepan, bring to a boil and cook for 15 minutes until syrupy. Divide cloves and cinnamon sticks, tie up in 3 cheesecloth bags and add to peaches along with syrup. Let stand overnight.

2. Drain peaches; boil syrup and pour back over peaches. Repeat process on 2 more days. On the fourth day, return to the stove and boil for 30 minutes, watching carefully so that the peaches do not stick. Cool and place in sterilized jars.

Holidays
Holidays

143

Turkey Fritters Grandmere

Serves 8 to 10

After a long Thanksgiving weekend at the farm in Vermont, Grandma always made a batch of these before we all loaded in the car for the long ride back to Connecticut – the last of the best!

2 cups flour
2 teaspoons salt
$\frac{1}{2}$ teaspoon paprika
$\frac{3}{4}$ teaspoon thyme
2 teaspoons baking powder
4 eggs, separated
$\frac{2}{3}$ cup milk
3 tablespoons sherry (optional)
3 cups cooked diced turkey
1 cup leftover vegetables, whatever is left, peas, beans, squash
3 cups vegetable oil (safflower or canola)

1. Sift the flour together with the salt, herbs and baking powder.

2. Beat the egg yolks until creamy, then beat in the milk and sherry. Slowly beat the flour mixture into the liquid. Beat the egg whites until they are stiff; fold into the batter. Fold in the turkey and vegetables.

3. Heat the oil in a deep skillet to 375°. Drop batter in small batches by the spoonful and cook until golden, turning to brown completely. Drain on paper towels and keep hot in a low oven. Serve hot with leftover gravy, hot sauce or tartar sauce.

Lil's Figgy Easter Ham

Serves 10

From the kitchen of one of Noank's fine artists.

1 large ham, butt or shank
cloves
1 cup dark rum
2 cups Coca-Cola
4 tablespoons dry mustard
$1\frac{1}{2}$ cups brown sugar
juice of 3 lemons
1 10-ounce package figs

1. With a sharp knife, score ham and stud with cloves. Combine rum and Coca-Cola.

2. In a separate bowl, combine mustard, brown sugar, lemons and just enough of the rum-Coca-Cola mixture to make a thick paste. Spread mixture on ham and bake in a 325° oven for 2 to 3 hours, depending on size of ham and directions on packaging. Baste ham every half-hour and, during last 30 minutes, top ham with figs, basting well. Remove to a platter, pour juices overtop and surround with figs.

Easter Special Stuffed Leg Of Lamb

Serves 6 to 8

1 leg of lamb, deboned, about 4 to 5
  pounds
salt
pepper
2 bags of fresh spinach, lightly steamed
4 ounces goat cheese
$\frac{1}{2}$ cup chopped black olives
$\frac{1}{2}$ cup chopped sun-dried tomatoes
3 garlic cloves, slivered
2 teaspoons herbes de Provence or 1
  tea spoon rosemary and $\frac{1}{2}$ teaspoon
  thyme
$\frac{1}{4}$ cup olive oil

1. Preheat oven to 400°. Put a large
   sheet of plastic wrap on your work
   surface and open the leg of lamb and
   lay out flat, the long edge toward
   you. Sprinkle generously with salt and
   pepper. Layer the lamb with half the
   spinach, then the goat cheese, black
   olives and sun-dried tomatoes. Top
   with the rest of the spinach.

2. Roll the lamb away from you and tie
   with kitchen twine. Make slits in the
   roast and insert garlic. Sprinkle with
   the herbes de Provence or rosemary
   and thyme and lightly salt and pepper.
   Spread the olive oil over the surface
   and place the leg in a roasting pan.
   Roast for 1 hour and 15 minutes, or
   until the meat thermometer registers
   145° for medium-rare or 160° for

medium. Remove and let stand for
about 10 minutes, then slice thickly
and serve.

Sunday Morning Yorkshire Eggs

Serves 4
**After the busy holidays, try this easy
one-dish breakfast.**

$\frac{1}{3}$ cup butter
2 eggs, beaten
1 cup milk
1 cup flour
1 teaspoon baking powder
$\frac{1}{2}$ teaspoon salt
4 hard-boiled eggs, peeled and sliced
your favorite breakfast meat, cooked (a
  few sausages, strips of bacon or ham)

1. Grease the sides and bottom of a 9-
   inch casserole with butter. Place the
   casserole in a preheated 450° oven for
   a minute to melt.

2. Beat eggs and milk thoroughly. Add
   flour, baking powder and salt, beating
   until smooth. Remove hot pan from
   oven, make a layer of sliced eggs and
   top with meat. Pour batter into pan
   and bake at 425° for 30 to 40 minutes
   until puffed and brown.

Marta's Valentine Chicken

Serves 4

This recipe was the first meal I ever cooked for my husband-to-be on February 1, 1992. After dinner he handed me a present and announced "Happy Valentine's Day!" I replied, "Thanks, but you are a week too early." To this day we still celebrate Valentine's Day on both dates – I'm a lucky gal.

1 red pepper, seeded and sliced
1 medium onion, sliced
2 tablespoons olive oil
1 pound boneless chicken breast, cut into 2-inch strips
salt and pepper
$\frac{1}{2}$ pound mushrooms, sliced
1 tomato, chopped
$\frac{1}{4}$ cup chopped fresh basil plus sprigs for garnish
$\frac{1}{2}$ cup cream
$\frac{1}{2}$ cup sour cream
$\frac{1}{2}$ cup Parmesan cheese

1. In a large skillet, sauté pepper and onion in 1 tablespoon oil until soft, about 5 minutes, remove from pan. Season chicken pieces with salt and pepper and add to pan with remaining tablespoon of olive oil. Brown on both sides.

2. Add mushrooms, tomato and chopped basil to pan, cook until mushrooms are soft, another 5 minutes. Add peppers and onions; stir in cream, sour cream and Parmesan cheese. Simmer over low heat until heated through. Serve over hot, buttered noodles, garnished with basil sprigs.

Aunt Marion's Gourmet Potatoes

Serves 8 to 10

This is made for every holiday and family celebration at our house – make it a day ahead if you can.

6 medium potatoes
2 cups grated cheddar cheese
$\frac{1}{4}$ cup butter or margarine, plus 2 tablespoons
$1\frac{1}{2}$ cups sour cream or plain yogurt
$\frac{1}{3}$ cup finely chopped onion
1 teaspoon salt
$\frac{1}{4}$ teaspoon pepper

1. Cook potatoes in skins, cool, peel and coarsely grate. In a saucepan, combine cheese, $\frac{1}{4}$ cup butter and melt over low heat, stirring occasionally. Remove from heat and blend in sour cream, onions, salt and pepper. Gently fold in potatoes.

2. Pour potatoes into a lightly buttered 2-quart casserole, dot with butter and bake at 350° for 25 minutes until browned and bubbly. If made ahead and refrigerated, increase heat to 375° and bake for an additional 10 minutes.

Super Bowl "Big Kick" Casserole

Serves 8

Our friends are addicted to this – never any left over! I often double or triple the batch, and serve it hot at different times during the game as guests stop in.

8 ounces lean sausage
1 pound mushrooms, sliced
$\frac{1}{2}$ pound Ricotta cheese
3 ounces cream cheese, at room temperature
1 tablespoon baking powder
$\frac{1}{2}$ teaspoon salt
black pepper
$\frac{1}{2}$ cup flour
9 eggs, lightly beaten
$\frac{1}{4}$ pound grated sharp cheddar cheese
$\frac{1}{2}$ pound grated Monterey Jack cheese
2 bunches scallions, chopped (about 2 cups)

1. Cook sausage until browned, about 5 minutes. Add mushrooms to pan and cook until just softened; remove from heat.

2. In a large bowl, cream Ricotta and cream cheese. Add baking powder, salt, pepper and flour, mixing well. Whisk in beaten eggs, add sausage-mushroom mixture, grated cheeses and scallions. Pour mixture into a well-greased 9-by-13-inch baking pan and cook in a 350° oven for 45 minutes until puffed and brown.

After Easter Deviled Ham And Eggs

Serves 8

Not everything has to go into pea soup...

3 cups chopped ham (this can be done in a food processor)
$\frac{1}{4}$ cup (4 tablespoons) butter
$\frac{1}{2}$ cup chopped onion
2 tablespoons flour
$\frac{1}{4}$ cup chicken broth
1 cup light cream
4 tablespoons Dijon mustard
1 tablespoon horseradish
$\frac{3}{4}$ cup sliced stuffed olives
salt and freshly ground black pepper
16 slices buttered toast, crusts trimmed
8 hard cooked eggs, sliced

1. Preheat the oven to 350°. In a saucepan, brown the ham and onion in the butter. Add the flour and cook, stirring, for 3 minutes. Remove from the heat.

2. Blend in the broth, cream, mustard and horseradish. Cook, stirring, until thickened. Add olives, salt and pepper.

3. For each serving, gently press 1 slice of toast in the bottom of a buttered ramekin or custard cup. Top with $\frac{1}{2}$ cup of sauce and 1 sliced egg. Cut another slice of toast into triangles and place around edges of ramekins. Bake for 10 to 12 minutes until bubbly and brown.

Hanukah Holiday Brisket

Serves 6

A family tradition, modernized a bit to prepare in advance. Serve with latkes, applesauce or potato kugel.

4 to 5 pounds brisket of beef
2 medium leeks, white part only, chopped
3 cups mini carrots
2 cups chopped celery
2 bay leaves
salt and pepper to taste
1 1.4-ounce package Knorr dry vegetable soup mix
$\frac{1}{2}$ teaspoon paprika
1 cup red wine
$\frac{1}{2}$ cup water
roux: $\frac{1}{2}$ cup flour with enough water to make a thick paste

1. Wash brisket. Place leeks in the bottom of a Dutch oven, place brisket on top. Place carrots and celery around brisket, add bay leaves, season with salt and pepper. Sprinkle dry soup mix over meat, add paprika and pour wine and water into pan.

2. Cover pan with aluminum foil, do not use pot cover. Place in middle rack of a preheated 325° oven and bake for 3 hours. Remove from oven and leave covered for $\frac{1}{2}$ hour. Uncover and place meat on a platter.

3. Strain vegetables from gravy into a medium bowl. Heat gravy, whisk in roux and cook until thickened, adding more wine or water as needed. Add strained vegetables back to gravy and re-season to taste with salt and pepper. Slice meat into $\frac{1}{4}$-inch thick slices and arrange in a 9-by-13-inch casserole. Pour gravy and vegetables over brisket, cover with foil and keep warm in a 275° oven until ready to serve.

Sweet Potato Festival Fritters

Makes 20 fritters

A family Kwanzaa tradition for the "First Fruits of the Harvest" celebration.

$1\frac{1}{2}$ cups grated sweet potato
$\frac{1}{2}$ cup chopped scallions
$\frac{1}{2}$ cup grated coconut
2 teaspoons finely minced fresh ginger root
2 eggs, lightly beaten
$\frac{2}{3}$ cup fine, dry, plain bread crumbs
salt and pepper to taste
vegetable oil for deep frying

1. Combine all ingredients in a large bowl.

2. In a large heavy skillet, heat oil on high. In small batches, drop the sweet potato mixture into the oil by tablespoons; fry for about 2 minutes on each side or until golden brown and tender. Transfer the fritters to paper towels to drain. Serve warm.

Linguini With Fennel And Sardines

Serves 6
A Sicilian addition to celebrate a Christmas Eve feast.

$2\frac{1}{2}$ cups sliced fennel with tops
2 tablespoons extra virgin olive oil
$\frac{1}{2}$ cup chopped onion
4 cloves garlic, minced
1 29-ounce can tomato sauce
$\frac{1}{8}$ teaspoon sugar
crushed red pepper to taste
1 4.2-ounce can sardines in oil
1 pound linguini, cooked and drained
freshly grated Parmigiano-Reggiano
   cheese and fennel leaves for garnish

1. Place fennel in 1 inch of water in a saucepan, cover and steam until wilted, about 3 to 4 minutes. Reserve water and add to pasta water for extra flavor.

2. Heat oil in a large saucepan over medium-high heat. Add onion and garlic, and sauté until translucent, about 4 to 5 minutes. Add tomato sauce, fennel, sugar and season with salt and pepper. When the sauce begins to boil, cover and lower heat to medium. Add crushed red pepper, stir and simmer for 20 more minutes. Add sardines, stir and simmer for 10 minutes.

3. Toss sauce with linguini. Sprinkle with Parmigiano-Reggiano cheese just before serving. Garnish with snipped fennel leaves.

Signature Corn Custard Pudding

Serves 8
Mother always served this with her wonderful Sunday roast chicken dinners, and the pudding always found its way to every holiday table.

4 eggs
1 12-ounce can evaporated milk
2 teaspoons sugar
$\frac{1}{2}$ teaspoon salt
$\frac{1}{4}$ to $\frac{1}{2}$ teaspoon black pepper
1 15-ounce can cream style corn
1 15-ounce can corn niblets
2 tablespoons butter, melted, plus 1
   tablespoon unmelted

Beat eggs with milk, sugar, salt and pepper to taste. Mix in corn and melted butter. Pour into a greased 2-quart casserole and dot with butter. Refrigerate for at least 1 hour or overnight. Bake at 325° for 50 to 60 minutes or until custard is set.

Pell's Fish Market Scalloped Oysters

Serves 4

A much heralded Thanksgiving and Christmas tradition, adapted from a fish market in Greenport, Long Island, over 25 years ago.

1 pint oysters
2 cups medium-coarse cracker crumbs
$\frac{1}{2}$ cup butter, melted
$\frac{3}{4}$ cup light cream
$\frac{1}{4}$ cup oyster liquor
$\frac{1}{4}$ teaspoon Worcestershire sauce
$\frac{1}{2}$ teaspoon salt
dash of pepper

1. Drain oysters, reserving $\frac{1}{4}$ cup liquor. Combine cracker crumbs and butter. Spread $\frac{1}{3}$ of crumbs in a well greased 8-by-1$\frac{1}{4}$-inch round pan. Cover with half the oysters and sprinkle with pepper.

2. Using another third of the crumbs, spread a second layer, cover with remaining oysters and sprinkle with pepper. Mix cream-oyster liquor, Worcestershire sauce and salt; pour over oysters. Top with last of the crumbs and bake at 350° for 40 minutes and serve immediately.

Roberto's Calamari With Red Sauce

Serves 6 as an appetizer

This is a traditional part of the Christmas Eve "Primi Piatti" or first course – always a seafood dish.

1 pound cleaned squid
  (fresh or frozen and defrosted)
1 tablespoon extra-virgin olive oil
1 cup chopped onion
3 cloves garlic, minced
2 cups tomato sauce
salt and freshly ground pepper to taste
1 teaspoon dried oregano
1 teaspoon dried basil
$\frac{1}{3}$ cup dry red wine
1 teaspoon brown sugar
2 tablespoons fresh chopped parsley
Italian bread, sliced and toasted

1. Cut squid across body and tentacles into $\frac{1}{2}$-inch pieces. (Some stores may carry pre-cleaned, boxed squid in the frozen food section.) Heat oil in a nonstick skillet over medium-high heat. Add onion and garlic; sauté until onion is translucent, about 4 to 5 minutes.

2. Lower heat to medium. Sauté squid for 10 minutes, stirring occasionally. Add tomato sauce, salt and pepper, oregano, basil, red wine, and brown sugar. Simmer for 20 minutes. To serve, ladle into wide-rimmed bowls. Sprinkle with parsley and serve with Italian bread.

Concetta's Christmas Risotto

Serves 12 to 20

From a long lineage of cooks, this is unlike any risotto you have ever tasted.

the broth from 1 dead old hen (original recipe) or 3 48-ounce cans chicken broth
2 medium onions, chopped
4 celery stalks, $\frac{1}{2}$-inch diced
1 8-ounce can tomato paste
salt and pepper
$\frac{1}{2}$ pound salt pork, diced
1$\frac{1}{2}$ pounds ground pork
1 pound ground beef
red pepper flakes
3 cloves garlic, chopped
2 7-ounce cans sliced mushrooms, drained
1$\frac{1}{2}$ pounds brown rice
1 cup grated Parmesan or Romano cheese

1. In a large pot, combine broth, onion, celery, tomato paste, and salt and pepper. Bring to a boil and simmer for 15 minutes.

2. In a large skillet or Dutch oven, fry salt pork for 10 minutes or until brown. Add pork, ground beef and red pepper flakes to taste. Cook over medium-low heat for 20 minutes, add garlic and mushrooms; continue cooking for another 20 minutes. Add the rice and cook, stirring for 10 minutes.

3. Pour in enough hot broth just to cover rice, reduce heat to low and simmer, adding more broth, until rice is done (about 20 minutes). When rice is done, add the rest of the broth and grated cheese. Let the mixture rest until all the broth is absorbed.

4. Spoon risotto into a large, buttered casserole and cover with foil. It may either be refrigerated or frozen at this point. To heat, bake covered in a 350° oven for 1 to 1$\frac{1}{2}$ hours, adding extra broth if needed.

Canterbury Pork And Potato Pie

Serves 6 to 8

A generations-old recipe in our family, always a tradition on New Year's as a sign of a good and prosperous year to come.

1 pound ground pork
1 pound ground beef
3 medium onions, finely chopped
1 teaspoon salt
$\frac{1}{2}$ teaspoon black pepper
1 teaspoon garlic powder
4 medium russet potatoes, peeled and diced
$\frac{1}{4}$ cup milk
$\frac{1}{2}$ teaspoon cloves
$\frac{1}{4}$ teaspoon cinnamon
dash nutmeg
2 9-inch pie crusts, homemade or frozen and defrosted

1. In a large skillet, brown pork and ground beef. Add onion, salt, pepper, and garlic powder; cook until onions are soft, about 5 minutes.

2. Cook potatoes until soft, 10 to 12 minutes, and drain well. Add milk (using a little more if you need to) and mash. Fold in the meat and onion mixture; add cloves, cinnamon, and nutmeg to taste.

3. Place 1 piecrust in a 9-inch pie pan and pour in meat filling. Top with remaining crust, crimp edges and vent top by piercing crust with a fork. Bake at 400° for 35 to 45 minutes until light brown. Let sit for 10 minutes before cutting into wedges.

Sweet Potato Apple Bake

Serves 6 to 8

My large family always shares in preparing for our massive Christmas dinner. I always ask to prepare this dish as my assignment. I am grateful that this melt-in-your-mouth dish is labeled in my recipe box with the word "Mom" in the corner. Thanks, Mom!

3 medium sweet potatoes
3 medium apples, peeled and sliced
$\frac{1}{4}$ cup sugar
2 tablespoons butter or margarine
salt and pepper to taste
$\frac{1}{4}$ cup orange juice

1. Cook potatoes, skin on, in boiling water until just tender, about 15 minutes. Drain, peel and slice.

2. Layer potatoes and apples in a buttered 2-quart baking pan, sprinkling each layer with sugar, dotting with butter and seasoning with salt and pepper.

3. Pour orange juice over casserole, cover and bake at 375° for 45 minutes to 1 hour until apples are tender.

Oh-So-Sweet Potato Casserole

Serves 8

Christmas – Thanksgiving – Easter – a tradition.

3 pounds cooked sweet potatoes, canned or fresh
$\frac{1}{2}$ cup (4 tablespoons) butter or margarine, melted
$\frac{1}{2}$ cup sugar
1 egg, beaten
1 teaspoon vanilla

In a large mixing bowl, mash sweet potatoes, adding melted butter, sugar, egg and vanilla. Beat until smooth. Pour into a lightly greased 8-by-11-inch baking dish and sprinkle with topping.

TOPPING
$\frac{1}{2}$ cup coconut
$\frac{1}{2}$ cup brown sugar, firmly packed
$\frac{1}{2}$ cup butter or margarine, melted
$\frac{1}{2}$ cup chopped pecans
1 tablespoon flour

In a medium bowl, combine all ingredients. Spread over potatoes and bake at 350° for 30 minutes until lightly browned and crisp.

Berry Mallow Yam Bake

Serves 8

My first Thanksgiving with my husband's family was my introduction to this dish which had been part of their tradition at dinner for over 35 years – whoever hosts the dinner must include this special dish. Don't wait until Thanksgiving; it is great with roast pork or ham.

$\frac{1}{2}$ cup flour
$\frac{1}{2}$ cup brown sugar
$\frac{1}{2}$ cup old-fashioned oats
1 teaspoon cinnamon
$\frac{1}{3}$ cup butter
2 17-ounce cans yams
2 cups fresh cranberries
$1\frac{1}{2}$ cups mini marshmallows

1. Combine flour, brown sugar, oats and cinnamon. Add butter, cut into pieces, mixing until it looks like coarse crumbs.

2. In a large bowl, toss yams, cranberries and 1 cup of crumb mixture. Place yams in a buttered $1\frac{1}{2}$-quart casserole and sprinkle with remaining crumbs. Bake at 350° for 35 minutes. Top with marshmallows and broil until browned.

Braised Red Cabbage With Chestnuts

Serves 10 to 12

1 3-pound red cabbage
12 chestnuts
$\frac{1}{4}$ pound salt pork, cut into small cubes
1 medium onion, chopped
3 apples, peeled, cored, and quartered
  (about 1 pound)
1 cup dry white wine
salt and freshly ground pepper to taste
$\frac{1}{3}$ cup brown sugar
2 tablespoons butter
2 tablespoons red wine vinegar

1. Pull off and discard any wilted outside leaves from the cabbage. Quarter the cabbage and shred finely.

2. Using a sharp paring knife, make an incision around the perimeter of each chestnut, starting and ending at either side of the "topknot" or stern end. Place the chestnuts in one layer in a baking dish just large enough to hold them. Place the pan in a preheated 450° oven and bake the chestnuts about 10 minutes or until they crack open. Let the chestnuts cool until they can be handled, and peel them while they are hot.

3. Heat the salt pork in a heavy oven-proof saucepan large enough to hold the cabbage. When the salt pork is rendered of its fat, about 5 minutes, add the onion and apples; sauté for 5 more minutes until onion is soft.

4. Pour in the wine and bring the mixture to a boil. Add the cabbage, salt, pepper, brown sugar and chestnuts; cover and simmer for 10 minutes. Stir the mixture occasionally making sure the bottom does not stick and get too brown. Place the saucepan in the oven and bake at 375° for 30 minutes. Reduce the temperature to 325° and continue baking for 1 hour until cabbage is tender. Remove from oven and stir in the butter and vinegar.

Finnish Holiday Bread

Makes 4 braids

When I was a little girl a wonderful family from Finland lived next door. Every Christmas the mother would knock on our door and deliver a loaf of this wonderful bread, warm from the oven. Now a tradition in our home with even the children helping out with kneading and braiding the dough.

3 cups whole milk, scalded
1 cup sugar
1 teaspoon salt
9 plump whole cardamom, pounded fine
  (or $\frac{1}{2}$ teaspoon ground cardamom)
$11\frac{1}{2}$ cups flour
2 packets dry yeast or $\frac{1}{3}$ yeast cake
4 eggs
$\frac{1}{2}$ cup melted butter

GLAZE
$\frac{1}{2}$ cup confectioners' sugar
$\frac{1}{2}$ cup milk or half-and-half

1. Place milk, sugar, salt and cardamom in a large bowl. Add 5 cups flour, beat with an electric mixer until smooth. Dissolve yeast in a little warm water and add to dough.

2. Beat in eggs, one at a time. (You will not be able to use mixer any further as dough will be too stiff.) With your hands, work in remaining $6\frac{1}{2}$ cups flour, kneading well. Add melted butter, $\frac{1}{3}$ at a time, kneading well after each addition (dough should leave your hands). Cover with a towel, let rise in a warm place until doubled in size.

3. Divide dough into 4 pieces. Divide each piece in thirds. Braid pieces into a loaf and place each on a well-greased baking sheet. Let rise again, about 1 hour or until light. Bake for 20 minutes at 375° until golden brown. Mix glaze ingredients in a small bowl and brush on top.

Holiday Sweet Bread

Makes 4 large or 8 mini loaves

As a little girl, I always enjoyed baking our Holiday Sweet Bread with my mom – the smell of it baking just invades the house. Now I bake it with my 3 children and they will surely carry on their grandmother's tradition.

1 package dry yeast
$\frac{1}{4}$ cup lukewarm water
1 teaspoon sugar
5 eggs, at room temperature
$1\frac{3}{4}$ cups sugar
$1\frac{3}{4}$ cups warm milk
$\frac{1}{2}$ teaspoon salt
1 tablespoon vanilla
9 cups flour, sifted
12 tablespoons unsalted butter, melted at room temperature

1. Sprinkle yeast over lukewarm water in a measuring cup, stir, and when it gets foamy, add 1 teaspoon of sugar to activate the yeast.

2. Place eggs in a large bowl. Beat until foamy and gradually add $1\frac{3}{4}$ cups sugar. Add milk, salt, vanilla and yeast mixture, combining well. A little at a time, add 5 cups flour, using a wooden spoon. Add melted butter and beat well.

3. Add remaining 4 cups of flour and mix. The dough should be stiff to handle. Cover and let sit until dough is doubled in size, at least 2 hours or overnight.

4. Punch down dough and remove from bowl. Knead the dough and divide evenly between the baking pans which have been lightly greased. Let the dough rise, uncovered for $1\frac{1}{2}$ hours. Bake in a 325° oven for 30 to 35 minutes for the large pans or 15 to 20 minutes for the smaller ones. Check with a cake tester so as not to over-bake. Remove to a cake rack and let cool before slicing.

Heirloom Coffee Filling

This was the traditional cake filling for all birthdays in our family. It was usually a 3-layer white cake, and the recipient would choose either a white or chocolate frosting. It wasn't a birthday cake without this filling!

$\frac{3}{4}$ cup boiling water
2 heaping teaspoons instant coffee
$\frac{1}{4}$ cup milk **OR** 1 cup strong perked coffee
3 to 4 tablespoons flour
3 or 4 egg yolks
$\frac{1}{2}$ teaspoon vanilla
2 tablespoons butter or margarine

In a small saucepan, boil water and add instant coffee and milk or perked coffee; thicken with flour, stirring constantly. Slightly beat the egg yolks and to them add, a little at a time, the coffee mixture. Continue heating the mixture for at least 2 minutes and remove from heat. Add vanilla and butter or margarine. Cool slightly before applying to your favorite cake.

Danbury News-Times Pumpkin Cake

Serves 10

I cut this recipe out of the newspaper years ago and bake it for both Thanksgiving and Christmas. My husband and sons are not breakfast eaters, but devour this cake whenever it is around.

CAKE
2 cups flour
2 cups sugar
1 15-ounce can pumpkin
1 cup oil
4 eggs
2 teaspoons baking soda
2 teaspoons baking powder
1 teaspoon salt
2 teaspoons cinnamon

FROSTING
8 tablespoon butter or margarine
1 8-ounce package cream cheese
1 1-pound box confectioners' sugar
1 teaspoon vanilla
1 cup chopped nuts

1. In a large bowl, combine all cake ingredients and mix thoroughly. Pour batter into a greased Bundt pan and bake at 350° for 45 minutes. Cool completely.

2. Combine frosting ingredients and frost cooled cake. Refrigerate before serving.

Aunt Yolanda's Holiday Spice Cake

Makes 2 cakes

My Canadian grandmother came to this country with her sisters as a young child. During the Depression, my Aunt Yolanda prepared her cake at the coffee shop where she worked. We have made this rich cake every holiday (except December 1983) celebrated in the United States.

$\frac{1}{2}$ cup butter
1 cup dark brown sugar
$\frac{1}{2}$ cup white sugar
$\frac{1}{2}$ cup dark molasses
2 eggs
$2\frac{1}{2}$ cups flour
$1\frac{1}{2}$ teaspoons baking soda
2 teaspoons cinnamon
$\frac{1}{2}$ teaspoon nutmeg
$\frac{1}{2}$ teaspoon allspice
$\frac{1}{2}$ teaspoon ground cloves
1 pint (16 ounces) sour cream
$\frac{1}{4}$ cup raisins
$\frac{1}{4}$ cup chopped nuts

1. Cream butter with brown sugar, white sugar and molasses. Beat in eggs. Sift flour, baking soda and spices; mix with butter mixture.

2. Add sour cream, raisins and chopped nuts to batter. Divide mixture into 2 buttered loaf pans and bake in a 350° oven for 50 to 60 minutes or until toothpick inserted in center comes out clean. Remove from oven and cool completely before frosting with:

MAPLE ICING

1 1-pound box confectioners' sugar
$\frac{1}{2}$ pound soft butter
2 teaspoons milk
2 teaspoons maple extract

Soften butter and sugar together. Add maple extract and blend. To make icing smoother, gradually add milk for desired consistency. Refrigerate unused icing.

Bløtkake

Serves 8 to 10

Bløtkake was the dessert always served for birthdays and special occasions in my father's home in Norway. In 1994, my mother, daughter, and I traveled to Spangeried and Lyngdal (where my parents grew up) and were always served generous portions of this with coffee when visiting relatives.

3 eggs
1 cup sugar
1 cup flour
3 teaspoons baking powder
$\frac{1}{4}$ cup water
club soda
1 package vanilla pudding mix, prepared according to directions, chilled
apricot jam
1 pint heavy cream, whipped

1. Cream eggs and sugar, beat well. Blend in flour, baking powder and water. Grease and flour 2 9-inch round pans. Pour batter into pans and bake at 350° for 30 minutes and cool completely in pans.

2. With a long, sharp knife, split each cake in half and sprinkle each piece with club soda. Layer cake as follows: bottom layer spread with vanilla pudding, remaining layers spread with apricot jam and whipped cream, ending with whipped cream on top. Refrigerate for several hours before slicing.

Pineapple Delight "A La Nana"

Makes 12 to 14 $\frac{1}{2}$-cup servings

This is our grandmother's special Christmas recipe. Everyone always wants to know her secret and we (Chenoa, Tashalena and Adam) are happy to share it with you.

1 cup cooked rice
2 tablespoons sugar or to taste
2 16-ounce cans crushed pineapple, drained
3 pints heavy cream
Maraschino cherries (optional)

1. When rice has cooled add sugar; mix and refrigerate for 1 hour. In a large bowl, mix rice with pineapple and refrigerate for several hours.

2. Whip cream at high speed until it is thick, adding sugar to taste, 8 to 10 minutes. Gently fold the pineapple-rice mixture into the whipped cream. Refrigerate until ready to serve. Garnish with cherries.

Mary Hunt's Fruit Cake

Makes 4 loaf-size cakes

My husband's mother, along with raising 9 children, was a wonderful baker. This fruitcake was served as a Christmas dessert at their home in New York, and is one that even your "non-fruitcake" guests will adore.

$\frac{1}{2}$ pound figs, cut into small pieces
$\frac{1}{2}$ cup raisins
1 8-ounce package dates, chopped
$\frac{1}{2}$ pound citron
$\frac{3}{4}$ pound currants
1 apple, chopped
2 bananas, chopped
1 cup grape juice
$\frac{1}{2}$ cup brandy or any type whiskey
1 cup ($\frac{1}{2}$ lb) butter
3 cups brown sugar
6 eggs, beaten
4 cups flour
$\frac{1}{2}$ teaspoon salt
2 teaspoons baking soda
2 tablespoons cinnamon
2 teaspoons cloves
2 teaspoons nutmeg
2 tablespoons molasses
1 cup walnuts, chopped

1. Soak figs, raisins, dates, citron, currants, apple and bananas in grape juice and brandy, stirring gently to coat the fruit.

2. Cream butter, add sugar and beat in eggs. Mix in flour and all dry ingredients.

3. Fold into the soaked fruit, add molasses and nuts, mix well. Generously butter loaf pans and place a double layer of wax paper on the bottom of each. Pour in batter and bake at 300° for 2 to 2$\frac{1}{2}$ hours. Cool in pans, remove and wrap tightly.

Patriotic Trifle

Serves 10 to 12
What better for a Fourth of July picnic?

1 quart strawberries, sliced, saving a few
    whole berries for the top
1 pint blueberries
2 cups seedless grapes, halved
$\frac{1}{3}$ cup rum (optional)
1 package instant vanilla pudding mix
    prepared according to package directions
1 6-ounce container frozen whipped
    topping, thawed
1 sponge or angel cake, sliced

In a trifle bowl or deep, clear glass dish,
layer ingredients as follows:

cake slices, sprinkled with rum, pudding,
strawberries, topping

cake slices, sprinkled with rum, pudding,
grapes, topping

cake slices, sprinkled with rum, pudding,
blueberries and topping

Garnish with reserved whole strawberries
and chill for at least 2 hours.

Gruyère Noel

Makes about 48 puffs
**These tasty bites are always a great success,
so easy but elegant.**

1 cup milk
4 tablespoons unsalted butter
$\frac{3}{4}$ teaspoon salt
pepper to taste
1 cup flour
4 large eggs plus 1 egg yolk
$\frac{1}{2}$ cup grated Gruyère cheese
$\frac{1}{4}$ cup freshly grated Parmesan cheese,
    plus 3 tablespoons for sprinkling on top
4 ounces cooked asparagus, chopped
2 tablespoons sun-dried tomatoes,
    chopped (drained well if packed in oil)

1. Bring milk and butter to a boil, add salt
   and pepper to taste. Lower heat, add
   flour; beat mixture for 1 minute until
   mixture pulls away from sides of the
   pan. Add whole eggs, one at a time,
   beating well after each addition.

2. Add Gruyère and Parmesan cheeses,
   stirring constantly over low heat until
   cheese has melted. Stir in asparagus and
   sun-dried tomatoes.

3. Drop rounded teaspoonfuls of batter on
   a buttered baking sheet, 1 inch apart.
   Brush tops with remaining egg yolk that
   has been thinned with a few drops of
   water. Sprinkle tops with reserved
   Parmesan cheese and bake puffs 1 sheet
   at a time on the middle rack of a 400°
   oven for 20 to 25 minutes until golden
   brown. Serve immediately with a nice
   glass of Burgundy.

Thanksgiving Steamed Pudding

Serves 6 to 8

During my childhood, Thanksgiving always included Grammie de Coster's delicious steamed pudding with your choice of hard sauce, or her unique sweet and sour hot molasses sauce. Today my family prefers the hard sauce, but I can't help making the molasses sauce for my own once a year treat!

$1\frac{7}{8}$ cups flour
$\frac{1}{2}$ teaspoon salt
1 teaspoon baking soda
$\frac{1}{4}$ teaspoon cloves
1 teaspoon allspice
$\frac{1}{2}$ teaspoon nutmeg
3 tablespoons butter or margarine, melted
$\frac{1}{2}$ cup molasses
$\frac{1}{2}$ cup milk
1 cup raisins and/or chopped nuts

1. Sift flour, salt, baking soda, cloves, allspice and nutmeg in a large bowl. Add melted butter, molasses and milk, stir until smooth. Add raisins and/or nuts, mixing well.

2. Spoon batter into a well-greased steamer or one-pound coffee can. Cover tightly with buttered aluminum foil or use cover of steamer. Place on a rack in a saucepan with at least 2 inches of boiling water. (If you don't have a rack that fits the pan, a folded washcloth is fine.) Cover saucepan and simmer for 2 to 3 hours. Check water, adding more as needed, keeping a constant 1-inch level of simmering water. Remove from pan and serve warm with hard sauce or "Old Fashioned Sauce."

HOT MOLASSES SAUCE
$\frac{2}{3}$ cup sugar
1 heaping tablespoon flour
cold water
$\frac{1}{2}$ cup molasses
$\frac{1}{2}$ to $\frac{3}{4}$ cup boiling water
$\frac{1}{3}$ cup vinegar
$\frac{1}{2}$ tablespoon nutmeg
$\frac{3}{4}$ teaspoon cinnamon

Add small amount of cold water to sugar and flour in a non-aluminum 1-quart saucepan. Stir in enough water to form paste. Add molasses and boiling water. Stir and cook over medium heat until mixture thickens. Add up to $\frac{1}{4}$ cup more water, if needed, but keep sauce thick. Add vinegar and spices and simmer for 5 minutes. Serve hot over hot steamed pudding. Top with whipped cream.

Sticky Toffee Pudding

Serves 8

Whenever my English grandmother from Henley-on-Thames would visit over the holidays, she would complain that there was never enough time for all of the baking and other preparations. There was, however, always enough time for her to prepare our favorite dessert often twice, both Christmas Eve and New Year's.

$1\frac{1}{4}$ cups boiling water
$\frac{3}{4}$ cup chopped dates
1 teaspoon baking soda
$\frac{1}{4}$ cup (4 tablespoons) butter
$\frac{3}{4}$ cup sugar
1 egg
1 teaspoon vanilla
1 cup plus 1 tablespoon flour
1 teaspoon baking powder

TOFFEE SAUCE
$\frac{1}{2}$ cup (8 tablespoons) butter
$\frac{1}{2}$ cup heavy cream
1 cup light brown sugar

1. In a bowl, mix boiling water, dates and baking soda. Let cool. Preheat oven to 350° and generously butter an 8-by-8-inch baking dish.

2. In a large bowl, beat butter and sugar until fluffy. Beat in egg and vanilla. Slowly beat in the flour and baking powder; add the date mixture. Pour batter into baking pan and bake for 35 minutes.

3. In a small saucepan, boil remaining butter, heavy cream and brown sugar, stirring over medium-low heat until slightly thickened, about 8 minutes.

4. Preheat broiler. Spread $\frac{1}{3}$ cup sauce over pudding and broil 1 minute until crisp. Spoon pudding into bowls and top with remaining sauce and lots of fresh whipped cream.

Mom's Italian Cream Pie

Makes 1 10-inch pie

My mother, who was not much of a baker, had this special recipe for a cream pie that she made on holidays. It was a favorite of my husband and children. Every holiday when she baked this pie, my husband would make a fuss over it, and she loved every minute of it. He made her feel as though she was the greatest baker in the world.

Now that Mom is gone, it is a must on Christmas and Easter. My husband loves the pie and enjoys it immensely but says it will never be quite the same as hers.

CRUST
4 cups flour
1 cup sugar
$\frac{1}{2}$ cup shortening
4 eggs
1 teaspoon baking powder

CREAM
$\frac{3}{4}$ cup flour
$\frac{3}{4}$ cup sugar
6 egg yolks
4 cups milk
1 teaspoon vanilla
1 14-ounce can sliced peaches in heavy
  syrup, drained
1 8-ounce jar maraschino cherries, drained
2 egg whites

1. Make a well with the flour and in the center add the shortening, sugar, eggs and baking powder. Mix well and knead until smooth. (May be frozen for future use.)

2. Combine the flour, sugar, egg yolks, milk and vanilla in a pan and cook over a moderate heat, stirring constantly, until thickened and smooth. Allow the cream to cool. Cut the crust mixture in half and roll out half the crust and place in a 10-inch pie plate.

3. Add some cream and layer the peaches and cherries, then add more cream and use the rest of the peaches and cherries. Roll out the other half of the crust and place it on top of the cream. Flute the edge of the crusts.

4. Whip the egg whites and brush over the top of the crust. Cover the edges of the crust with tin foil and bake in a 325° oven for approximately 20 minutes; remove the tin foil and bake for another 25 minutes or until top is light brown.

Grammie Morgan's Christmas Cookies

Makes about 4 dozen

This recipe dates back perhaps as far as the 1850s on my husband's side of the family. My 8 children all got their paint brushes out to decorate these at Christmas time, and we now share the tradition with 22 grandchildren, using a variety of cookie cutters (some hand-made) passed down from grandmothers in the past.

4 cups flour ($4\frac{1}{2}$ cups if using butter)
2 cups sugar
1 teaspoon salt
4 teaspoons baking powder
1 cup shortening or butter
4 eggs, beaten
$1\frac{1}{2}$ tablespoons milk
1 teaspoon vanilla or almond extract
  (or both)

1. Mix flour, sugar, salt and baking powder together in a large bowl. Work in shortening a little at a time. Add eggs, milk and vanilla and mix until combined, adding a small amount of flour if dough seems too sticky.

2. Knead until all ingredients are mixed in. Roll dough, in small batches, on a floured surface $\frac{1}{4}$-inch thick. Cut with cookie cutters and bake at 350° for 8 to 12 minutes or until the edges are light brown. If dough becomes hard to handle, refrigerate for 10 minutes before re-rolling. Remove cookies to a rack to cool before frosting and decorating with coconut, cinnamon shots or candies.

COOKIE PAINT

5 egg yolks
10 teaspoons water
5 food coloring colors

Place 1 egg yolk in each of 5 cups, add 2 teaspoons water and mix with a fork. Drop several drops of food coloring in each cup and decorate cookies using small paintbrushes. (Have cups of water on hand to clean brushes between batches.)

Almond Sand Tarts

Makes about 6 dozen

I am convinced that cookie baking is an inherited gene. Some of my fondest memories of my grandmother are wrapped up in cookies. She always had at least three different kinds, all carefully separated by wax paper in old containers. I shared many happy moments with my mother while she cut out the Christmas cookies and I decorated them. My children's friends always loved to come to our house for the home baked cookies (as well as the aroma). Few of my friends bake, so their children, and now their grandchildren, look forward to a plate of my Christmas cookies arriving on Christmas Eve.

1 cup butter or margarine
2 cups sugar
2 eggs
3 cups flour
2 teaspoons baking powder
$\frac{1}{2}$ teaspoon cinnamon
1 to $1\frac{1}{2}$ cups blanched and split almonds
cinnamon/sugar mixture: (2 teaspoons
    cinnamon - $\frac{1}{4}$ cup sugar)

1. Cream butter and sugar in a large bowl until light and fluffy. Beat in eggs, one at a time. Add 1 cup flour, baking powder and cinnamon; mix well. Add remaining 2 cups flour gradually, preferably mixing by hand. Form dough into 1 piece, wrap in plastic wrap and refrigerate for several hours or overnight.

2. Working with $\frac{1}{4}$ of the dough at a time, roll out to $\frac{1}{8}$-inch thickness on a lightly floured surface. Cut into 3-inch rounds or hearts with a cookie cutter. Place on a very lightly greased baking sheet. Arrange 3 pieces of almonds, pointed side towards the center on each cookie. Sprinkle with cinnamon/sugar mixture and bake at 350° for 8 to 9 minutes. Remove immediately to a wire rack to cool.

Loretta's Buckeyes

Makes 8 dozen

This makes a big batch and is always part of my cookie making marathon for holiday gift boxes.

1 pound butter, at room temperature
2 1-pound jars peanut butter, chunk or
    creamy
3 1-pound boxes confectioners' sugar
1 teaspoon vanilla
$1\frac{1}{4}$ pounds semi-sweet chocolate chips
    ($1\frac{1}{2}$ 12-ounce bags)
1 bar paraffin wax

1. In a large bowl, cream butter and peanut butter. Add confectioners' sugar and vanilla, mixing well. Roll into 1-inch balls.

2. In a double boiler, melt chocolate chips and paraffin. Stick a toothpick into each ball and dip halfway into heated chocolate (top half should not be coated). Place on waxed paper to harden and refrigerate until ready to serve.

My Grandmother's Christmas Sugar Cookies

Makes about 3 dozen

Mother and I have followed in her footsteps and have been baking and delivering these fresh out of the oven for years.

$\frac{1}{2}$ cup butter, softened
1 cup sugar
1 egg
1 teaspoon vanilla
1 tablespoon light cream
$1\frac{3}{4}$ cups flour
$1\frac{1}{2}$ teaspoons baking powder

1. Cream butter and sugar together until light and fluffy. Add egg, vanilla and cream. Sift together dry ingredients and stir into butter/sugar mixture. Chill at least 4 hours or best overnight.

2. Dust cutting board with a light mixture of flour and sugar to keep dough from getting too sticky. Break off about $\frac{1}{6}$ of the dough; refrigerate remainder. Continue rolling out 5 more batches of dough, keeping unused dough refrigerated as you work, for easier handling. Roll out to $\frac{1}{8}$- to $\frac{1}{4}$-inch thickness and cut with your favorite holiday cookie cutters. Place on a lightly greased cookie sheet, decorate with sprinkles, jimmies or colored sugar, if you like, and bake for 5 to 6 minutes at 350° until lightly browned. Carefully remove with a spatula and let cool on a rack.

Oslo Twists

Makes about 2 dozen

A holiday recipe from a dear great aunt.

3 egg yolks
$\frac{1}{2}$ teaspoon salt
$\frac{1}{4}$ cup confectioners' sugar
1 tablespoon whiskey or rum
vegetable oil

1. Beat egg yolks until creamy, add salt, sugar and whiskey. Turn dough out onto a well-floured board, knead until surface of dough is blistered in appearance (about 5 to 8 minutes).

2. Divide dough in half and roll each piece out very thin, about $\frac{1}{8}$ inch. With a knife, cut dough into 4-by-2-inch rectangles. Make a slit down the center and draw the long point of the dough through the cut to form a bow. Preheat oil in a heavy skillet to 375° and fry until lightly browned, about $\frac{1}{2}$ minute on each side. Drain on paper towels and sprinkle with additional confectioners' sugar.

Finfancy Gingerbread Men

Makes 4 to 5 dozen men, depending on thickness rolled

My son, Greg, is now nearly 30 years old and lives some distance away, but every Christmas, wherever he is, he impatiently awaits his delivery of Gingerbread Men. He has been known to hoard or hide the cookies to avoid having to share their soft spicy goodness! I suspect he has even used them for barter on occasion! I hope your family will enjoy them as much as we do.

1 cup shortening
1 cup sugar
1 egg
1 cup molasses
2 tablespoons cider vinegar
5 cups sifted flour
$1\frac{1}{2}$ teaspoons baking soda
$\frac{1}{2}$ teaspoon salt
2 to 3 teaspoons ground ginger
1 teaspoon cinnamon
1 teaspoon ground cloves

1. Thoroughly cream together shortening and sugar. Stir in egg, molasses and vinegar and beat well. Sift dry ingredients together. Blend completely into creamed mixture.

2. Divide into balls of dough (4 to 5), cover and refrigerate for up to 3 hours which allows the spices to blend and makes it easier to roll out the dough. One ball at a time, roll cookie dough to a thickness of $\frac{1}{4}$ to $\frac{1}{2}$ inches. These cookies are to be thick and cake-like. Do not over-handle or roll too thin. Use dusted flour as necessary to manage dough. Cut gingerbread men with 5-inch cookie cutter and bake on a greased cookie sheet for 6 to 9 minutes in a preheated 375° oven. Cookies should just begin to brown at the edges. Thicker cookies require longer baking time, but be careful not to over-bake.

3. Remove sheet from oven and allow to cool for a couple minutes then carefully move gingerbread men to a cooling rack. Continue to roll and cut cookies, baking them one sheet at a time.

4. When cookies are cool, decorate with confectioners' frosting. Using a pastry tube (or roll a triangle of waxed paper into a cone shape with a sharp point, fill with some frosting, cut the tip to desired thickness), outline gingerbread man with curly cues and draw in eyes, smile and buttons.

FROSTING
confectioners' sugar
milk or cream

Whisk 1 cup of confectioners' sugar with just enough liquid to make thick, creamy frosting. It should not be runny, but of a consistency to work through a pastry tube and hold its design on the cookie. Candies and raisins can be used to decorate cookies, but simple is often best!

Pineapple Cheese Baklava

Serves 16

As an experiment on an Easter recipe, two sisters came up with this terrific combination.

1 $14\frac{1}{2}$-ounce can crushed pineapple
1 8-ounce package cream cheese, softened
1 cup ricotta cheese
1 cup sugar, divided into $\frac{1}{2}$ cups
2 egg yolks
1 teaspoon grated lemon rind
1 teaspoon vanilla
8 sheets thawed phyllo dough
$\frac{1}{2}$ cup ($\frac{1}{4}$ pound) melted butter
$\frac{2}{3}$ cup coarsely ground walnuts
1 teaspoon lemon juice

1. Drain pineapple and reserve $\frac{1}{2}$ cup juice in a small saucepan. In mixing bowl combine cream cheese, ricotta, $\frac{1}{2}$ cup sugar, egg yolks, lemon rind and vanilla. Blend at medium speed until well blended. Stir in drained pineapple.

2. On a well-greased 9-by-13-by-2-inch baking pan, place first sheet of phyllo dough. Brush with melted butter and sprinkle with ground walnuts. Repeat this procedure with the next 3 sheets of dough.

3. Spoon on the pineapple-cheese mixture and spread evenly over the dough. Top mixture with 3 more sheets of dough, brushing each with butter and sprinkling with nuts. Place last sheet of dough on top, brush with butter and using the tip of a sharp knife, carve a diamond pattern on the entire pastry. Bake about 50 minutes at 350° until golden brown.

4. Combine the reserved juice, remaining $\frac{1}{2}$ cup sugar and lemon juice in saucepan and cook until it forms a thick syrup, about 10 minutes. Cook slightly and then drizzle evenly over the entire pastry. Let cool in pan before cutting into triangles.

Haunted House Halloween Brownies

Makes 16

FIRST LAYER:
2 squares unsweetened chocolate
$\frac{1}{2}$ cup ($\frac{1}{4}$ pound) butter
1 cup sugar
2 eggs, beaten
1 teaspoon vanilla
1 teaspoon grated orange rind
$\frac{1}{2}$ cup flour
$\frac{1}{8}$ teaspoon salt
$\frac{3}{4}$ cup chopped walnuts

Combine the chocolate and butter; melt in a microwave or in the top of a double boiler over hot water. Beat in sugar, eggs, vanilla and orange rind. Stir in flour, salt, and nuts. Bake in a greased 8-inch square baking pan in a 325° oven for 30 to 35 minutes until done. Cool in pan.

SECOND LAYER:
1 cup sifted confectioners' sugar
2 tablespoons soft butter
2 teaspoons orange juice
$\frac{1}{2}$ teaspoon vanilla
3 or 4 drops orange food coloring
   (or mix red and yellow to make orange)

Combine the sugar, butter, orange juice and vanilla to make a smooth frosting. Tint with the orange food coloring. Spread over cooled brownies in pan. Chill for 30 minutes.

THIRD LAYER:
$\frac{1}{4}$ square unsweetened chocolate
$1\frac{1}{2}$ teaspoons butter

Combine chocolate and butter and melt in a microwave or double boiler. Drizzle over chilled brownies. Cut into 2-inch squares.

M&M's Pecan Sweets

Makes 6 cups

4 cups pecans
2 egg whites
1 cup sugar
dash of salt
8 tablespoons butter

Toast pecans on cookie sheet for 10 minutes at 300°. Beat egg whites until stiff. Fold in sugar, nuts and salt. Coat nuts well. Melt butter on cookie sheet in oven. Spread nuts on cookie sheet and bake approximately 25 to 30 minutes at 300°, stirring every 10 minutes until butter is absorbed. Cool and enjoy.

Red And White Christmas Fudge

Makes 36 squares
Serve this on your favorite holiday plate, garnished with sprigs of holly.

$2\frac{1}{2}$ cups confectioners' sugar
$\frac{2}{3}$ cup milk
$\frac{1}{4}$ cup (4 tablespoons) butter
12 ounces white chocolate, coarsely
  chopped
$\frac{1}{2}$ teaspoon almond extract
$\frac{3}{4}$ teaspoon dried cranberries or cherries,
  coarsely chopped
$\frac{3}{4}$ cup almond slices, lightly toasted

1. Line an 8-inch square pan with foil or plastic wrap. Spray with nonstick cooking spray.

2. In a heavy 3-quart saucepan, whisk together confectioners' sugar and milk. Add butter and bring to a boil, stirring constantly. Boil without stirring for 5 minutes.

3. Reduce heat to low and add chocolate and almond extract. Stir with a whisk until chocolate melts and mixture is smooth. Add the dried fruit and toasted almonds. Pour mixture into prepared pan and chill, covered, for at least 4 hours until firm. Invert pan on the counter, peel off wrap and cut into 1-inch squares.

Swedish Christmas Nuts

Makes 4 cups
Everyone loves to receive these over the holidays – a 30 year old tradition.

2 cups pecan halves
2 cups walnut pieces
1 cup sugar
dash of salt
2 egg whites, stiffly beaten
$\frac{1}{2}$ cup (8 tablespoons) butter, melted

1. Spread nuts on a jelly roll pan (15-by-10-by-1-inch) and toast at 325° for 10 minutes, shaking pan several times to avoid burning, watch carefully.

2. Add sugar to egg whites, a little at a time and beat until mixture forms a meringue, about 8 to 10 minutes. Drizzle butter over nuts, toss to coat and spread meringue on top. Bake at 325° 25 to 30 minutes, turning every 10 minutes, until nuts are nicely toasted. Cool completely before placing in decorative containers.

World's Best Chocolate Fudge

Makes $1\frac{1}{4}$ pounds

This old family fudge recipe came from my great-grandfather, Midshipman (later Captain) Philip R. Alger, of Annapolis, who made it for his classmates over gas lights, at the Naval Academy, from 1876 to 1880! I consider it to be the world's best fudge. My Dad, The Hon. John R.M. Alger, passed it down to me. He's been making it for as long as I can remember. We loved it so much as kids, that he used to stay up and make it after we'd gone to bed (so we couldn't get at it and eat it all in one sitting). Once when he left on a business trip, he hid the batch he'd just made. We found it while he was gone, and when he returned and looked in the cupboard there were only crumbs left!

2 cups sugar
1 cup milk
$\frac{1}{2}$ teaspoon salt
2 squares unsweetened chocolate
2 tablespoons white corn syrup
2 tablespoons butter
$\frac{1}{2}$ teaspoon vanilla
$\frac{1}{2}$ to 1 cup chopped nuts, walnuts or pecans

1. In a medium saucepan, combine sugar, milk, salt, chocolate and corn syrup. Stir over low heat until sugar dissolves. Continue cooking over medium heat, stirring occasionally until mixture reaches 238° on a candy thermometer. A little drop of the mixture should form a soft ball when dropped into cold water. Remove from heat.

2. Add butter; do not stir. Cool without stirring to 110°. (You should be able to rest your hand on the bottom of the pan.) Add vanilla and nuts, beat with a spoon until mixture loses its gloss. Pour into a greased 9-by-5-by-3-inch pan and cool thoroughly before cutting into squares.

NOTE:
When checking the temperature of the fudge, measure in the middle of the mixture, not at the bottom of the pan.

Glazed And Spiced Pecans

Makes 3 cups

I like to serve these at each place setting for a holiday meal, in old individual salt dishes that belonged to my great-grand-mother.

2 tablespoons butter
3 cups pecan halves
$\frac{1}{2}$ cup light brown sugar
1 teaspoon paprika
2 teaspoons chili powder
1 tablespoon ground cumin
3 tablespoons apple cider or white wine vinegar
coarse salt to taste

1. Melt butter in a large skillet over medium heat. Add pecans and sauté lightly, until browned, about 3 minutes. Add sugar and cook until lightly caramelized.
2. Stir in paprika, chili powder and cumin. Add vinegar and continue cooking until all liquid is evaporated. Season with salt. Spread pecans on a cookie sheet and bake at 350° until crisp, about 3 to 5 minutes. Serve as a cocktail nibble or as an addition to a mixed green salad. These may be stored in the freezer for unexpected guests.

Ruby Red Port Wine Jelly

Makes 2 cups

Make this early in December as a gift for special friends – a perfect condiment for ham, lamb, or game.

2 cups port wine
3 cups sugar
$\frac{1}{4}$ teaspoon powdered cinnamon
$\frac{1}{4}$ teaspoon powdered cloves
6 whole cloves
$\frac{1}{2}$ bottle liquid pectin

1. Place the wine into a medium saucepan. Stir in sugar and spices and mix well. Heat and stir constantly until the sugar is dissolved.
2. Add the pectin and bring to a boil for one minute. Remove from heat and skim off the foam. Pour into sterilized jelly jars (4 small jars) and seal with $\frac{1}{8}$-inch of paraffin wax or use canning lids.

Apple Nut Sage Stuffing

Makes 8 cups
No need for the bird... serve cooked stuffing in baked apple or acorn squash halves. This custard-like stuffing is an excellent vegetarian holiday accompaniment.

1 1-pound loaf white bread, torn or diced into small pieces
3 cups chicken or vegetable broth
6 tablespoons butter
3 medium onions, chopped
$1\frac{1}{2}$ cups chopped celery
1 cup slivered almonds, toasted
1 cup walnuts, toasted
2 teaspoons dried sage
1 teaspoon dried thyme
1 cup chopped apple
salt and pepper to taste
6 eggs

1. Place bread in a large mixing bowl. Pour chicken broth over and let stand for 5 minutes until most of broth is absorbed.

2. Melt butter in a large heavy skillet and sauté onions and celery over medium heat until tender. Stir in almonds, walnuts and seasonings. Sauté 5 or more minutes. Add mixture to bread. Stir in apples and season with salt and pepper.

   Beat eggs with a fork until well blended and pour over stuffing; toss lightly until bread is well coated. Transfer mixture to a buttered 13-by-9-inch baking pan and bake at 325° uncovered until golden brown and cooked through, about 1 hour. Serve immediately.

Rhubarb Chutney

Makes 1 quart
If you usually freeze some of your spring harvest, try this rich, tart chutney over the winter holidays.

2 pounds brown sugar
2 cups cider vinegar
2 pounds rhubarb, chopped into $\frac{1}{2}$-inch pieces
1 pound golden raisins
1 large fresh ginger root, peeled and grated
6 cloves garlic, peeled and minced
3 lemons, seeded and thinly sliced
$\frac{1}{2}$ teaspoon cayenne pepper

Place the sugar and vinegar in a heavy-bottomed saucepan and bring to a boil. Add the other ingredients and lower the heat to a simmer. Cook, stirring occasionally for 2 to $2\frac{1}{2}$ hours until mixture is thick and dark. Put in sterilized jars and seal.

Peabody Punch

Serves 50+

For a while in the late 1980s and early 1990s, my brother hosted a Solstice Feast that was attended by old college friends and acquaintances from the New London area. These parties were quite festive (some would say wild), made more so perhaps by the consumption of this punch. This punch was originally served by Salem, Massachusetts merchant Joseph Peabody (1751 – 1844), and has been known to make you "waltz into eternity!"

1 pot strong tea (1 quart, use 4 teabags)
1 13-ounce jar apple or guava jelly
3 1-liter bottles dark rum, Bacardi or
    Barbancourt
1 1-liter bottle Taylor Tawny Port
1 1-liter bottle new red table wine
½ cup French brandy
4 cups orange juice
2 cups lime juice
6 tablespoons lemon juice
½ cup grenadine syrup
ginger ale, seltzer
thinly sliced fruit, lemon, lime, orange

1. Make tea in a saucepan, let steep 6 minutes. While tea is still hot, dissolve jelly in tea and let cool. Mix all liquors in a large pot, add fruit juices, grenadine and tea. Transfer punch to bottles and refrigerate until ready to serve.

2. Fill a large punch bowl with ice and mix punch half and half with ginger ale or seltzer. Float fruit slices on top and propose a toast.

Posset

Serves 24

This is a traditional 18th century Christmas drink – a family tradition here in Boston. Served before dinner.

3 pints cream, whipped
juice of 10 lemons
1 gallon dry white wine
sugar to taste
ground cinnamon

Fold whipped cream into lemon juice and wine in a large, chilled punch bowl. Season as you wish with sugar, usually about 1 cup. Ladle into punch cups and sprinkle with cinnamon.

Trinity Church Wassail

Serves 12
From an Old Concord family.

2 cups sugar
2 cups water
6 whole cloves
2 cinnamon sticks
1 piece crystallized ginger about as large
   as a quarter
5 oranges, cut into slices
4 lemons, cut into slices
2 cups cider

Boil sugar and water for 10 minutes to make a syrup. Add spices, ginger and fruit. Let stand for 1 hour to infuse. Add cider, bring to a boil and turn off heat. Serve warm.

Beacon Hill Eggnog

Serves 6
Make your own for the holidays, it is well worth it.

6 egg yolks
$\frac{1}{4}$ cup sugar
2 cups cream or half-and-half
2 cups milk
1 teaspoon vanilla
$\frac{1}{2}$ cup liqueur, dark rum, brandy or
   bourbon
whipped cream
freshly grated nutmeg

1. Beat egg yolks and sugar in a saucepan. Stir in cream and cook, stirring over medium heat until mixture reaches 160° and is thick enough to coat the back of a spoon. Do not boil.

2. Remove saucepan from heat and stir in milk, vanilla and liqueur. Chill at least 4 hours and pour into your best punch bowl. Ladle into cups and top with a dollop of whipped cream. Sprinkle with freshly grated nutmeg.

Berries,
Bogs & Bark

Cranberry French Toast Bake

Serves 6
A breakfast from the "Burdick boggs."

6 slices wide white bread
  (Texas Toast style), cubed with crust
$\frac{1}{2}$ cup dried cranberries
3 ounces cream cheese, cubed
3 eggs
1$\frac{1}{2}$ cups milk
$\frac{1}{2}$ cup maple syrup
1 teaspoon vanilla
1 teaspoon cinnamon
2 tablespoons sugar

Lightly grease or spray with nonstick cooking spray an 11-by-7-inch baking pan. Layer bread, cranberries and cream cheese in dish. Beat eggs, add milk, syrup and vanilla, pour over bread. Cover and refrigerate overnight. When ready to bake, sprinkle with cinnamon and sugar. Bake, uncovered, in a 350° oven for 40 to 45 minutes until puffed and golden brown. Serve warm with maple syrup.

To gauge the freshness of a berry, gently drop it on a work surface. Due to their inner air pocket, ripe cranberries bounce.

Fresh cranberries should be tightly wrapped and refrigerated for up to weeks. They can be frozen for up to a year.

Apple Maple Oven Pancake

Serves 4
A favorite East Haddam Sunday breakfast – great on those cold and snowy winter mornings.

4 tablespoons butter
$\frac{1}{2}$ cup maple syrup
4 Macintosh apples, peeled, cored and
  sliced $\frac{1}{4}$-inch thick
1 cup flour
2 teaspoons baking powder
2 tablespoons sugar
$\frac{1}{2}$ teaspoon salt
1 cup milk
1 egg
1 cup flour
2 teaspoons lemon juice

1. Preheat oven to 350°. In a 10-inch ovenproof skillet, melt 2 tablespoons butter, add $\frac{1}{4}$ cup maple syrup and apples. Cook over medium heat for 10 to 12 minutes until caramelized.

2. Mix flour, baking powder, sugar and salt. Add milk, egg and remaining 2 tablespoons butter (melted). When apples are done, remove from heat and add remaining $\frac{1}{4}$ cup maple syrup and lemon juice. Pour batter over the apples and bake for 15 minutes until puffed and brown. Remove from oven and serve with warm maple syrup and butter.

Apple Cranberry Breakfast Pudding

Serves 8 to 12

4 cups milk
¾ cup firmly packed brown sugar (divided use)
½ teaspoon salt
1 cup fresh cranberries, halved, plus extras for garnish
8 ounces golden raisins
2 cups rolled oats
4 to 5 Red Delicious or other apples, not peeled, cored and sliced thin
1 cup chopped almonds
sour cream, lowfat or regular
cinnamon sugar

1. Preheat oven to 350°. Combine milk, ½ cup brown sugar and salt in a large microwave-safe bowl. Heat on high until very hot but not boiling, about 6 to 8 minutes.

2. Mix in the cranberries, raisins, oats, apples and nuts; mix well. Sprinkle with remaining ¼ cup brown sugar. Place in a 3-quart casserole that has been lightly buttered and bake for 30 minutes. Stir before serving. Mix sour cream with a little cinnamon sugar and top each serving with a dollop and a few extra cranberries.

To reheat: If made ahead of time and refrigerated, warm for 30 minutes in a preheated 325° oven.

Mountain Maple Granola

Makes about 6 cups
Sprinkle on fresh fruit or yogurt, or as a snack. Your friends will want this recipe.

4 cups old-fashioned rolled oats
¼ cup shelled sunflower seeds
¼ cup chopped nuts – walnuts, pecans, or almonds
¾ cup thawed, undiluted apple juice concentrate
¼ cup pure maple syrup
1 tablespoon vegetable oil
½ cup dried cranberries
½ cup golden raisins

1. Preheat oven to 350°. Spray or lightly oil a large baking sheet. Combine oats, sunflower seeds and nuts in a large bowl. Drizzle with apple juice, maple syrup and oil. Toss until well coated. Spread on baking sheet and bake for 30 to 35 minutes, stirring every 5 minutes, until lightly browned and fragrant. Remove from oven and let cool.

2. Place mixture into a large bowl, add dried fruit and mix well. Place in a tightly sealed container.

Early each Spring, weeks before the buds on the maples begin to swell, the Vermont farmer plows through the snow to drill holes in the sapwood. Into each hole he hammers an iron spout onto which he hangs a covered bucket so that the sap drips in, but the rain and melting snow stay out.

Spicey Orange And Cranberry Salad

Serves 4

4 cups mixed salad greens, spinach included
4 naval oranges, sectioned
$\frac{1}{4}$ cup chopped fresh parsley
$\frac{1}{4}$ cup chopped fresh cilantro
$\frac{1}{3}$ cup pecans, broken
$\frac{3}{4}$ cup fresh chopped cranberries

DRESSING:
3 cloves garlic, minced
$\frac{1}{4}$ cup olive oil
$\frac{1}{4}$ cup orange juice
1 teaspoon cumin
2 tablespoons balsamic vinegar
$\frac{1}{2}$ teaspoon cayenne pepper
salt and pepper to taste

1. Toast pecans for 10 minutes in a 350° oven. Toss greens in a large salad bowl or on a platter. Arrange orange sections on top of greens and sprinkle with parsley, cilantro, pecans and cranberries.

2. Whisk together the dressing ingredients in a small bowl until well blended. Drizzle over salad and serve.

To freeze fresh berries, tightly wrap unwashed berries in plastic or store in a tightly sealed container.

Frozen berries do not need to be thawed before use.

Cranberry Salad Mold

Serves 8 to 10

This Thanksgiving recipe from my aunt has been a tradition for years. As a child, I remember grinding the ingredients in a meat grinder with a large bowl below to catch everything. Thank goodness for modern technology and the food processor!

2 cups cranberries
1 apple, seeded and quartered
1 orange, seeded and sliced
1 cup chopped celery
$\frac{1}{2}$ cup chopped walnuts
1 package lemon Jell-O
$1\frac{1}{4}$ cups boiling water
$1\frac{1}{2}$ cups sugar

1. In a food processor with a metal blade, chop the cranberries, apple and orange. Combine with the celery and walnuts.

2. Dissolve Jell-O in boiling water, add sugar and stir until well blended. Refrigerate for at least 1 hour until partially set. Fold in fruit mixture and pour into a 2-quart decorative mold. Chill for 4 hours or more. To serve, dip mold in warm water for 30 seconds and unmold onto a lettuce lined serving platter.

Gram's Cranberry Ambrosia Salad

Serves 12 to 14

This recipe has been in the family "since before I was born," says Mary. Always served as the "last" dessert at both Thanksgiving and Christmas.

1 12-ounce bag fresh cranberries, minced
1 16-ounce can crushed pineapple, drained
1 cup sugar
1 cup chopped pecans plus halves for garnish
1 pint heavy cream, whipped, or 2 cups Cool Whip
fresh mint

1. In a large bowl, combine cranberries, pineapple, sugar and chopped pecans. Fold the whipped cream into the cranberry mixture one quarter at a time.

2. Pour the salad into your favorite glass bowl (a trifle bowl looks great) and refrigerate, covered, overnight. Before serving, decorate top with fresh mint and reserved pecan halves.

When the settlers of New England landed, they found bright red berries – cranberries – growing along the damp shore. The Indians called them sassamanesh and not only ate them raw or cooked, but were known to rub the pulp onto a wound to "draw the poison" out.

Maple-Ginger Candied Sweet Potatoes

Serves 12

Nonstick cooking spray
6 medium sweet potatoes, about $3\frac{1}{2}$ pounds
1 cup pure maple syrup
1 cup orange juice
1 tablespoon chopped fresh ginger
1 medium onion, finely chopped
$\frac{1}{4}$ cup chopped parsley
salt and white pepper to taste

1. Preheat oven to 325°. Lightly coat a 3-quart baking pan with nonstick cooking spray. Peel the potatoes and cut into $\frac{1}{2}$-inch slices. Arrange, overlapping slices, in prepared pan.

2. In a small saucepan, combine the maple syrup, orange juice, ginger, onion, parsley, salt and pepper. Bring to a boil and pour the hot syrup over the potatoes. Bake for 1 hour and 15 minutes, basting occasionally with the syrup. This can be prepared up to 3 days in advance. To reheat, cover with foil and bake for 20 to 25 minutes at 325°.

Pumpkin Soup With Cranberries And Sage

Serves 6

1 pound sugar pumpkin or butternut
squash
2 tablespoons olive oil
$\frac{1}{2}$ cup onion, chopped
$\frac{1}{2}$ cup celery, chopped
$\frac{1}{2}$ cup carrots, chopped
2 cups peeled apple, chopped
$\frac{1}{2}$ cup fresh cranberries
2 teaspoons fresh grated ginger
pinch EACH: cinnamon, nutmeg, and allspice
salt and pepper to taste
2 tablespoons fresh chopped sage
$2\frac{1}{2}$ cups chicken stock
1 cup cranberry juice

1. Prick the pumpkin with a fork in several
   spots, place on a cookie sheet and bake
   at 350° in a preheated oven for one hour
   until soft. When cool enough to handle,
   separate flesh from the skin, discard skin.

2. Heat oil in a large saucepan over medium
   heat and add vegetables, including
   pumpkin, apples and cranberries, stirring
   constantly. Add seasonings, stock and
   juice; bring to a boil, reduce heat and
   cook until vegetables are tender.

3. Cool slightly and purée in blender or
   food processor in batches and return to
   saucepan to heat. Adjust seasonings and
   serve hot with a dollop of whipped
   cream or sour cream.

Cranberry And Rosemary Glazed Brie

Serves 20

1 Brie cheese wheel, 10 inches in diameter

MARMALADE:
2 cups cranberries
$\frac{3}{4}$ cup brown sugar
$\frac{1}{3}$ cup golden raisins
$\frac{1}{3}$ cup water
1 teaspoon dry mustard
1 teaspoon ground allspice
pinch of ground cloves and ground ginger
3 tablespoons fresh chopped rosemary

Preheat oven to 300°.

TO PREPARE MARMALADE:
Combine all ingredients in a medium
saucepan and simmer until berries pop.

TO PREPARE CHEESE:
Using a sharp knife, cut a circle in the top
of the rind, being careful to leave a $\frac{1}{2}$-inch
border of rind. Remove the center of the
rind being careful not to cut into the
cheese. Spread the marmalade over the
top and place the cheese in a baking dish.
Bake until soft, about 15 minutes. Cool
slightly and serve with apple slices and
crackers.

Cranberry Nut Wild Rice Stuffing

Makes 10 cups

When asked to bring a dish for a "Leftover Thanksgiving Party," I found that neither I, nor anyone else, had any stuffing left. For a quickie version, you may substitute wild rice pilaf mix, adding just the fruits, nuts and vegetables.

$\frac{1}{2}$ cup (8 tablespoons) butter
2 large onions, chopped
1 garlic clove, minced
6 cups chicken broth
2 cups wild rice
2 cups long grain brown rice
2 cups dried cranberries
$\frac{1}{2}$ cup chopped fresh parsley
2 tablespoons chopped fresh thyme
$1\frac{1}{2}$ cups hazelnuts, toasted, husked and coarsely chopped (you may substitute chestnuts)
1 cup chopped green onions

1. Melt butter in large heavy saucepan over medium-high heat. Add onions and garlic and sauté until tender, about 4 minutes. Add chicken broth, bring to a boil and add wild rice. Reduce heat to medium, cover and simmer for 30 minutes. Mix in brown rice, cover and simmer until rice is just tender and most of liquid is absorbed, about 30 minutes.

2. Stir cranberries, parsley and thyme into rice. Cover and cook until remaining liquid is absorbed, about 5 minutes. Mix in hazelnuts and green onions, seasoning generously with salt and pepper.

TO BAKE STUFFING IN TURKEY:
Loosely fill main cavity with stuffing, placing any extra stuffing in a buttered casserole. Cover with buttered foil and bake alongside turkey until heated through, about 30 minutes.

TO BAKE ALL OF STUFFING ON THE SIDE:
Preheat oven to 350°. Butter a 15-by-10-by-2-inch glass or ceramic baking pan, transfer stuffing to pan. Cover with buttered foil and bake stuffing for 40 minutes.

Hot Spiced Cranberry Apple Cider

Serves 4

2 cups cranberry juice
2 cups apple cider
2 cinnamon sticks
8 whole cloves
$\frac{1}{2}$ teaspoon ground allspice
$\frac{1}{4}$ cup brown sugar
3 tablespoon lemon juice
$\frac{1}{3}$ cup orange juice
cinnamon sticks and orange slices for garnish

Combine all ingredients in a large saucepan. Bring to a boil and turn down to simmer. Steep for 15 minutes until flavors blend and sugar is completely dissolved. Pour into mugs and garnish with cinnamon sticks and an orange slice.

Provincetown Blueberry Pudding

Serves 6

My Grandmother, Alice F. Dunham, handed down one recipe to me when I was just a boy. I spent my summers in Provincetown and my favorite dessert was her "Blueberry Pudding." It was cooked with local blueberries picked by my brother and I. This may have been why it tasted so good. We lived (my brother, my grandmother and I) in the Dunham Family summer house. The Dunhams were a prominent whaling family in the late 1800s, early 1900s. The Dunham whaling ship, "William A. Grozier," sailed out of P-town for twenty to twenty-five years before it finally sank off Cape Hatteras in 1919 with all hands.

1 quart blueberries
$\frac{1}{2}$ cup of sugar
1 cup or so of water
pinch of nutmeg
2 tablespoons of cornstarch
2 cups sifted flour
3 teaspoons baking powder
$\frac{1}{2}$ teaspoon salt
4 tablespoons butter
$\frac{1}{2}$ cup milk

1. In a large bowl, toss blueberries with sugar, water, nutmeg and cornstarch. Pour into a 2-quart baking pan that has been buttered both on the sides and around the rim.
2. Mix flour, butter, baking soda and salt. Add about $\frac{1}{2}$ cup milk or enough to make a good dough consistency. Roll into a circle large enough to cover baking dish, place on top and seal the edges. Prick crust and bake pudding at 400° for 20 minutes. Serve warm with sweet sauce.

Cranberry Muffin Puddings

Serves 8

A must during the Thanksgiving to Christmas season; decorate with a piece of holly and a red candle – make them ahead and freeze them.

$1\frac{1}{2}$ tablespoons butter
$\frac{1}{2}$ cup sugar
$\frac{1}{2}$ cup evaporated milk
1 cup flour
$1\frac{1}{2}$ teaspoons baking powder
$\frac{1}{2}$ teaspoon salt
$1\frac{1}{2}$ cups whole fresh cranberries

In a medium bowl, cream butter and sugar. Combine with remaining ingredients, mixing well. Pour batter into 8 paper-lined muffin tins and bake for 30 minutes at 350°. Serve warm with vanilla sauce.

VANILLA SAUCE
$\frac{1}{2}$ cup (8 tablespoons) butter
$\frac{1}{2}$ cup medium or heavy cream
1 cup sugar
1 teaspoon vanilla

Combine all ingredients in a small saucepan and cook for 5 to 7 minutes until slightly thickened. Spoon over warm cranberry puddings.

Cranberry Pudding With Orange Sauce

Serves 8 to 10

For many years, I have had a passion for all things cranberry. During the holiday season when they are readily available, I often experiment with new ways to craft, decorate or consume these delightful berries. The orange sauce compliments the sweet and tangy flavor of this dessert.

CRANBERRY PUDDING
$1\frac{1}{3}$ cups flour
2 teaspoons baking powder
$2\frac{1}{2}$ cups fresh cranberries
1 egg
$\frac{1}{2}$ cup molasses
$\frac{1}{3}$ cup hot water

1. In a large mixing bowl, sift flour and baking powder; set aside. Sort, rinse and drain cranberries. Cut each cranberry in half. Gently stir berries into flour mixture to coat.

2. In a small mixing bowl, beat egg with a fork, add molasses and hot water. Add to flour/cranberry mixture and gently mix until evenly moistened. Pour into a greased 4- to 5-cup pudding mold. Cover loosely with foil. Place in a steamer with a wire rack. Pour in boiling water to just below level of rack, cover and steam for $1\frac{1}{2}$ hours or until springy to the touch. Let stand 5 minutes before unmolding; cool to room temperature and serve with warm sauce.

ORANGE SAUCE
Makes 1 cup

$\frac{1}{4}$ cup sugar
1 tablespoon cornstarch
1 tablespoon finely grated orange peel
1 cup orange juice
2 teaspoons lemon juice

In a small saucepan, stir sugar, cornstarch, orange peel, and orange juice. Over medium heat, cook until thickened and bubbly. Remove from heat and add lemon juice. Serve immediately over cranberry pudding. Refrigerate any remaining sauce.

As a symbol of New England cuisine, cranberries may have been served at the Pilgrims' first Thanksgiving dinner in October, 1621. It was not until trade with the West Indies was established that the tart and sour berries were cooked with sugar.

Tabor Cranberry Cake

Serves 8 to 10

My husband works for the largest cran-berry grower in Massachusetts, and picks a box of berries for me each fall. This cake-like pie is our favorite recipe.

2 cups fresh cranberries, whole or
  chopped
$\frac{1}{2}$ cup walnuts, coarsely chopped
$1\frac{1}{2}$ cups sugar
2 eggs
$\frac{3}{4}$ cup butter (12 tablespoons), melted and
  cooled
1 cup flour
$\frac{1}{4}$ teaspoon salt
$\frac{1}{4}$ teaspoon almond extract

1. Preheat oven to 350°. Chop cranber-ries if desired, and mix with walnuts and $\frac{1}{2}$ cup sugar. Spread in a lightly buttered 10-inch pie plate.

2. Mix eggs, butter, remaining 1 cup sugar, flour, salt and almond extract until well blended. Pour over cranber-ry mixture and bake on the middle rack of oven for 40 minutes, or until a tooth pick inserted in the middle comes out clean. Serve with a dollop of ice cream on top.

Cranberry Cake Ring

Makes 1 9-inch cake

This recipe originated from my great aunt, Anna Dunbar Rivers, who was born in 1889 in Wallingford, Connecticut. She shared it with many friends; always a popular dessert.

$\frac{1}{2}$ cup butter or margarine
$\frac{3}{4}$ cup sugar
1 egg
1 teaspoon vanilla
1 16-ounce can jellied cranberry sauce
2 cups flour
$\frac{1}{2}$ teaspoon cinnamon
$\frac{1}{4}$ teaspoon cloves
2 teaspoons baking soda
chopped walnuts

1. In a medium bowl, cream butter and sugar. Add egg, vanilla, and cranberry sauce. Mix until well blended.

2. Sift flour, cinnamon, cloves and baking soda, add to butter mixture. Pour bat-ter into a greased 9-inch tube pan and bake in a 350° oven for 1 hour or until a toothpick inserted in the center comes out clean.

3. Make a frosting. Cream 2 tablespoons butter and gradually beat in 1 cup confectioners' sugar. Add $1\frac{1}{2}$ to 2 tablespoons milk, the frosting should be thin enough to drip down the sides of the cake. Frost, and sprinkle with chopped walnuts.

Cranberry Apple Cake Clapp

Serves 12

$2\frac{1}{4}$ cups flour
1 teaspoon baking powder
1 teaspoon cinnamon
$\frac{3}{4}$ teaspoon salt
$\frac{1}{2}$ teaspoon baking soda
$1\frac{3}{4}$ teaspoons sugar
$1\frac{1}{4}$ cups vegetable oil
2 eggs
$\frac{1}{4}$ cup milk
1 teaspoon vanilla
2 cups apple, peeled and chopped
$\frac{1}{2}$ cup sweetened dry cranberries
1 teaspoon grated lemon peel
1 to 2 tablespoons confectioners' sugar
whipped cream

1. Preheat oven to 350°. Grease and flour a 12-cup Bundt cake pan. Mix flour, baking powder, cinnamon, salt and baking soda in a medium mixing bowl.

2. Combine sugar, oil, eggs, milk and vanilla in a large mixing bowl. Beat at medium speed with an electric mixer until blended. Add dry ingredients slowly, scrapping bowl after each addition. Stir in the apples, lemon rind and cranberries. Pour into prepared pan and bake for 1 hour 15 minutes until a toothpick inserted in center comes out clean. Let stand 10 minutes and invert onto a cake plate. Sift confectioners' sugar onto cake and serve warm, topped with whipped cream.

Creamy Maple Rice Pudding

Serves 4

As a child in Pennsylvania, on some lucky days, I would find a dish of this pudding waiting for me when I came in from sledding or winter chores. Comfort food supreme!

4 cups whole milk
$\frac{1}{3}$ cup white or brown rice
$\frac{1}{3}$ cup maple syrup
$\frac{1}{2}$ cup raisins
$\frac{1}{2}$ teaspoon cinnamon

Warm milk in a medium saucepan and add remaining ingredients, mixing thoroughly. Pour into a buttered $1\frac{1}{2}$-quart baking pan and place in a 275° oven for 2 hours and 15 minutes. Stir gently after 1 hour and again after 2 hours. Serve warm from the oven or cold with whipped cream.

No one seems to know for sure if the Indians were the first to tap sugar maples. Some say they hacked gashes in the bark with their tomahawks, making an upward cut to make the sap run down the tree trunk into a rawhide container.

Cranberry Chocolate Bread Pudding

Serves 6 to 8

This recipe has all the fine qualities for an interesting holiday offering – easy, warm, rich, attractive, comforting, and portable.

4 croissants, torn into bite-size pieces
8 ounces high quality bittersweet
  chocolate (a bar of Ghiardelli Dark
  is fine)
2 cups fresh cranberries
6 eggs
$\frac{3}{4}$ cup sugar
$1\frac{1}{2}$ cups milk
1 cup heavy cream
$\frac{1}{2}$ teaspoon vanilla
$\frac{1}{2}$ teaspoon almond extract
2 tablespoons butter, cut into bits
pinch salt

1. Place croissant pieces on a baking sheet and dry in oven at 250° for 1 hour, turning several times. Chop chocolate into chunks (not too fine). Chop cranberries in food processor.

2. Spread half of croissant mixture in the bottom of a buttered $1\frac{1}{2}$-quart shallow baking pan. Top with half of the chocolate and all of the cranberries. Finish with rest of bread. Whisk eggs with sugar, milk and $\frac{1}{2}$ cup cream and add vanilla and almond extract. Pour evenly over bread. Dot with butter, cover with foil and refrigerate for at least 1 hour.

3. Preheat oven to 350°. At baking time, if the pudding appears too dry, add up to $\frac{1}{2}$ cup more milk. Bake covered until puffy, about $\frac{1}{2}$ hour, uncover and continue baking for 15 more minutes. In a small pan, melt remaining 4 ounces chocolate. Whisk in remaining $\frac{1}{2}$ cup cream, add a pinch of salt. Serve pudding warm or at room temperature with chocolate sauce spooned on top or served on the side.

It is known that colonial ships carried barrels of cranberries on long voyages as a scurvy prevention for the crew. When reaching the continent, the "Cape Cod Bell Cranberry" became a popular delicacy in the capitals of Europe.

Pear and Dried Cranberry Crostata

Serves 8 to 10

Serve this as a surprise out of an old-fashioned hatbox if you have one on the shelf.

$2\frac{1}{2}$ cups all-purpose flour
$\frac{1}{4}$ cup sugar
1 teaspoon salt
$\frac{3}{4}$ cup (12 tablespoons) unsalted butter, chilled, cut into $\frac{1}{2}$-inch pieces
6 tablespoons water (about)

FILLING
$\frac{1}{2}$ cup plus 1 tablespoon sugar
3 tablespoons all-purpose flour
$\frac{1}{4}$ teaspoon ground cardamom
$\frac{1}{4}$ teaspoon ground allspice
3 pounds firm but ripe Anjou pears (about 6 small), peeled, halved, cored, cut into $\frac{1}{4}$-inch-thick slices
$\frac{3}{4}$ cup dried cranberries
3 tablespoons Poire Williams (clear pear brandy)
1 large egg, beaten to blend (for glaze)

WHIPPED CREAM
2 cups chilled whipping cream
2 tablespoons powdered sugar
additional dried cranberries (optional)

CRUST
Mix flour, sugar and salt in a food processor. Add butter. Using on/off turns, process until mixture resembles coarse meal. Add 5 tablespoons ice water; process until moist clumps form, adding more water by tablespoonfuls if mixture is dry. Gather into ball; flatten into disk. Wrap in plastic. Chill until firm, about 1 hour. (Can be made 1 day ahead. Keep chilled. Let soften slightly before rolling out.)

FILLING
Combine $\frac{1}{2}$ cup sugar, flour, cardamom and allspice in large bowl. Add pears and cranberries and toss to coat. Mix in pear brandy.

1. Position rack in center of oven and preheat to 375°. Roll out dough on floured parchment paper to 14- to 15-inch round. Transfer dough still on parchment paper to large baking sheet.

2   Spread filling into center of dough, leaving 2-inch border. Fold dough border over fruit, pleating loosely and pinching to seal any cracks. Brush border with egg glaze; sprinkle with 1 tablespoon sugar.

3   Bake tart until crust is golden, about 1 hour. Cover edges of crust with foil and continue baking until filling bubbles thickly, about 15 minutes longer. Transfer baking sheet to rack; run a long knife under tart to loosen from parchment and let cool. Using the tart pan as an aid, transfer tart to a platter. (Can be made 6 hours ahead and kept at room temperature).

FOR WHIPPED CREAM
Beat cream and powdered sugar in large bowl until peaks form. Place in a decorative bowl and sprinkle with dried cranberries, if desired, and serve with tart.

Mamouth Mountain Maple Apple Crisp

Serves 6

This dessert is served at our favorite ski resort, great after a long day on the slopes.

1 pound tart, crisp cooking apples
juice of $\frac{1}{2}$ lemon
3 tablespoons maple syrup
$\frac{3}{4}$ cup all-purpose flour
$\frac{1}{4}$ teaspoon salt
4 tablespoons maple sugar or light
   brown sugar
2 teaspoons cinnamon
6 tablespoons butter

1. Core apples and cut into slices about $\frac{3}{4}$-inch thick at widest part. Toss in bowl with lemon juice to prevent browning.

2. Place apples in a lightly buttered 9-inch pie pan. Drizzle maple syrup evenly over the apples.

3. In a small bowl, combine flour, salt, sugar and cinnamon; cut in butter as if making a pie crust. Distribute mixture evenly over apples. Bake in preheated 375° oven 30 minutes or until juices are bubbling and topping is crisp. Serve hot, warm or at room temperature with vanilla or coffee ice cream.

Aunt Mary's Blueberry Buckle

Serves 6 to 8

From a Mystic Seaport volunteer, a favorite from her 90 year-old aunt – still cooking!

$\frac{3}{4}$ cup sugar
$\frac{1}{4}$ cup shortening
1 egg
$\frac{1}{2}$ cup milk
2 cups flour
2 teaspoons baking powder
$\frac{1}{2}$ teaspoon salt
2 cups blueberries

TOPPING
$\frac{1}{2}$ cup sugar
$\frac{1}{2}$ teaspoon cinnamon
$\frac{1}{4}$ cup butter or margarine
$\frac{3}{4}$ cup flour

1. Mix sugar and shortening. Add egg and milk, mixing well. Sift flour, baking powder and salt, add to sugar/egg mixture. Gently fold in blueberries. Pour batter into a greased and floured 9-inch square baking dish.

2. Combine topping mixture ingredients and sprinkle over batter. Bake at 375° for 45 to 50 minutes. Serve warm with whipped cream or vanilla ice cream.

Craisin Cranberry-Pecan Bread

Makes 1 loaf

2 eggs
1¼ cups sugar
1½ teaspoons vanilla extract
¾ cup (12 tablespoons) butter, melted and
  cooled slightly
1½ cups bread flour
1 cup dried cranberries
½ cup golden raisins
1½ cups coarsely chopped pecans

1. Preheat oven to 350° and place oven
   rack in middle position. Generously
   grease and lightly flour a loaf pan. In a
   large bowl with an electric mixer, beat
   eggs and sugar together on medium
   heat until light yellow and thickened.

2. Beat in the vanilla and melted butter.
   On low speed, thoroughly mix in the
   flour; add cranberries, raisins and nuts.
   Stir mixture to combine all ingredients
   (mixture will resemble lumpy mashed
   potatoes).

3. Spoon batter into prepared pan and
   smooth top with a rubber spatula. Bake
   until firm and golden brown, about 1
   hour 15 minutes, rotating pan during
   baking for even browning. Transfer to a
   wire rack to cool in pan for 10 minutes.
   Run a sharp knife along the edge of the
   pan, remove bread from pan and place
   on a rack to cool completely.

Holiday Cranberry Bread

Makes 1 9-by-5 loaf

**My mother was a small town librarian who
had a habit of purchasing cookbooks for her-
self after she'd seen them in the library cata-
logues. This recipe, which was one of her
holiday favorites, came from a collection of
Pillsbury contest winners she acquired this
way. It has always been something special,
and she received several requests for it as
her daughter and nieces grew up and started traditions of their own.**

2 cups sifted all-purpose flour
1 cup sugar
1½ teaspoon baking powder
1 teaspoon salt
½ teaspoon baking soda
1 orange, juiced, rind grated
2 tablespoons shortening
1 egg, well beaten
1 cup nuts, chopped
1 cup cranberries, cut in half

1. Sift together flour, sugar, baking powder,
   salt and baking soda in a large bowl.

2. Combine orange juice with enough
   boiling water to measure ¾ cup. Add
   shortening and egg, mixing well.
   Combine with dry ingredients, adding
   nuts, cranberries and reserved orange
   rind.

3. Pour batter into a greased 9-by-5-by-3-
   inch loaf pan and bake at 350° for 55 to
   65 minutes. Cool before slicing.

Ruby Red Upside-Down Gingerbread

Serves 9

1 cup firmly packed brown sugar
$\frac{1}{4}$ cup (4 tablespoons) butter or
  margarine, melted
1 8-ounce can pineapple chunks, drained
$\frac{3}{4}$ cup fresh cranberries
$\frac{1}{3}$ cup chopped pecans
1 $\frac{1}{3}$ cup flour
$\frac{1}{2}$ teaspoon baking powder
$\frac{1}{2}$ teaspoon baking soda
$\frac{1}{4}$ teaspoon salt
1 teaspoon cinnamon
1 teaspoon ginger
$\frac{1}{2}$ teaspoon allspice
$\frac{1}{2}$ cup (8 tablespoons) butter or margarine,
  softened
$\frac{1}{2}$ cup boiling water
$\frac{1}{2}$ cup molasses
1 egg, slightly beaten

1. Preheat oven to 350°. In a small bowl, combine $\frac{1}{2}$ cup brown sugar and melted butter. Blend well and spread in bottom of an ungreased 8- or 9-inch square pan. Arrange pineapple in 3 rows over sugar mixture and sprinkle cranberries and pecans around pineapple.

2. In a large bowl, combine flour, baking powder, baking soda, salt, cinnamon, ginger, allspice; mix well. Add remaining $\frac{1}{2}$ cup brown sugar, softened butter, water, molasses and egg; blend well. Pour batter evenly over pineapple in prepared pan.

3. Bake for 45 to 55 minutes or until toothpick inserted in center comes out clean. Cool upright for 2 minutes. Run sharp knife around edge of pan and invert onto serving plate. Cool at least 30 minutes before cutting. Serve warm with whipped cream.

Laura Moore's Maple Pumpkin Bread

Makes 2 loaves

A tribute to my dear friend. Her recipe serves as a treat to the classes at the Parkway School in Greenwich, Connecticut.

4 eggs
2 cups sugar
$\frac{1}{2}$ cup vegetable oil
$\frac{1}{2}$ cup applesauce
$\frac{2}{3}$ cup pure maple syrup
1 15-ounce can pumpkin
3 cups flour
2 teaspoons baking soda
1 teaspoon salt
2 teaspoons cinnamon
$\frac{1}{4}$ teaspoon nutmeg
$\frac{1}{4}$ teaspoon allspice

1. In a medium bowl, beat eggs. Add sugar, vegetable oil, applesauce, maple syrup and pumpkin, mix well.

2. Sift flour, baking soda, salt, cinnamon, nutmeg and allspice. Pour liquid ingredients into flour mixture and blend until just mixed, being careful not to over-beat. Pour batter into 2 loaf pans that have been sprayed with nonstick cooking spray. Bake in a preheated 350° oven for 1 hour or until toothpick inserted in center comes out clean. This bread may be made ahead and frozen.

Vermont Maple Cream Pie

Makes a 9- or 10-inch pie

Use only 100% maple syrup – we like grade A, "Medium Amber."

pastry dough for a single crust
    9- to 10-inch pie
3 large eggs
3 tablespoons flour
$1\frac{1}{2}$ cups pure maple syrup plus extra
    for finishing desert
$\frac{3}{4}$ cup heavy cream
whipped cream

1. Preheat oven to 450°. Line pie shell with wax paper and weight with raw rice, dry beans, or pie weights. Bake pie shell in middle of oven for 12 minutes. Carefully remove paper and weights and cool pie shell on a rack.

2. Reduce oven temperature to 350°. In a bowl, beat eggs with an electric mixer until foamy, add flour, 1 tablespoon at a time, beating until well combined. Beat in maple syrup and cream slowly and pour filling into shell. Bake pie in middle of oven about 45 minutes until a knife inserted in the middle comes out clean. Cool pie to room temperature and serve topped with whipped cream, drizzle a bit of maple syrup over each piece.

"By glory, after all is said and done, sugaring is fun!" (the sugar-makers claim)

Blueberry Streusel Sour Cream Pie

Serves 8

You may never settle for a traditional blueberry pie again – the almond scented filling is a show stopper.

CRUST:
$1\frac{1}{4}$ cups all-purpose flour
$\frac{1}{2}$ cup ($\frac{1}{4}$ pound) chilled unsalted butter, cut into pieces
2 tablespoons sugar
pinch of salt
4 tablespoons (about) ice water

FILLING:
1 cup sour cream
$\frac{3}{4}$ cup sugar
$2\frac{1}{2}$ tablespoons all-purpose flour
1 egg, beaten
1 teaspoon almond extract
$\frac{1}{4}$ teaspoon salt
2 cups fresh blueberries

TOPPING:
6 tablespoons all-purpose flour
$\frac{1}{4}$ cup (4 tablespoons) chilled unsalted butter, cut into pieces
$\frac{1}{2}$ cup chopped pecans
2 tablespoons sugar

1. For crust: blend flour, butter, sugar and salt in a food processor until coarse meal forms. With machine running, add water by tablespoons until clumps form. Gather into a ball, flatten, wrap in plastic and refrigerate until firm, about 30 minutes.

2. Preheat oven to 375°. Roll out the dough on a floured surface to a 13-inch round. Transfer to a 9-inch glass pie plate. Trim edge to $\frac{1}{2}$-inch overhang, fold under and crimp. Line crust with foil, fill with beans or pie weights and bake until sides are set, about 10 to 12 minutes. Remove foil and beans.

3. For filling: Mix first 6 ingredients in a medium bowl to blend. Gently stir in the blueberries and spoon into crust. Bake for 30 minutes until filling is set.

4. For topping: With a fork or fingertips, mix flour and butter in a medium bowl, add pecans and sugar and mix well. Sprinkle topping over pie and bake until topping browns lightly, 10 to 12 minutes. Cool pie to room temperature before serving.

Figgy Cranberry Bars

Makes 28 bars

1 12-ounce package fresh cranberries
1 cup snipped dried figs
6 tablespoons honey
1 teaspoon vanilla
2 cups all-purpose flour
2 cups oatmeal
$1\frac{1}{2}$ cups light brown sugar, packed
$\frac{1}{2}$ teaspoon baking soda
$\frac{1}{2}$ teaspoon cinnamon
$\frac{1}{4}$ teaspoon salt
1 cup ($\frac{1}{2}$ pound) butter, melted
$1\frac{1}{2}$ cups sifted powdered sugar
2 tablespoons lemon juice

1. In a large saucepan, combine cranberries, figs, and honey. Cook, covered, over low heat for 15 minutes until cranberries pop, stir often. Add vanilla.

2. In a large mixing bowl, stir together flour, oatmeal, brown sugar, baking soda, cinnamon, and salt. Blend in melted butter. Pat half of mixture into an 8-by-13-by-2-inch baking pan. Bake at 350° for 8 minutes.

3. Spread fruit filling over baked layer and sprinkle remaining dry mixture evenly on top. Pat gently. Return to oven and bake 20 minutes longer until golden brown.

4. In a medium bowl, combine powdered sugar with lemon juice, gradually adding lemon juice until mixture has spreading consistency. Drizzle over top and let rest for at least 1 hour before cutting.

Vermont Applesauce Cookies

Makes about 3 dozen
My friendly 100-year old neighbor, a native of County Cork, Ireland, came over to show me how to make her famous cookies.

1 cup sugar
$\frac{1}{2}$ cup shortening
2 eggs
1 cup applesauce
2 cups flour
1 teaspoon baking powder
$\frac{1}{2}$ teaspoon salt
1 teaspoon baking soda
2 teaspoons cinnamon
$\frac{1}{2}$ teaspoon nutmeg
1 teaspoon cloves
1 cup raisins
$\frac{1}{2}$ cup walnuts

1. In a medium bowl, cream sugar and shortening, add eggs, and beat well. Stir in the applesauce.

2. Sift the flour, baking powder, soda and spices. Add to the applesauce mixture along with the raisins and walnuts, mixing well. Drop by teaspoonfuls on an ungreased cookie sheet and bake in a 350° oven for 12 to 15 minutes until light brown. Cool on a rack.

Pond Road Cranberry Nut Squares

Makes 24 pieces

I requested this recipe from a friend after watching my husband consume nearly half a platter of these at a party – a great "in a hurry" dessert.

$1\frac{1}{2}$ cups flour
$\frac{1}{2}$ teaspoon baking soda
$\frac{1}{2}$ teaspoon baking powder
2 eggs
$1\frac{1}{2}$ cups sugar
8 tablespoons butter, melted
2 tablespoons vegetable oil
2 cups cranberries, rinsed and dried
2 cups chopped walnuts
powdered sugar

1. Mix together flour, baking soda and baking powder. In a large bowl, beat eggs with a mixer, add sugar and continue beating until mixture is lemon-colored. Alternate adding flour, melted butter and oil to the beaten eggs and sugar.

2. Mix in the cranberries and walnuts by hand, the mixture will be very stiff. Spread batter into a 9-by-13-inch baking dish that has been sprayed with nonstick cooking spray. Bake in a 350° oven for 40 minutes and when cool, sift powdered sugar on top before cutting into squares.

Maple Popcorn

Serves 6

Two native New England foods combine to make this tempting snack.

$\frac{1}{3}$ cup popcorn kernels
$\frac{2}{3}$ cup sugar
$\frac{2}{3}$ cup water
$\frac{1}{8}$ teaspoon cream of tartar
$\frac{2}{3}$ cup maple syrup
2 tablespoons butter
$\frac{1}{2}$ teaspoon salt

1. Pop popcorn kernels in a hot air popper and put aside in a large bowl. Generously grease a baking sheet.

2. In a 2-quart saucepan, heat sugar, water and cream of tartar to boiling over high heat, stirring occasionally. Brush side of pan with warm water to dissolve any crystals forming on the edge. Reduce heat to medium and continue cooking, without stirring, until mixture becomes a deep golden brown, about 10 minutes.

3. Carefully stir in maple syrup and cook 2 minutes longer. Remove from heat and stir in butter and salt. Immediately pour maple mixture over popcorn to coat. (Do not mix with hands, syrup is very hot.)

4. Spread popcorn onto greased baking sheet to cool. Serve this treat shortly after it is made or store in an airtight container.

Nantucket Cranberry Bread Stuffing

Makes 10 servings

$1\frac{1}{2}$ cups fresh cranberries, coarsely
  chopped
$\frac{1}{4}$ cup sugar
$\frac{1}{4}$ cup (4 tablespoons) butter or margarine
$1\frac{1}{2}$ cups chopped celery
1 large onion, diced
$1\frac{1}{2}$ teaspoons poultry seasoning
$\frac{1}{4}$ teaspoon salt
$\frac{1}{8}$ teaspoon black pepper
4 cups white bread cubes
4 cups whole wheat or cornbread cubes
1 to $1\frac{1}{4}$ cups chicken broth

1. In a mixing bowl, stir together
    cranberries and sugar. In a medium
    skillet, melt butter and sauté celery
    and onion until tender, 4 to 5 minutes.
    Remove from heat and stir in poultry
    seasoning, salt and pepper.

2. In a large bowl, combine bread
    cubes; add celery-onion mixture and
    cranberries; toss to mix. Add enough
    chicken broth to moisten and let cool.
    Use to stuff a 10- to 14-pound turkey.
    Bake remaining mixture in a covered
    dish at 325° for 45 minutes to 1 hour.

Spiced Cranberry Orange Chutney

Makes 5 cups

$2\frac{1}{4}$ cups brown sugar, firmly packed
$1\frac{1}{2}$ cups cranberry juice
$\frac{1}{2}$ cup apple cider vinegar
$\frac{1}{2}$ teaspoon ground ginger
$\frac{1}{4}$ teaspoon ground allspice
2 12-ounce packages cranberries
2 oranges, peeled and white pith
  removed, sectioned
1 Granny Smith apple, peeled, cored,
  and coarsely chopped
$\frac{1}{2}$ cup dried currants
$\frac{1}{2}$ cup dried apricots
2 tablespoons grated orange rind

1. Combine first 5 ingredients in a large
    heavy saucepan. Cook, stirring, over
    medium heat until sugar dissolves.
    Increase heat and bring to a boil.

2. Stir in remaining ingredients; bring to
    a boil. Reduce heat and simmer until
    mixture is thick, about 40 minutes.
    Cool completely, cover and chill. This
    may be made 3 days before serving.

Wild cranberry vines thrive along the rugged dunes of Cape Cod, where the Pilgrims probably found them growing close to the roaring surf. The sturdy plant does not object in the least to the salt spray, and gradually takes possession of the bare sand, building up a dense mat of vine.

Patti Ann's Cranberry Chutney

Makes 10 to 12 half pint jars

As my family is scattered all over the United States, I enjoy making this in mid-November and sending it off for the holidays to friends and relatives. It helps rekindle fond memories as we all share it on Christmas Day.

3 12-ounce bags cranberries
6 ounces apple jelly
3 apples, peeled and chopped
4 clementines, peeled and chopped, reserving 3 teaspoons grated peel
3 teaspoons grated lemon peel
1 teaspoon ground ginger
1 teaspoon coarse salt
$\frac{1}{4}$ teaspoon ground nutmeg
$1\frac{1}{2}$ cups brown sugar
$\frac{1}{2}$ cup apple cider vinegar
1 cup chopped walnuts
1 cup golden raisins
1 cup dark raisins
1 cup dried cherries
2 cups water

Mix all ingredients in a large, heavy saucepan. Bring to a boil, reduce to a simmer and cook for $1\frac{1}{2}$ to 2 hours, uncovered, until thickened. Pour into sterilized jars, seal and process in a hot water bath for 10 minutes. Chutney will keep refrigerated for 2 weeks without processing.

Cranberry Apple Rum Mincemeat

Makes 5 quarts

Without the traditional lard, this has a fruity, fermenty flavor. It makes a big batch so plan to freeze some for use throughout the winter. Great for pies and puddings.

6 cups Granny Smith apples, peeled and chopped
4 cups dark brown sugar
4 cups dark rum
6 cups cranberries
$2\frac{1}{2}$ cups raisins
3 cups currants
$\frac{1}{2}$ cup raspberry vinegar
1 tablespoon nutmeg
1 tablespoon allspice
1 teaspoon ground cloves

Mix all ingredients in a large heavy-bottomed saucepan and bring to a boil, stirring constantly. Reduce heat and simmer, uncovered, for one hour or until thick. The mincemeat may also be place in sterilized jars and sealed for holiday gifts.

"The Indians and English use cranberries much, boyling them with sugar as sauce to eat with their meat, and it is indeed a delicate and tangy taste."
   John Josselyn, on visiting New England in 1663.

Melting Pot

Old Country Lamb Meat Loaf With Olives

Serves 6

Having been raised on my Greek grandmother's version of this "All-American Standby," my family would never expect a beef meat loaf as a substitute.

$1\frac{3}{4}$ pounds ground lamb or lean minced lamb from the leg or loin
1 egg, lightly beaten
1 teaspoon oregano
$\frac{1}{4}$ teaspoon cayenne pepper
2 cloves garlic, minced
1 small onion, diced
2 tablespoons chopped fresh parsley
12 oil-cured black olives, pitted and chopped
$\frac{1}{2}$ cup bread crumbs
4 tablespoons Parmesan cheese
1 tablespoon red wine vinegar
1 8-ounce can tomato sauce
salt and pepper

1. In a large bowl combine all ingredients, using only $\frac{1}{2}$ cup of the tomato sauce. Season with salt and pepper.

2. Pour half of the remaining tomato sauce into a loaf pan and place the mixture in pan, spreading evenly into the corners. Cover the top with remaining tomato sauce, and bake in a 350° oven for one hour until nicely browned. Rather than serving with mashed potatoes, try buttered orzo instead.

Mémères Pork Pies

Serves 12

My family is descended from French Canadians who continuously migrated to New England mill towns since the 1850s. We have always greeted the New Year with a family gathering serving our traditional pork pie dinner. New Year's Day just doesn't feel right without a pork pie, and a pork pie doesn't feel right if it is eaten on any other day!!

$2\frac{1}{2}$ pounds lean ground pork
1 pound ground beef
1 medium onion, chopped
1 cup finely chopped celery
4 slices white bread torn into small pieces
$\frac{1}{2}$ teaspoon poultry seasoning
salt and pepper
2 9-inch pie crusts

Mix all ingredients in a large saucepan. Add enough water, just to cover, and cook stirring frequently until meat is cooked through. Drain off any excess liquid and divide mixture between 2 9-inch pie pans. Bake at 400° for 25 to 30 minutes until browned. Cut into wedges and toast the New Year.

O'Malley's Irish Stew

Serves 8

Thomas Anthony O'Malley, a widower, left County Cork, Ireland in 1860 with his three sons aboard a steam liner heading for Boston, Massachusetts. Upon arrival in Boston Harbor the men were questioned by custom officials. Hearing that Irish immigrants were discriminated against and given "lesser paying jobs" in this country, the men were faced with a difficult decision. They knew that recognition of their Irish ancestry might bring them discrimination in the work force. Yet, for centuries, this family had proudly carried the name: O'Malley. Their hearts were saddened when they told the custom officials that their name was: Malley. Who would think that dropping the letter "O" from the front of one's name would cause such anguish and hurt? My great-grandfather, however, instilled in his sons to never forget that they were born "Irish Men."

8 slices of ham, $\frac{1}{4}$-inch thick, cubed
6 pork sausage links, cut into small pieces
2 tablespoons freshly chopped thyme
3 to 4 teaspoons ground black pepper
pinch salt
4 tablespoons freshly chopped parsley
4 large onions, sliced
2 pounds potatoes, peeled and sliced
2 tablespoons catsup
2 cups water

1. Place ham and pork pieces in a plastic bag. Add thyme, black pepper and salt to bag and shake until meat is well coated.

2. In a large 2-quart casserole, line the bottom with a layer of sliced potatoes. Cover with a layer of ham and sausage chunks, sprinkle with parsley and top with a layer of sliced onions. Finish filling the casserole with another layer of potatoes, meat, parsley, onions, finishing with a layer of potatoes.

3. Heat water to a boil and add catsup. Pour mixture over casserole and cover with aluminum foil. Bake in a 325° oven for one hour or until potatoes and onions are soft. You may like to remove the foil during the last 15 minutes to brown the potatoes. Sprinkle with additional chopped parsley before serving.

Cornish Pastries

Serves 4 to 6

Originally prepared by housewives as a hearty meal, served hot with any extras carried in lunch pails by the coal miners. This recipe was brought with ancestors from Cornwall, England to homes in the area of Mineral Point, Wisconsin. Today they have become somewhat of a local favorite, usually made in large batches for family reunions and ordered ahead by other "aficionados."

CRUST
2 cups flour
1 teaspoon salt
$\frac{2}{3}$ cup shortening
5 to 6 tablespoons cold water

FILLING
1 cup diced potatoes
$\frac{1}{2}$ cup diced carrots
$\frac{1}{2}$ cup sliced onion
$\frac{1}{2}$ pound round steak, cut into $\frac{1}{8}$ inch
  cubes (ground beef may be substituted)
2 teaspoons salt
black pepper
$\frac{1}{2}$ cup finely diced turnip or rutabaga
  (optional)

1. Mix flour and salt, cut in shortening, adding enough water to make a stiff dough. Roll out on a lightly floured board and cut into triangular or square pieces (5-by-7 inches, approximately).

2. Mix filling ingredients in a medium bowl, seasoning with black pepper to taste. Place a spoonful of filling in center of each piece of crust, fold over to enclose mixture, dab edges with water and pinch to seal. Place on a baking sheet and bake at 350° for 25 to 35 minutes until crust is golden brown. Serve hot or cold.

Halupsi Brackman

Serves 6 to 8

Just before the outbreak of the Russian Revolution this recipe was brought to the United States by my grandmother from Odessa, Russia.

HALUPSI
1 large head cabbage
1 onion, finely chopped
1 tablespoon olive oil
1 teaspoon fresh thyme or $\frac{1}{2}$ teaspoon dried
1 teaspoon salt
$\frac{1}{2}$ teaspoon cayenne pepper
1 tablespoon chopped fresh parsley
1 teaspoon cinnamon
1 pound ground beef
$\frac{1}{2}$ cup uncooked white rice
1 egg, beaten
1 4-ounce can mushrooms

SAUCE
1 14-ounce can plum tomatoes, drained and chopped
juice of 1 lemon
$\frac{1}{4}$ cup brown sugar, firmly packed
1 10-ounce can beef consommé
$\frac{1}{2}$ cup raisins

1. Wash and core cabbage, place in a saucepan of boiling salted water and boil for 10 to 15 minutes until leaves begin to loosen. Drain and cool.

2. Meanwhile, sauté onion in olive oil. Add the seasonings and ground beef and cook until nicely browned. Mix in the rice, egg and mushrooms, combining well.

3. Separate cabbage leaves and trim off the thick stem end. Put a spoonful of the filling on each leaf, fold in sides, and roll up, securing with a toothpick as needed. Place seam or toothpick-side down in a 9-by-13-by-2-inch baking pan.

4. In the same pan as the meat was cooked, place all of sauce ingredients and bring to a simmer. Pour sauce over halupsi rolls and bake in a 350° oven for 30 to 40 minutes or until bubbly. These may be prepared in advance and refrigerated.

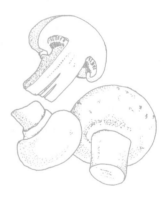

Zouzoukakia

Serves 6 as an entrée or 12 as an appetizer
In the early 1970s, Channel 2 in Boston had a cooking show called, "Theonie, Greek Island Cooking." I remember jotting this recipe on the back of an envelope and trying it out at my next cocktail party – I wish I had a dollar for each one of these I have made in 30 years!!

1 cup soaked and squeezed stale bread
   (Italian, Greek, or Sourdough)
2 pounds lean ground beef
2 eggs, lightly beaten
4 garlic cloves, minced
$\frac{1}{4}$ cup chopped fresh parsley
3 tablespoons grated Kephalotiri or
   Parmesan cheese
1 teaspoon cumin
salt and pepper to taste
1 cup flour to roll sausages in
$\frac{3}{4}$ cup olive oil to fry sausages

FOR SAUCE:
2 cloves garlic, minced
2 cups tomato sauce
$\frac{3}{4}$ cup dry red wine
salt and hot pepper flakes to taste
flat leaf parsley, chopped

1. Soak stale bread in water, squeeze out excess liquid, and break into small pieces. In a large bowl, mix bread, meat, eggs, garlic, parsley, cheese, cumin, salt and pepper. Knead with hands until well mixed.

2. Take small (walnut-size) pieces of mixture and form into 2-inch long sausage shaped meatballs. Roll in flour and fry in hot oil on both sides (about 5 minutes per side), until brown. Drain and set aside.

3. If there is no oil left in pan, add an additional 2 tablespoons olive oil to pan. Add garlic and cook 2 minutes, scraping all of the brown bits from the bottom of the pan. Add tomato sauce, wine, salt and pepper flakes; bring to a boil, add sausages, cover and reduce heat. Cook over low heat for 30 minutes and sprinkle with a generous amount of chopped parsley before serving. These make a great appetizer or as a meal served with a traditional orzo pilaf or crispy fried potatoes.

Father Bartholomew's Best Bolognese

Serves 8 to 10

The kitchen at our parish house in Boston's South End was always full of many great cooks, young and old – as Father also shared the stoves on many occasions. I remember bowls of his robust sauce over hot pasta with plenty of cheese – so close to heaven!

1 pound lean ground beef
1 pound sweet Italian sausage, crumbled
4 tablespoons olive oil
2 large onions, diced
4 stalks celery, diced
2 carrots, diced
8 cloves garlic, minced
8 ounces smoked ham, coarsely chopped
2 cups water
2 13$\frac{1}{2}$-ounce cans whole tomatoes packed with purée
2 teaspoons salt
$\frac{1}{2}$ teaspoon black pepper
2 teaspoons thyme
$\frac{1}{2}$ cup chopped fresh parsley
1 teaspoon oregano
$\frac{2}{3}$ cup dry red wine

1. In a large skillet or saucepan, sauté ground beef and sausage in 2 tablespoons oil until browned. Transfer to a bowl.

2. Add remaining 2 tablespoons of olive oil to skillet (or less if there is enough fat from the meat). Sauté the onion, celery, carrot and garlic until soft but not browned.

3. Return the browned meat to the pan, add the ham and remaining ingredients. Cover and simmer over medium-low heat for 1 hour, stirring occasionally, adding a bit more water if sauce thickens too quickly. Serve over your favorite hot pasta or make a double batch and freeze some for another night.

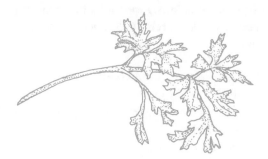

Olde Stonington Meatballs

Serves 6

This was my grandmother's recipe, a young mother and wife of the Episcopal minister at Calvary Church in Stonington, Connecticut. A generation later, my mother said this was a "Godsend" during World War II when meat was rationed. The recipe is in my mother's handwritten recipe book, dated 1895, and has been adapted over the years.

2 cups ground round steak
   (about $1\frac{1}{2}$ pounds)
1 cup finely crumbled fresh bread crumbs
1 teaspoon salt
1 teaspoon black pepper
2 tablespoons grated onion
1 teaspoon sage
$\frac{3}{4}$ cup canned tomatoes or equal amount
   of condensed tomato soup
2 eggs
$\frac{1}{2}$ cup flour
2 tablespoons butter

1. Combine ground beef and bread crumbs in a large bowl. Add remaining ingredients, except flour, and mix well. Shape mixture into 8 to 10 oval croquette shaped patties, and roll in the flour.

2. Heat butter in a heavy skillet (preferably cast iron) and brown meatballs on both sides until nice and crispy, about 20 minutes. If you wish to make gravy, remove meatballs and keep warm.

Add 2 teaspoons Worcestershire sauce and 1 cup beef broth (or 1 beef bouillon cube and 1 cup boiling water) to the pan. Bring to a boil, scraping all of the browned bits from the bottom of the pan and cook until thickened.

Mom's Casserole Stuffed Cabbage Deluxe

Serves 6 to 8

My mom, Florence Wincze, is of Polish descent as well as a Connecticut native. She devised this recipe over 40 years ago as an easy alternative to the traditional stuffing and rolling of each cabbage leaf. Everything goes in one pan and it is especially good reheated the next day.

1 to 2 teaspoons butter
$\frac{1}{4}$ cup diced salt pork or bacon
$\frac{3}{4}$ cup diced onion
$\frac{2}{3}$ cup long grain white rice
1 pound ground beef
1$\frac{3}{4}$ teaspoons salt
$\frac{1}{8}$ teaspoon pepper
1 medium head of cabbage
1 15-ounce can condensed tomato soup
1$\frac{1}{4}$ cups tomato sauce
$\frac{1}{4}$ cup water

1. Melt 1 tablespoon butter in a skillet; add salt pork and onion. Cook over medium heat until onion is soft, about 5 minutes, adding more butter if needed. Par boil rice in boiling water for 10 minutes, drain well. In a large bowl, mix rice with salt pork, onion, ground beef, salt and pepper.

2. Rinse cabbage; cut in half and remove core. Slice halves into 1-inch wide strips. Drop strips into a pot of boiling salted water and cook for 5 minutes. Remove with a slotted spoon and drain well.

3. In a mixing bowl, mix tomato soup, tomato sauce and water. Spread $\frac{3}{4}$ cup of the tomato mixture on the bottom of a 9-by-13-inch baking pan. Layer cabbage on bottom of pan. Spread ground beef-rice mixture on top and with the handle of a wooden spoon, poke 8 to 9 holes, going to the bottom of the pan. Add remaining soup mixture. Cover dish with aluminum foil and bake in a 350° oven for 50 to 60 minutes until browned.

Ceylonese Fried Fish

Serves 4

During World War II my father, Paul Hobson, was an officer in the Royal Navy. He spent most of 1943 in Tricomalee, Ceylon (now Sri Lanka) where he picked up this recipe. It has been somewhat modified from the original, but is a family favorite.

1 to 1$\frac{1}{2}$ pounds of a variety of fish and seafood to include any of the following: cod, smelt, halibut, shrimp, scallops, squid (cut into rings), shucked oysters and/or clams
$\frac{1}{2}$ cup oil
4 shallots, chopped
4 cloves garlic
2 chili peppers, seeded and chopped
1 teaspoon mace
1 tablespoon fresh ginger, grated
2 tablespoons lime juice
1 tablespoon cider vinegar
$\frac{1}{2}$ teaspoon brown sugar
salt and pepper to taste

1. Cut fish into bite-size pieces. Reserving 1 tablespoon oil, heat oil 1 tablespoon at a time in a wok or frying pan, and fry seafood in several batches for 2 to 3 minutes until lightly browned. Drain fish on paper towels and keep warm.

2. In a food processor or blender, purée shallots, garlic, chilies, mace and ginger. Put reserved tablespoon of oil in wok or frying pan, add paste and cook for 1 minute. Add lime juice and vinegar, cook for 2 minutes. Sauce should be thin; add a little water if it seems too thick.

3. Stir in sugar, salt and pepper and gently mix cooked seafood into sauce. Cook for 2 to 3 minutes until heated through. Serve with fluffy white rice.

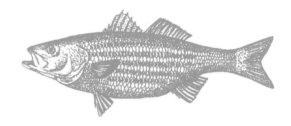

On his way to Florida from Connecticut in 1774, William Bartram described his trailside dinner: "I collected a sufficiency of dry wood to keep a lit fire during the night, and to roast some fish which I caught descending the river. Their heads I stewed in the juices of oranges, which with boiled rice, afforded me a wholesome and delicious supper."

Fennel Olive Stuffing

Serves 10

The flavors of the Mediterranean enhance an American favorite.

$\frac{3}{4}$ pound firm crusty white bread,
  cut into $\frac{1}{2}$-inch cubes
2 medium fennel bulbs, trimmed and
  coarsely chopped
2 cups chopped red onion
$\frac{1}{4}$ cup olive oil plus 2 tablespoons
1$\frac{1}{2}$ cups Kalamata olives, pitted, rinsed
  and coarsely chopped
1 tablespoon dried oregano
1 teaspoon fennel seed, crushed
$\frac{3}{4}$ teaspoon salt
1$\frac{1}{2}$ cups chicken broth

1. Spread the bread cubes on a baking
   sheet and bake at 400° for 6 to 10
   minutes until lightly toasted. Transfer
   to a large bowl and set aside.

2. In a large skillet, sauté fennel and
   onion in $\frac{1}{4}$ cup olive oil over medium
   heat until tender. To the bread cubes
   add olives, oregano, fennel seed and
   salt. Add chicken broth, a little at a
   time, until stuffing is lightly moist,
   but not packed together.

3. Stuff turkey or spoon into a greased
   13-by-9-inch casserole. Drizzle with
   remaining 2 tablespoons olive oil and
   bake for 30 to 45 minutes at 350°.
   (Stuffing may be prepared ahead and
   frozen.)

Swedish Cheese Potatoes

Serves 4 to 6

Another Tuckie Road favorite

4 large baking potatoes
$\frac{1}{3}$ cup (5$\frac{1}{3}$ tablespoons) butter, melted
1 cup grated Swiss or sharp cheddar
  cheese
2 tablespoons fine cracker crumbs
1 teaspoon salt
1 teaspoon paprika
pepper to taste

Peel potatoes, cut in half lengthwise and
then into 1-inch wedges. Arrange in a
single layer in a shallow baking pan.
Drizzle butter on top, sprinkle with
cheese, crumbs, salt, paprika and pepper.
Bake at 325° for 1 hour until brown and
crispy.

Kartoffel Suppe – Potato Soup

Serves 2 to 4

It was worth being ill to have a favorite meal prepared just for you. Most German heritage people appreciate root vegetables and the delicious meals prepared from them. My favorite was and is Kartoffel suppe (just plain potato soup). My mother and other family members all made potato soup, but no two of them made it the same. After 68 years, regardless of the pain or illness, nothing makes me well until I have my potato soup. I get out of bed to prepare it!

2 medium white potatoes, peeled and diced
1 carrot, diced
1 stalk celery and a few leaves, chopped
dash of salt
2 tablespoons butter
2 cups whole milk
3 tablespoons flour
black pepper
2 eggs, hard-boiled, peeled and chopped

1. Place potatoes, carrot, celery and salt in a medium saucepan, cover with water and cook for 15 to 20 minutes until vegetables are tender. Remove from heat and drain thoroughly.

2. Mash potatoes and vegetables with a hand masher, add butter and milk; return to stove. Mix the flour with a little milk and stir into the potato mixture. Cook over low heat until soup has thickened. Season to taste with pepper, ladle soup into soup bowls and garnish with chopped egg.

Old World Fried Potatoes

Serves 4

Ever since I was a young boy, my mother (who came from Finland) told us the story about how she and her sisters were always served these potatoes and plenty of fish – the only two foods the family could afford. I, in turn, grew up loving her wonderful fried potatoes.

2 tablespoons butter
6 medium potatoes, peeled and sliced
1 large onion, sliced
2 cloves garlic, minced
2 tablespoons olive oil
4 tablespoons Worcestershire sauce
$\frac{1}{2}$ teaspoon salt
$\frac{1}{8}$ teaspoon black pepper

1. Melt butter in a large skillet; add sliced potatoes, top with onions and sprinkle garlic on top. Cover pan and cook over medium-low heat for 10 minutes. Stir potatoes around in pan, add olive oil, cover and cook for 10 more minutes.

2. Add Worcestershire sauce, season with salt and pepper, cover and cook for 15 minutes on low heat. Serve hot from the pan.

Sauerkraut Pirogues

Makes about 40

This recipe was passed down to me from Mary Yacek who immigrated to the United States from Poland in 1910. She settled in Wallingford, Connecticut, where she lived for 85 years. Mary was born February 25, 1893 and passed on February 6, 1995. Mary was my grandmother who we called Babci (grandma in Polish). Babci would make pirogues every Christmas and Easter. My brother Bill and I always looked forward to going to Babci's on these holidays. There was always a lot of different Polish food, but we liked pirogues the best. Like Babci, I make a batch of pirogues every Christmas.

$\frac{1}{2}$ cup vegetable oil
4 tablespoons butter
2 pounds sauerkraut, rinsed
1 medium onion, chopped
2 teaspoons mushroom powder
1 teaspoon garlic powder

Melt butter with oil in a large frying pan. Add sauerkraut, onion, mushroom powder and garlic powder. Sauté over medium heat for 30 minutes until soft and golden. Refrigerate overnight.

PIROGUES DOUGH
2 pounds flour
4 eggs
2 cups warm water
1 teaspoon salt
$\frac{1}{4}$ teaspoon black pepper
3 tablespoons oil

1. In a large mixing bowl, mix flour, eggs, water (mix a little at a time), salt, pepper, and oil. Make dough like bread dough, consistency-wise. Add a little more flour if it is too sticky to roll. Roll out dough, cut into circles with a coffee can and fill with cold sauerkraut mixture. Fold in half and pinch edges together with a fork.

2. Boil in water with 1 teaspoon salt for 5 minutes. Let cool. (Wrap individually and freeze if wanted.) Fry pirogues in a skillet with butter and chopped onions until golden brown. To cook a large amount of pirogues: Sauté several cups of sliced onions in butter. Place pirogues in a baking pan, pour onion and butter mixture over the pirogues, bake at 350° for 1 hour.

Old World Danish Pancakes

Makes 16 7-inch pancakes

This recipe has been in my family for as long as I can remember. My grandmother made it for my mother and my aunt in Denmark when they were children. When my mother's family moved to the United States, it continued to be something that reminded them of home, I imagine. It's just my all-time favorite recipe and if I'm ever in the mood for something special or want to remember family memories, this always does the trick!

4 eggs
1 tablespoon sugar
$\frac{1}{4}$ teaspoon salt
1 cup flour
1 cup milk
1 tablespoon butter

1. Beat eggs with a whisk in a large bowl, add sugar and salt; mix well. Add flour and mix until evenly blended. Add milk, a little at a time, until evenly blended. Melt butter and mix into batter.

2. Pour a $\frac{3}{4}$-full ladle of the batter onto a lightly greased skillet and spread to cover. Cook for about 2 minutes per side (flip with spatula) or until slightly browned. Repeat until batter is gone and you've got a stack of delicious pancakes!

Since they are similar to crêpes, they can be served with just about anything imaginable, but I highly recommend butter, any type of preserves or jam, and sugar (powdered or otherwise). Fresh fruit and cream cheese are also wonderful! Spread a thin layer of butter and jam (for example) onto a pancake, lightly sprinkle with sugar, roll as you would a crêpe and enjoy!

Warm German Potato Salad

Serves 10

$2\frac{1}{2}$ pounds waxy potatoes, such as red skin or Yukon Gold
6 sliced bacon, diced
$\frac{1}{4}$ cup vegetable oil
2 tablespoons brown mustard
$2\frac{1}{2}$ cups chicken broth
$\frac{1}{4}$ cup white wine vinegar
1 cup diced onion
1 teaspoon sugar
1 teaspoon salt
freshly ground black pepper
$\frac{1}{2}$ cup chopped fresh parsley

1. Quarter and slice potatoes, leaving the skins on if you prefer. Simmer in salted water for 8 to 10 minutes until just tender. Meanwhile prepare the dressing.

2. In a heavy saucepan, cook the bacon until crisp, remove and drain, reserving the bacon fat. Combine the oil, bacon fat and mustard, pour over hot potatoes. Bring the chicken broth, vinegar, onions, sugar, salt and pepper to a boil and pour over potatoes. Mix to coat. Just before serving, add the bacon and parsley, toss gently and serve warm with your favorite knockwurst, bratwurst or boiled pig's knuckle.

French Pancakes / Crêpes

Makes 20

My parents arrived in this country from France and Belgium through Ellis Island. With four small mouths to feed, things were not always easy for Mom and Dad, so crêpes became a basic part of our menu for any meal of the day.

1 cup sifted all-purpose flour
$\frac{1}{2}$ teaspoon salt
3 large eggs, beaten
2 cups milk
2 tablespoons melted butter
1 tablespoon vanilla

1. Sift flour and salt, set aside. Combine eggs and milk, stir into the flour mixture. Mix in melted butter and vanilla and stir until batter is well mixed.

2. For each crêpe, pour 2 tablespoons of batter into a hot, lightly-greased, 6-inch skillet. Brown lightly on the bottom until bubbles form on the top. Flip over and brown for 20 to 30 seconds. Stack pancakes as you make them on a plate and keep warm until ready to serve. Top with butter, sprinkle with sugar or any other topping of your choice.

Norwegian Sweet Bread

Makes 3 loaves

This recipe was brought from Norway by my husband's family when they first came to New York in 1920. Whenever my father-in-law bakes this bread, he shares it with all of us.

3 eggs
3 cups milk
$\frac{1}{2}$ cup butter or margarine
1 cup sugar
2 packages dry yeast
$\frac{1}{2}$ teaspoon salt
6 cups flour
$\frac{1}{2}$ cup raisins

1. Take eggs out of the refrigerator at least 6 hours before making dough. It is important that they be room temperature. Warm milk in a saucepan, add butter and heat until melted.

2. Mix sugar, yeast and salt. Beat eggs, add to sugar mixture, mixing well. Combine milk mixture and sugar/egg mixture. Slowly add flour, 2 cups at a time. Add raisins and place batter in a large bowl. Cover with foil, keep warm and let rise until dough rises to the top of the bowl.

3. Divide dough into 3 pieces and place in loaf pans that have been greased and buttered. Cover again and let rise again. Bake at 350° for 30 minutes until golden brown. When done, remove from pans and cool on a wire rack.

Caraway "Seedy" Cake

Makes 1 loaf

This recipe was one of several brought to America with my grandmother, Mabel Daisy Patterson from Cheltenham, England shortly before the turn of the last century. She was only 12 years old at the time. It makes a fair-size loaf cake, somewhat like a pound cake – always a favorite on my birthday.

$\frac{1}{2}$ cup solid shortening
1 cup sugar
2 eggs
1 teaspoon (or more) caraway seeds
1 teaspoon lemon extract or freshly grated lemon rind
2 cups flour
2 teaspoons baking powder
$\frac{3}{4}$ cup milk
pinch of salt

Cream shortening and sugar, add eggs, caraway seeds and lemon extract or rind and mix well. Sift dry ingredients together and add, alternately, with milk to shortening mix. Mix well. Pour batter into a greased 9-by-5-inch loaf pan and bake at 350° for 30 to 35 minutes or until a toothpick inserted in center comes out clean. Remove to a cooling rack. Slice and serve plain, or as a "tea cake" with butter or cream cheese.

Nanny's Swedish Coffee Bread

Makes 2 loaves

My grandmother, Ellen Nilsson, arrived in America from Sweden in 1898 at age 13 and was sent to live with an older sister. After marrying, she set up housekeeping on Swede Hill in New Haven and often took in laundry and Yale students. She baked extensively and was rumored to feed hobos on the back step.

1 cup sugar
1$\frac{1}{2}$ cups milk
12 tablespoons butter
5 teaspoons dry yeast
$\frac{1}{4}$ cup warm water
1 tablespoon ground cardamom
6$\frac{3}{4}$ cups flour
3 eggs, beaten
1 teaspoon salt
1 beaten egg white
sugar

1. Heat sugar, milk and butter in a saucepan until butter melts. Proof yeast in warm water, add to milk with cardamom and $\frac{3}{4}$ cup flour. Pour into a large bowl. Add eggs and mix in salt and remaining flour gradually. Cover and let rise until dough has doubled.

2. Remove to a floured board and knead well. Separate dough into 4 equal pieces. Cut each piece lengthwise into thirds and braid. Grease two 9-by-13-inch pans. Place 2 braids in each pan.

Cover and let rise until double. Brush tops with egg white and sprinkle liberally with sugar. Bake at 400° for 5 minutes, reduce heat to 325° and continue baking for 17 to 20 minutes. Cool for 5 minutes before removing to a wire rack. Serve warm with sweet butter.

Moke's Apple Cake

Makes 1 10-inch cake

My husband's aunt and uncle, Mildred and Les Morse ("Moke" and "Pop" to the numerous nieces and nephews) ran The Cape Cod Diner in Batavia, New York, for many years until they "retired" to Winter Park, Florida, where they promptly opened The Green Lantern Inn. In the early '60s, as a newlywed, I sought Moke's recipes for my own whenever they came to visit. She graciously complied, but was spare with details... she figured anyone with half a brain could put together a simple recipe! This cake was a family favorite – simple to make, wonderful with fresh fall apples, and as good for breakfast as at any other time of day.

1 cup oil
1 cup granulated sugar
1 cup brown sugar
3 eggs
2 cups flour
1 teaspoon cinnamon
1 teaspoon baking soda
1 teaspoon salt
2 cups finely chopped apples
  (any good variety will do)
1 cup chopped walnuts, pecans, hazelnuts or
  a combination

In a large mixing bowl, mix oil, sugars and eggs; beat until smooth. Sift together flour, cinnamon, baking soda and salt. Add dry ingredients to the bowl and beat well. Fold in apples and nuts. Pour into a prepared Bundt pan (10-cup size) or large rectangular baking pan. Bake at 375° for 45 minutes. Serve with cream, whipped cream, ice cream, sliced apples and applejack, or "sliced plain, to eat out of hand."

Swedish Apple Pie

Makes 1 9-inch pie

Four women, now in their '70s, all went to school together since grade 1. This recipe has been shared and passed back and forth to many others over the last 40 years, a token of their friendship.

6 to 8 apples, peeled and sliced
1 tablespoon sugar
1 tablespoon cinnamon
$\frac{1}{2}$ cup walnuts, chopped
$\frac{1}{3}$ cup ($5\frac{1}{3}$ tablespoons) melted butter
1 cup sugar
1 cup flour
1 egg

1. Lightly butter a 9-inch pie plate. Combine apples, tablespoon of sugar, cinnamon and walnuts. Pour into pie plate (the apples should fill the plate up $\frac{2}{3}$ full).

2. In a small bowl, combine remaining ingredients and beat until creamy. Spread batter over apples and bake in a 350° oven for 45 minutes. Serve warm or cold with a dollop of whipped cream.

Matzo Apple Kugel

Serves 12

For a festive holiday side dish, serve this with your best brisket and latkes.

4 squares matzo, crushed
warm water
6 large eggs
$1\frac{1}{2}$ cups sugar
$1\frac{1}{2}$ cups coarsely chopped walnuts
1 cup raisins
$\frac{1}{4}$ cup orange juice
1 teaspoon freshly grated orange peel
5 tart apples, peeled and sliced
$\frac{1}{4}$ cup sugar mixed with $1\frac{1}{2}$ teaspoons cinnamon
$\frac{1}{4}$ cup melted butter or margarine

1. Preheat oven to 350° and grease a 9-by-13-inch baking pan. Place the matzos in a bowl and pour in enough water to cover. Let the matzos soak for 5 minutes and drain.

2. In a large bowl, using an electric mixer, beat the eggs until frothy. Add $1\frac{1}{2}$ cups sugar, beating until well combined. Stir in the drained matzo, nuts, raisins, orange juice and peel.

3. In another bowl, toss the apples with the sugar and cinnamon mixture. Spread half the apples in the prepared pan, top with the matzo mixture and finish with the remaining apples. Drizzle the melted butter over the top and bake for 45 to 50 minutes, or until the kugel is set. Serve warm or at room temperature.

Lemon Sponge Pie

Makes 1 9-inch pie

This recipe is from my great-grandmother and is Pennsylvania Dutch in origin. It is light and refreshing.

$\frac{1}{4}$ cup softened butter
1 cup sugar
3 tablespoons flour
3 eggs, separated
6 tablespoons fresh lemon juice
1 teaspoon grated fresh lemon rind
$1\frac{1}{2}$ cups milk
1 prepared pie crust

1. Line a 9-inch pie plate with dough (homemade or store bought). Chill pie shell while preparing custard.

2. With an electric mixer, cream butter. Gradually add sugar and flour; mix thoroughly. Add the egg yolks, lemon juice, rind, and milk; beat well.

3. In another bowl, beat the egg whites until they form stiff peaks. Gently fold egg whites into egg yolk mixture. Pour mixture into prepared pie shell and bake in a 425° oven for 15 minutes. Reduce heat to 325° and bake for an additional 30 minutes, or until toothpick inserted into the center comes out clean.

VARIATION:
Omit pie shell and bake in a buttered baking pan (lemon sponge pudding). Serve with a dollop of whipped cream.

Mrs. Fleming's Plum Pudding

Makes 1 pudding

This recipe was brought to this country from Granton, Scotland, by my grandmother in 1895. My father tells that grandmother would occasionally rent a room to any newly arrived Scotsman, one of whom was David Hood, a carpenter, and a very religious gentleman. The first Thanksgiving he shared at her house was started with a prayer from David and ended with the serving of this Plum Pudding. After 3 helpings of the hard sauce, David was advised as to the secret ingredient, a heavy dose of brandy – this story still brings us many laughs as we retell it every year.

$1\frac{1}{2}$ cups suet, finely chopped or grated
2 cups raisins, cut in half
2 cups currants, soaked in water overnight
    and drained
1 cup orange rind, minced
$\frac{1}{2}$ cup brown sugar, firmly packed
$\frac{1}{3}$ cup flour
1 teaspoon nutmeg
1 teaspoon cinnamon
$\frac{1}{2}$ teaspoon cloves
$\frac{1}{2}$ teaspoon ginger
6 eggs, lightly beaten
$\frac{1}{2}$ cup light cream or milk
grated rind of 1 lemon
juice of 1 lemon
1 cup fresh bread crumbs

1. Thoroughly mix suet, raisins, currants, orange rind, brown sugar, flour and spices. Mix in beaten eggs. Add cream, lemon rind, lemon juice and bread crumbs, mixing well. Batter will be somewhat stiff.

2. Grease a 2-quart pudding mold or other container that can be tightly covered. Pour batter into mold (it should be about $\frac{3}{4}$ full), cover tightly with lid or aluminum foil, secured with a string. Place on a rack in a large saucepan and pour in enough boiling water to come $\frac{2}{3}$ up the side of the mold. Cover saucepan when water is boiling vigorously, reduce heat and steam for 6 hours, adding water as needed.

3. When pudding is done, remove lid and let cool before removing from mold. Serve warm with hard sauce. The pudding may be wrapped and refrigerated at this point and reheated later.

David's Brandy Hard Sauce

Makes $1\frac{1}{2}$ cups

8 tablespoons unsalted butter, softened
$1\frac{1}{2}$ cups superfine granulated sugar
1 teaspoon vanilla
3 tablespoons brandy (or more to taste)

Beat butter and sugar until light and fluffy. Add vanilla and brandy, cover and chill. Remove from refrigerator $\frac{1}{2}$ hour before serving and fluff up with a fork.

Nana's Filled Cookies

Makes $4\frac{1}{2}$ dozen

Nana came to America from Cork, Ireland, when she was just 22 years old. With minimal skills and money, she cleaned homes and cooked for others to get by. I believe this recipe was created from whatever was left on her kitchen shelves, as she was a genius at turning out culinary masterpieces from scratch.

1 cup unsalted butter, softened
1 cup sugar
1 egg, beaten
$2\frac{1}{3}$ cups flour
1 $7\frac{1}{2}$-ounce package almond paste*
1 egg white mixed with 1 teaspoon milk

1. Cream butter. Gradually add sugar, mixing until fluffy. Beat in egg, stir in flour until dough forms into a ball in the bowl. Chill 1 hour.

2. Roll out dough to $\frac{1}{4}$-inch thickness and cut into 2-inch rounds. Place $\frac{1}{2}$ teaspoon almond paste on each round, fold over and press edges together to make a crescent shape. Seal edges with a fork and brush lightly with egg wash. Bake at 350° for 8 to 10 minutes until edges are golden. Cool on a wire rack.

*You may substitute any favorite filling such as raspberry jam, apricot jam or pumpkin butter… any thick filling is delicious.

Babe's Angenetties

Makes 3 dozen

These delicious Italian cookies were always made for special occasions by my mother. The children always got the ones with the chocolate frosting first.

3 eggs
5 teaspoons baking powder
1 teaspoon vanilla
$\frac{1}{2}$ cup confectioners' sugar
grated rind of 1 orange
$\frac{1}{2}$ cup vegetable oil
$2\frac{1}{2}$ cups flour

1. Beat eggs until foamy. Add baking powder, vanilla, confectioners' sugar and orange rind. Mix in the oil and slowly add the flour, mixing until batter is smooth.

2. Drop batter by small teaspoonfuls onto a cookie sheet that has been sprayed with nonstick cooking spray. Bake at 400° for 8 to 10 minutes until golden; remove to a cookie rack, cool for 1 hour and finish as follows:

3. Sift $1\frac{1}{2}$ cups confectioners' sugar. Add either 1 teaspoon orange extract, lemon extract, or 1 tablespoon cocoa. Add enough water to make a frosting. Have a small bowl of chocolate shots, other colored holiday candies or chopped nuts on the side. Dip each cookie into the frosting so that only the top is covered and then dip them into the candies – watch them disappear.

Blarney Stones

Makes 24 squares

These small cakes are one of my mother's specialties. I remember on one occasion in the 1950s, when we were living in the Hague, Holland, she made batches of these for our church bazaar. They were a huge success with the Dutch women and sold out in no time. Mommy and I rushed home to make more and returned with overflowing platters of these delicacies which again disappeared.

4 eggs, separated
1 cup sugar
1 cup cake flour
$1\frac{1}{2}$ teaspoons baking powder
$\frac{1}{4}$ teaspoon salt
$\frac{1}{2}$ cup boiling water
1 teaspoon vanilla

FROSTING
3 cups unsalted peanuts
$\frac{1}{2}$ cup (8 tablespoons) butter
2 to $2\frac{1}{2}$ cups powdered sugar
1 teaspoon vanilla

1. Separate the egg whites and yolks. Beat the egg whites with $\frac{1}{2}$ cup of sugar until stiff. Beat yolks with remaining $\frac{1}{2}$ cup sugar and add vanilla.

2. Sift cake flour before measuring and re-sift with other dry ingredients. Add flour mixture to egg yolks, alternating with water. Fold in beaten egg whites. Pour batter into a greased 8-by-12-inch baking pan. Bake in a 325° oven for about 30 minutes or until cake begins to pull away from the edge of the pan. Cool.

3. To make frosting: Coarsely chop peanuts in a food processor or food grinder, being careful not to make them too fine. Cream butter, blend in powdered sugar and vanilla. Cut cake into 2-inch squares, cover with frosting and roll in the chopped peanuts.

Last
Bites

Hattie's Pound Cake

Makes 1 9-inch cake

The best thing about this rich, yet not too sweet cake is that it freezes so well; the challenge is not to eat it before it goes into the freezer!

1 cup milk
1 teaspoon vinegar
2 cups sugar
3 eggs
1 cup vegetable shortening
1 teaspoon vanilla
3 cups cake flour (or 3 cups all-purpose flour minus 6 tablespoons)
$\frac{1}{4}$ teaspoon baking powder
$\frac{1}{4}$ teaspoon salt
$\frac{1}{4}$ teaspoon baking soda
$\frac{1}{2}$ teaspoon mace

1. Before starting the cake, sour the milk by adding vinegar. Cream together sugar, eggs, vegetable shortening, and vanilla. Sift together flour, baking powder, salt, baking soda and mace. Mix together with electric mixer, alternating dry and wet ingredients.

2. Grease and flour a 9-inch tube pan. Pour batter into pan and bake at 350° for 1 hour 15 minutes until golden brown on top or until knife comes out clean. Remove from oven and, while still hot, run a knife around edge of pan to loosen cake from the sides of the pan. Cool before slicing. Serve with fresh berries or a dollop of lemon pie filling.

Gypson's Gingerbread Cake

Makes 1 9-by-13-inch cake

My husband's great-grandmother, Alice, was born in 1860. Her son (my father-in-law) remembered this special treat as a child. After finding Alice's recipe in the family bible, I was able to make it for him after 60 years!

$\frac{1}{2}$ cup shortening
$\frac{1}{2}$ cup sugar
1 egg, beaten
1 cup molasses
$2\frac{1}{2}$ cups flour
1 teaspoon baking soda
1 teaspoon cinnamon
1 teaspoon ginger
$\frac{1}{2}$ teaspoon cloves
$\frac{1}{2}$ teaspoon salt
1 cup boiling water
whipped cream

1. Preheat oven to 350°. In a medium bowl, cream shortening with sugar. Mix in beaten egg and molasses.

2. Sift flour with baking soda, spices and salt. Mix with shortening and molasses mixture, pour in boiling water and combine until batter is smooth. Bake for 45 minutes in a 9-by-13-inch baking pan that has been lightly greased and dusted with flour. Serve warm, topped with whipped cream.

Sour Milk Chocolate Cake

Makes 1 cake

I still have the handwritten recipe for this cake from my grandmother Cleaves. I remember my first attempt at making it with my mother, mine rose beautifully while my mother's cake fell! One of the original measurements was "a piece of shortening the size of an egg," but what size egg??

$\frac{1}{3}$ cup shortening
$\frac{1}{3}$ cup butter
5 ounces baking chocolate (5 squares)
2 cups sugar
1 tablespoon vanilla
3 eggs
$\frac{1}{2}$ teaspoons salt
1 teaspoon baking powder
2 teaspoons baking soda
3 cups flour
2 cups sour milk

1. Melt shortening, butter and chocolate in a saucepan over low heat or in the microwave. Cool. Add sugar, vanilla, and eggs, mixing well.

2. Combine salt, baking powder, baking soda, and flour; add alternately to batter with sour milk, mixing gently. Pour into a greased and floured 8-by-8-inch cake pan and bake at 325° for 30 to 35 minutes or until toothpick inserted in middle comes out clean. Cool on a rack for 10 minutes before removing from the pan. Frost with a white butter icing, if you like, or serve with vanilla ice cream. (This also freezes and makes great cupcakes.)

Ina's "Better Than Sin Cake"

Makes 1 cake

Not just for seniors! We serve this at our fall potluck dinner at The Grange in Mystic, and there is never a crumb left.

1 package yellow cake mix
1 package instant vanilla pudding
$\frac{1}{2}$ cup vegetable oil
$\frac{1}{2}$ cup water
4 eggs
1 8-ounce container sour cream
6 ounces chocolate chips
1 cup walnuts, chopped
1 cup coconut
1 8-ounce bar German sweet chocolate, grated

Mix cake mix, pudding, oil, water and eggs in a large bowl. Fold in sour cream, chocolate chips, walnuts, coconut, and chocolate. Pour batter into a lightly buttered Bundt or tube pan. Bake at 350° for 50 to 55 minutes.

Grandma Peckham's Buttermilk Nutmeg Cake

Makes 1 cake

In the mid 1800s, my great grandmother, Fannie Peckham, and her husband, Sam, a blacksmith, raised New Jersey cows on their farm in Middlefield, Connecticut. Fannie churned her own butter and often had buttermilk on hand. As a frugal New Englander living in the "Nutmeg State," she combined the best of both in this luscious cake.

$\frac{1}{2}$ cup shortening
$1\frac{1}{2}$ cups sugar
2 eggs
2 cups all-purpose flour
1 teaspoon baking powder
1 teaspoon nutmeg
1 teaspoon salt
1 cup buttermilk
$\frac{1}{4}$ teaspoon baking soda
3 teaspoons sugar
$\frac{1}{2}$ teaspoon cinnamon

1. Cream shortening and sugar; beat in eggs by hand. Mix flour, baking powder, nutmeg and salt. Stir baking soda into buttermilk.

2. Alternately add flour mixture and buttermilk to the egg/shortening mixture, beating well. Pour batter into a greased and floured 9-by-9-inch pan. Combine sugar and cinnamon in a small bowl, and sprinkle on top. Bake at 375° for 35 to 40 minutes.

Nutty Sour Cream Coffeecake

Serves 10 to 12

$\frac{1}{2}$ cup (8 tablespoons) butter
1 cup sugar
1 teaspoon vanilla
2 eggs, beaten, or $\frac{1}{2}$ cup Eggbeaters
$1\frac{1}{2}$ cups flour
1 teaspoon baking soda
1 teaspoon baking powder
8 ounces sour cream
$\frac{1}{3}$ cup sugar
$1\frac{1}{2}$ teaspoons cinnamon
$\frac{1}{2}$ cup chopped nuts

1. Cream butter and 1 cup sugar, add vanilla and eggs, mixing well. In a medium bowl, sift flour, baking soda, and baking powder. Add flour mixture and sour cream alternately to the butter mixture.

2. Combine remaining $\frac{1}{3}$ cup sugar, cinnamon, and walnuts. Pour half of the batter into a greased Bundt pan, top with half of the nut mixture and swirl with a knife. Pour the rest of the batter into pan and sprinkle with remaining nut mixture. Bake at 350° for 40 to 45 minutes.

Apple Nobby

Makes 1 cake

I found this hand-written recipe in an old Maine cookbook at our little red farmhouse in Bristol Mills. The local farmers' market had their first apples of the season at that time, so I tried it – knowing that whoever had written it down must have loved it. My husband claims this to be the best apple cake ever.

3 cups diced apples
1 cup sugar
$\frac{1}{4}$ cup butter or margarine
1 egg, beaten
1 cup flour
$\frac{1}{2}$ teaspoon baking powder
$\frac{1}{2}$ teaspoon baking soda
$\frac{1}{2}$ teaspoon salt
$\frac{1}{2}$ teaspoon cinnamon
$\frac{1}{2}$ teaspoon nutmeg
$\frac{1}{3}$ cup chopped walnuts
1 teaspoon vanilla

1. Peel apples and cut into $\frac{1}{2}$-inch cubes (the very word from the original recipe). Cream butter with sugar and add beaten egg.

2. Sift flour, baking powder, baking soda, salt, cinnamon and nutmeg. Add to the butter mixture. Stir in apples, walnuts, and vanilla; mix well. Pour batter into a greased 8-inch square baking pan. Bake in a 350° oven for 45 minutes. Serve warm topped with ice cream or vanilla yogurt.

Granny McAleer's Pound Cake

Makes 1 8-inch cake

This cake is truly addictive and always the first thing to go, wherever it is served. This recipe gives consistently fine results, but it is important to follow the directions closely – the ingredients must be at room temperature and the eggs beaten in one at a time.

$\frac{1}{2}$ pound butter, at room temperature
$1\frac{2}{3}$ cups sugar
5 large eggs, at room temperature
2 cups cake flour, measured after sifting
pinch of salt
$\frac{1}{4}$ teaspoon mace or nutmeg
1 teaspoon vanilla

1. In a medium bowl, cream the butter and sugar well. Add the eggs, one at a time, beating well after each addition, about 2 minutes. It is important to beat a lot of air into the mixture to assure a light cake.

2. Sift the flour (which has already been sifted before measuring), salt, and mace; repeat sifting 2 more times. Fold the dry ingredients into the butter/sugar/egg mixture; add the vanilla and mix well. Pour batter into a well greased 8-by-8-by-3-inch baking pan and bake for 1 hour in a 350° oven.

Not-So-Plain-Jane's Apple Cake

Makes 1 cake

A quick and easy recipe from a friend and chef at the Harbor View in Stonington, Connecticut.

8 tablespoons butter
1 cup sugar
1 cup flour
1 teaspoon baking soda
1 teaspoon baking powder
$\frac{1}{2}$ teaspoon salt
$1\frac{1}{2}$ teaspoons cinnamon
2 eggs
3 cups chopped apples, peeled or not, your choice
$\frac{1}{2}$ cup chopped pecans
confectioners' sugar

In a large bowl, cream butter and sugar. Add flour, baking powder, soda, salt, cinnamon and eggs; mix well. Stir in the apples and nuts; the batter will be stiff. Pour batter into a greased 8- or 9-inch baking pan and bake in a 350° oven for 35 to 45 minutes or until a toothpick inserted in the center comes out clean. Let cool, sprinkle with confectioners' sugar and cut into squares. Serve warm with whipped cream or vanilla ice cream.

Rose Gangemil's Cheesecake

Serves 8 to 10

So happy to share my mother-in-law's treasured and delicious recipe.

$\frac{2}{3}$ cup cornflake crumbs
3 8-ounce packages cream cheese, softened
4 large eggs
$1\frac{1}{2}$ cups sugar
2 teaspoons vanilla
1 cup sour cream

1. Generously butter an 8-inch springform pan. Shake the cornflake crumbs in pan to coat sides and bottom, adding a bit more if needed.

2. In a large bowl, using an electric mixer, beat cream cheese until smooth and fluffy. Add eggs, one at a time, mixing after each addition until well blended. Beat in 1 cup of sugar and 1 teaspoon vanilla; pour mixture into prepared pan. Bake cheesecake in a 350° oven for 45 minutes and remove to a wire rack for 25 minutes.

3. Meanwhile, combine sour cream, remaining $\frac{1}{2}$ cup sugar and remaining 1 teaspoon vanilla. Spread over top of cooled cheesecake, return to oven and bake for 15 minutes. Cool to room temperature and refrigerate for several hours until well chilled before slicing.

Grammy's Run-Away Apple Cake

Makes 1 9-by-13-inch cake

When we were children, my Grammy lived less than a mile away. On rather frequent occasions, my naughty big brother would let life's inequities overwhelm him, and he'd announce that he was running away from home. He'd phone Grammy to share this news, whereupon she'd suggest that he stop by on his way out of town to have a bite – he'd need his strength for his new life. In the time it took for him to pedal the distance, she would have thrown this cake together and would be taking it hot and fragrant from the oven as he arrived. After a comfy chat, she'd send him home with the leftovers.

For my Grammy, cooking came from her head, her hands, and her heart. Capturing any of her delicious concoctions in a written recipe was quite impossible, but this one comes pretty close to my recollection of her original cake.

$\frac{3}{4}$ cup sugar
$\frac{1}{4}$ cup shortening
1 egg, slightly beaten
$\frac{1}{2}$ cup milk
$1\frac{1}{2}$ cups flour
1 teaspoon salt
2 teaspoons baking powder
4 apples, peeled and sliced
1 teaspoon cinnamon
$\frac{1}{4}$ cup sugar
1 tablespoon butter

1. In a medium bowl, cream sugar and shortening. Add egg and mix well; stir in milk.

2. Sift flour, salt, and baking powder and combine with wet ingredients. Pour batter in a greased 9-by-13-inch baking pan and arrange apples, overlapping, to cover completely. Mix cinnamon with sugar, sprinkle over apples and dot with butter. Bake at 350° for 30 to 40 minutes or until apples are done.

Grandmother Merritt's Chocolate Cake

Makes 1 8-by-8-inch cake

This recipe has always been the standard birthday cake in our family, hence we are all <u>real</u> chocolate lovers. It makes a substantial cake, rich in flavor but not too heavy. Enjoy the cake alone or with ice cream, preferably hand-cranked.

3 squares unsweetened chocolate
4 tablespoons butter
$\frac{1}{2}$ cup boiling water
1 cup sugar
1 egg, well beaten
$\frac{1}{4}$ cup sour milk
1 cup flour
$\frac{1}{2}$ teaspoon baking soda
$\frac{1}{4}$ teaspoon salt
1 teaspoon vanilla

1. Melt chocolate and butter over low heat or in a double boiler. Add water and sugar, mix until sugar is dissolved. Add remaining ingredients in order, beating well after each addition.

2. Pour batter into a greased and floured 8-inch pan and bake in a 350° oven for 30 to 35 minutes. This recipe can be doubled for a 9-by-13-inch pan.

"Chocolate flatters you for awhile, warms you for an instant, then all of a sudden it kinders a mortal fever in you."
Julia Child

Black Ginger Cake

Serves 8
Dark molasses and strong coffee make a deep, rich-colored cake.

2 cups all-purpose flour
$\frac{1}{2}$ cup sugar
$1\frac{1}{2}$ teaspoons ground cinnamon
$\frac{1}{2}$ teaspoon ground ginger
$\frac{1}{2}$ teaspoon salt
$\frac{1}{4}$ cup finely chopped crystallized ginger
$1\frac{1}{2}$ teaspoons baking soda
$\frac{2}{3}$ cup strong hot coffee
1 cup molasses
1 egg white
1 tablespoon vegetable oil
confectioners' sugar for dusting

1. Preheat oven to 350° and lightly oil an 8-by-8-inch baking pan or coat it with nonstick spray. Line the bottom of the pan with a square of parchment or wax paper; oil or coat the paper with cooking spray.

2. Sift together flour, sugar, cinnamon, ground ginger and salt into a mixing bowl. Add crystallized ginger and mix well.

3. In another bowl, stir baking soda into hot coffee. Whisk in molasses, egg white and oil; pour into the dry ingredients. Do not overmix or the cake will be too dense. Pour into prepared baking pan and bake for 30 to 40 minutes or until firm to the touch. Dust with confectioners' sugar and cut into squares or triangles when cooled.

Scripture Cake

Makes 1 cake

From and old Stonington cookbook published by the Second Congregational Church in the Borough, dated 1911. Follow precisely for a direct road to heaven!

1 cup ($\frac{1}{2}$ pound) butter	Judges 2, 25
3$\frac{1}{2}$ cups flour	1 Kings, 22
3 cups sugar	Jeremiah 6, 20
2 cups raisins	1 Samuel 30, 12
2 cups figs	1 Samuel 30, 12
1 cup blanched almonds	Genesis 43, 11
1 cup water	Genesis 24, 17
6 eggs	Isaiah 10, 14
1 tablespoon honey	Exodus 16, 21
pinch of salt	Leviticus 2, 13
Spices to taste:	
cinnamon, nutmeg, allspice	1 Kings 10, 10

Follow Solomon's advice (Proverbs 13, 24) for making good boys and you will have a good cake. Or, combine all ingredients in a large bowl, mix well, and pour into a greased 13 x 9 x 2-inch baking dish. Bake at 350° for 45 – 55 minutes, or until a toothpick inserted in the center comes out clean.

Campers' Delight With Sunshine Sauce

Serves 10

The favorite dessert of the year in 1937 at Camp Anawan in Merideth, New Hampshire.

$\frac{1}{4}$ cup butter
1$\frac{1}{2}$ cups sugar
2 eggs, beaten
$\frac{1}{3}$ pound chocolate (about 5 ounces)
1$\frac{1}{2}$ cups milk
1$\frac{1}{2}$ cups flour
1 teaspoon baking powder

1. Cream butter and sugar. Add beaten eggs. Melt chocolate in a double boiler (or in a microwave) over medium heat; combine with milk and cook for 2 minutes.

2. Sift flour with baking powder and add to butter along with chocolate milk mixture. Pour batter into a greased 9-by-9-inch baking pan and bake for 40 minutes at 350°. Serve warm with sauce.

SUNSHINE SAUCE
2 egg yolks, beaten
1 cup sugar
1 cup heavy cream, whipped
1 teaspoon vanilla

Mix egg yolks and sugar until sugar is dissolved. Gently fold in whipped cream and vanilla. Spoon over warm cake.

Peach Macaroon Matthews

Serves 6

This recipe was one of my mother, Johanna's, best. As a registered nurse, she worked most of the school year, but in the summer when those "Jersey peaches" were ripe she would whip up this delight. Her secret?? – "The butter," she claimed.

$\frac{1}{4}$ pound (8 tablespoons) butter, plus 2 tablespoons additional
1 egg
1 cup flour
1 cup sugar
5 to 6 fresh ripe peaches, peeled and sliced
1 tablespoon cinnamon

1. Butter a 9- to 10-inch pie pan. Slice peaches, directly into the pan, dot with the 2 tablespoons of butter and sprinkle with cinnamon.

2. In a small bowl, mix butter, egg, flour and sugar; batter will be stiff. Spread batter over peaches and bake in a preheated 350° oven for 45 minutes until brown and bubbly. Serve warm with vanilla ice cream or whipped cream.

Baked Apples With Caramel Cream

Serves 6

This also may be made with gingersnaps or any spice cake crumbs.

$\frac{1}{2}$ cup sugar
$\frac{1}{4}$ teaspoon ground cinnamon
dash of freshly grated nutmeg
2 cups apple juice or cider
6 large Rome apples
$\frac{1}{4}$ cup coarsely chopped walnuts
$\frac{1}{2}$ cup vanilla wafer or cookie crumbs
$\frac{1}{4}$ cup golden raisins
$\frac{1}{4}$ cup heavy cream

1. Combine sugar, cinnamon, nutmeg and apple juice in a saucepan; bring to a boil. Reduce heat and simmer just until sugar dissolves, making a syrup.

2. Starting at stem end, peel 1/3 of each apple. Carefully core to within $\frac{1}{2}$-inch of the bottom. Mix nuts, crumbs and raisins, and spoon into apples. Press lightly to compact mixture.

3. Arrange apples in a shallow 8-by-11-inch baking pan. Pour the hot syrup over the top and bake in a 400° oven for 45 minutes, basting often. Transfer with a spatula to dessert dishes.

4. Pour baking juices into a saucepan and over medium heat, reduce to $\frac{1}{2}$ cup. Do not allow juice to caramelize. Whisk in the cream until well blended and drizzle over each baked apple.

Golden Delicious Apple Crisp

Serves 6

8 cups peeled and sliced Golden
  Delicious apples
$\frac{2}{3}$ cup orange juice
$\frac{1}{2}$ cup sugar
2 cups rolled oats
1 cup brown sugar, firmly packed
4 tablespoons butter or margarine, melted
$1\frac{1}{2}$ teaspoons cinnamon
1 teaspoon nutmeg

Preheat oven to 350°.

1. Combine apples, orange juice and
    sugar in a bowl and mix well. Spoon
    into a 2-quart baking pan that has
    been sprayed with nonstick cooking
    spray.

2. Combine the oats, brown sugar, but-
    ter, cinnamon and nutmeg in a bowl
    and mix well. Sprinkle over the apple
    mixture. Bake for 25 to 30 minutes or
    until the top is golden brown, and the
    apples are tender and bubbling. Serve
    warm with whipped cream or vanilla
    ice cream.

Frozen Peach Pie Filling

Makes enough for 4 pies

**As a true peach lover, I buy several bushel
baskets when the peaches are at their
peak and make enough pie filling to get
me through to the next harvest.**

4 quarts peeled and sliced peaches
  (16 cups, about 9 pounds peaches)
2 teaspoons "Fruit Fresh" (ascorbic acid)
$3\frac{1}{2}$ cups sugar
$\frac{1}{2}$ cup plus 2 tablespoons quick cooking
  tapioca
$\frac{1}{4}$ to $\frac{1}{2}$ cup lemon juice
1 teaspoon salt

1. Combine "Fruit Fresh" and sugar in
    a large bowl. Add peaches, tapioca,
    lemon juice and salt, mix well.

2. To freeze into pie shapes – divide
    peaches into 4 large plastic bags
    (about 4 cups filling each). Place bag
    in pie plate, pushing around to get a
    pie shape. Freeze until firm, takeout
    of pie plate and refreeze. Proceed
    with the remaining peaches.

3. To bake frozen pie filling: Prepare
    pastry for a 9-inch pie. Remove peach-
    es from bag and place in pie crust. Dot
    with 1 tablespoon butter, cover with
    top crust and make several slits in the
    top. Bake at 425° for 60 to 65 minutes
    until filling is bubbly and crust is
    brown.

Lemon Dainty

Serves 4

A tart cake and custard pudding – never a bite left.

3 tablespoons butter
$\frac{1}{8}$ teaspoon salt
$\frac{3}{4}$ cup sugar
2 tablespoons flour
2 egg yolks, slightly beaten
1 cup milk
juice of 1 lemon and grated rind
2 egg whites, beaten stiff
powdered sugar

1. Combine butter, salt, sugar and flour; mix well. Add egg yolks, milk, lemon juice and rind and beat with an egg beater until smooth.

2. Gently fold in the beaten egg whites and pour into a buttered baking pan, set in a pan of hot water. Bake at 350° for 45 minutes until golden brown. There will be cake on the top, pudding on the bottom. Dust with powdered sugar and serve warm.

Mimi's Butterscotch Russian Cream

Serves 6

Always on the holiday table at the Breed home in Melrose, Massachusetts. You can whip up this yummy dessert anytime.

2 cups milk
1 cup brown sugar
2 egg yolks, beaten
2 tablespoons butter
dash salt
1 teaspoon vanilla
1 envelope gelatin
2 tablespoons water
2 egg whites

1. Place milk, $\frac{3}{4}$ cup brown sugar, egg yolks and butter in a double boiler. Cook until thickened, stirring, about 8 to 10 minutes. Add salt and vanilla. Remove from heat and place in a bowl.

2. Soften gelatin in a cup with water. Beat egg whites until stiff with remaining $\frac{1}{4}$ cup brown sugar. Add gelatin to egg yolk mixture and gently fold in egg whites. Pour into a glass serving dish or individual cups.

Pumpkin Indian Pudding

Serves 10 to 12

A personal adaptation from *Fannie Farmer's Boston Cooking School Cookbook* – a classic.

5 cups milk
6 tablespoons cornmeal
2 tablespoons butter
1 14-ounce can pumpkin or 2 cups, cooked
1 cup molasses
2 eggs, beaten
1 teaspoon salt
1 teaspoon nutmeg
1 teaspoon cinnamon
2 teaspoons ginger

1. Scald 4 cups of milk in a medium saucepan (or microwave), add cornmeal and cook 15 to 20 minutes until thickened, stirring frequently. Add butter and pumpkin to cornmeal mixture and cook an additional 5 minutes.

2. In a separate bowl, mix the molasses, eggs, salt and spices. Add to cornmeal mixture.

3. Pour mixture into a buttered 2-quart casserole or 9-by-13-inch baking pan. Pour 1 cup of cold milk over the top and bake in a 325° oven for 50 minutes. Let cool to set for 15 minutes. Serve warm with vanilla ice cream. This may be reheated in the oven or microwave.

Apple Cider Indian Pudding

Serves 6 to 8

A favorite from an old Garden Club friend.

1 cup milk
$\frac{2}{3}$ cup cornmeal
3 cups cider
1 egg, slightly beaten
$\frac{1}{2}$ cup brown sugar, firmly packed
1 teaspoon cinnamon
1 teaspoon salt
$\frac{1}{4}$ cup (4 tablespoons) butter, cut into bits
$\frac{1}{2}$ cup raisins

1. In the top of a double boiler set over simmering water, scald $\frac{1}{2}$ cup of the milk. In a medium bowl, whisk together the cornmeal and the cider; stir the mixture into the scalded milk and cook, stirring occasionally, for 20 to 25 minutes until thickened. (The mixture may appear slightly curdled – don't worry.)

2. Remove from heat, whisk in the egg, brown sugar, cinnamon, salt, butter and raisins. Pour the mixture into a buttered 13-by-9-inch baking pan. Pour the remaining $\frac{1}{2}$ cup milk around the edges and bake in a 325° oven for 1 hour. Serve the pudding warm with vanilla ice cream.

Caramel Bread Pudding

Serves 6 to 8

This recipe has been in my husband's family for some 60 years, and I have now passed it on to my four children. It is delicious!

4 cups milk, scalded
$\frac{1}{2}$ cup sugar
2 cups cubed bread
2 eggs
$\frac{2}{3}$ cup sugar
$\frac{1}{2}$ teaspoon salt
1 teaspoon vanilla

1. In a small, heavy saucepan, cook $\frac{1}{2}$ cup sugar over medium heat until it caramelizes, watching carefully so that it does not burn. Add caramel to scalded milk and stir until sugar dissolves. Stir in the bread cubes and let soak for several minutes.

2. In a medium bowl beat eggs, add remaining $\frac{2}{3}$ cup sugar, salt, and vanilla. Combine with bread mixture. Pour into a buttered 2-quart baking pan and bake in a 325° oven for 1 hour. Turn off heat and let pudding rest in oven for 5 minutes. Cool and serve with fresh whipped cream.

Jo Dicianti's Indian Pudding

Serves 6 to 8

3 tablespoons corn meal
$\frac{1}{2}$ teaspoon salt
$\frac{1}{2}$ cup molasses
$\frac{1}{2}$ cup brown sugar
1 egg, slightly beaten
2 tablespoons butter
1 teaspoon cinnamon
$\frac{1}{2}$ teaspoon ginger
1 pint milk

1. Place all ingredients except milk in a medium saucepan and heat until butter is melted. Pour into a 2-quart baking pan.

2. Pour milk around the sides of the pan. Do not stir. Bake in a 250° oven for 4 to 5 hours, adding a bit more milk if the pudding becomes too firm. Serve at room temperature with whipped cream or vanilla ice cream.

Secret Walnut Pie

Makes 1 9-inch pie
This pie makes its own crust.

20 Ritz crackers, crumbled
⅔ cup chopped walnuts
1 teaspoon baking powder
3 egg whites
1 cup sugar
1 teaspoon vanilla
whipped cream
shaved chocolate

In a large mixing bowl, combine crackers, walnuts and baking powder. Beat egg whites until stiff, slowly adding sugar and vanilla. Fold egg whites into crumb mixture and pour into a buttered 9-inch pie pan. Bake at 350° for 30 minutes. Cool. Top with a dollop of whipped cream and sprinkle with chocolate.

Gooney Bird Pie

Makes 1 large pie
This recipe came from an old friend in Pensacola, Florida. It so intrigued my husband because of its name – he was stationed as a submariner on the USS ATULE in the Pacific during World War II. He had many occasions to see these comical birds, and this delicious pie brings back many memories.

8 tablespoons butter, melted
1 cup flour
1 cup chopped pecans
1 8-ounce package cream cheese
1 cup confectioners' sugar
2 cups Cool Whip
2 packages instant vanilla pudding mix
3 cups milk

1. Mix melted butter, flour and pecans, press into a 9-by-13-inch baking pan.

2. Combine cream cheese, confectioners' sugar and Cool Whip, beat with an electric mixer for 3 minutes until blended. Mixture will be very thick. Spread over crust.

3. Beat vanilla pudding with milk until well mixed and pour over second layer. Refrigerate for at least 6 hours before cutting into squares.

Pumpkin Ice Cream Pie

Serves 6

A nice change from the traditional pumpkin custard pie, serve this as a summer dessert and surprise your friends.

1 pint vanilla ice cream, softened
1 cup canned pumpkin
$\frac{3}{4}$ cup sugar
$\frac{1}{2}$ teaspoon salt
$\frac{1}{2}$ teaspoon ginger
$\frac{1}{2}$ teaspoon nutmeg
$\frac{1}{2}$ teaspoon cinnamon
1 cup whipping cream ($\frac{1}{2}$ pint), whipped
1 baked 9-inch pie shell or graham cracker crust

1. Spread softened ice cream over bottom of pie shell and place in the freezer while preparing filling.
2. Combine pumpkin, sugar, salt and spices; mix. Gently fold in the whipped cream until well blended. Remove pie shell from freezer and spread pumpkin mixture evenly over ice cream. Freeze for at least 6 hours before slicing.

Legendary Lemon Sponge Pie

Serves 8

My mother, Lena Poppe, always made this pie, and shared the recipe with me when I was married in 1928. It is my favorite pie and at 92 years old, I still prepare it at my home each Wednesday when my family comes for coffee and dessert. Lemon Sponge Pie is so special.

3 eggs, separated
juice and rind of 1 large lemon
1 cup sugar
3 tablespoons flour
pinch salt
1 cup milk
1 tablespoon butter, melted
1 prepared pie crust
confectioners' sugar

1. In a large bowl, beat egg yolks until creamy; add lemon juice, rind, sugar, flour, salt, milk, and melted butter, mixing well.
2. In a medium bowl, beat egg whites until stiff and gently fold them into the lemon mixture. Pour mixture into pie crust and bake for 40 minutes at 350°. Dust with confectioners' sugar before serving at room temperature.

A Major Pumpkin Pie(s)

Makes 1 10-inch pie and 1 8-inch pie
This pie can be successfully made lactose-free by substituting margarine and Lactaid for butter and milk with no loss of texture or flavor.

butter to grease pie pans
cornmeal
$3\frac{1}{2}$ cups canned pumpkin
$1\frac{1}{2}$ cups sugar
4 teaspoons cinnamon
1 teaspoon nutmeg
2 teaspoons ginger
1 teaspoon salt
lemon zest to taste
4 eggs, slightly beaten
3 cups milk

1. Butter the pie pans, shake cornmeal over them until they are completely covered. Discard any excess cornmeal. Combine pumpkin, sugar, cinnamon, nutmeg, ginger, salt and lemon zest. Add milk to slightly beaten eggs and strain this into the pumpkin mixture. Pour into the prepared pie pans.

2. Bake in 450° oven for 10 minutes, then reduce the heat to 350° and bake 50 to 60 minutes longer or until filling is firm and the dark ring in the center disappears.

Grandma's Lemon Butter

Makes 1 cup
A lovely tea time treat with toasted crumpets and a pot of tea, this recipe from my English grandmother is irresistible.

4 egg yolks
1 cup sugar
6 tablespoons lemon juice
$\frac{1}{4}$ cup butter

Beat egg yolks and sugar together until light. Add lemon juice and butter. Cook over hot water in a double boiler, stirring constantly until thickened, about 10 minutes. Pour into a pretty jar and refrigerate. (It will disappear quickly!)

Aunt Ebby's Frypan Cookies

Makes 2 to 3 dozen

My 90-year old aunt hated to cook and did so only when necessary. She did, however, make these great date cookies for the holidays. This recipe is for all of those who say they cannot bake.

2 eggs
1 cup sugar
$1\frac{1}{2}$ cups chopped dates
1 tablespoon butter
$\frac{1}{4}$ teaspoon salt
1 teaspoon vanilla
$\frac{1}{2}$ cup walnuts
2 cups Rice Krispies cereal
1 6-ounce bag flaked coconut

1. Beat eggs, add sugar and dates. Melt butter in a large skillet (electric is good) and add mixture. Cook over medium heat for 10 minutes, stirring very gently, like making scrambled eggs.
2. Remove from heat and add salt, vanilla, nuts and Rice Krispies. Stir until well mixed and form into 1-inch balls. Roll in coconut, coating outside generously. Store in an airtight container.

Gram's Spice Cookies

Makes about 4 dozen

With twelve grandchildren to make treats for, my grandmother made hundreds of these cookies. To press the cookies on the baking sheet, Gram used the top of an old cruet that left a wonderful star design on the top when baked.

10 tablespoons butter
1 cup sugar
2 eggs, beaten until fluffy
3 cups flour
3 scant teaspoons baking powder
$\frac{1}{4}$ teaspoon salt
2 teaspoons cardamom*

* To customize, you may use your own choice of ground anise, lemon peel, vanilla, or nutmeg instead of cardamom.

Cream together butter and sugar in a large bowl, add beaten eggs. Put flour, baking powder, salt and spices into a sifter and sift into wet ingredients. Mix well. Form dough into small balls, about 1-inch, and roll in sugar. Place dough on a cookie sheet and press down with a cruet top or glass. Bake at 350° for 8 to 10 minutes. Remove to a wire rack to cool.

Old Estate Sour Cream Drop Cookies

Makes 3 dozen

My mother's family is directly descended from Peter Folger, one of the original English settlers of Nantucket, Massachusetts. By the 1800s, the island was getting crowded and many Nantucketers, mostly all descendants of the original seven families, took part in the westward movement. They usually moved with groups of their neighbors establishing new communities in places like North Carolina and Indiana, building a new country and developing routes on the Underground Railroad as needs presented themselves. I know the importance of cookies fresh from the oven because I grew up smelling and tasting them. When I make these sour cream cookies which are from my Grandmother Folger's recipe, I still benefit from the love which was always so plentiful in her kitchen.

$\frac{1}{2}$ cup (8 tablespoons) butter
1 cup sugar
1 egg, well beaten
$\frac{1}{2}$ cup sour cream
$2\frac{1}{2}$ cups flour
$\frac{1}{4}$ teaspoon baking soda
$2\frac{1}{2}$ teaspoons baking powder
1 teaspoon vanilla

Cream butter and sugar, mix in beaten egg and sour cream. Sift dry ingredients and add to butter mixture along with vanilla*. Drop by rounded teaspoonfuls on a cookie sheet and bake in a 350° oven for 10 to 12 minutes.

* My grandmother often added raisins and nuts. I prefer a combination of chips – chocolate, vanilla, mint, etc. Sometimes I leave them plain and press a Hershey's Chocolate Kiss in the center before I take them out of the oven.

Joe Froggers

Makes 60 to 100 cookies,
depending on the size

**This cookie recipe was passed down to me
from my maternal grandmother, Sarah
Miranda Mattoon Isham. It is rather
unusual as it is made up, kept overnight,
and baked the next day.**

1 cup shortening
1 cup sugar
1 egg
2 cups molasses
2 tablespoons vinegar
6 to 7 cups flour
$\frac{1}{2}$ teaspoon cinnamon
$\frac{1}{2}$ teaspoon freshly ground nutmeg
1 teaspoon salt
2 tablespoons ground ginger
4 teaspoons baking soda
1 cup boiling water

1. Cream shortening, add sugar and egg.
    Beat together until light and fluffy.
    Add molasses and vinegar.

2. Add flour, starting with 6 cups, adding
    gradually. Mix in cinnamon, nutmeg,
    salt, and ginger. Dissolve baking soda
    in boiling water and add to flour
    mixture along with enough additional
    flour to form a stiff dough. Cover and
    let stand in a cool place overnight.

3. Roll dough out in small batches on a
    floured surface. Cut with cookie cut-
    ters (a scalloped edge round cutter is
    traditional) and place on an ungreased
    cookie sheet. Sprinkle lightly with
    sugar and bake at 350° for 8 to 10
    minutes. Cool on a wire rack. The
    cookies will be soft, not crisp.

NOTE:
The dough may also be rolled into small
walnut-size balls and dipped in sugar. If
they begin to get hard, put a few apple
slices in a sealed container with the cookies and they will become soft again.

Clifford Tea Cookies

Makes 2 dozen cookies

**A third generation delicacy – make these a
day ahead.**

$\frac{3}{4}$ cup butter
2 cups brown sugar
2 eggs
$\frac{1}{2}$ teaspoon salt
$3\frac{1}{2}$ cups flour
1 teaspoon baking soda
1 cup chopped walnuts

1. Cream butter and sugar. Add eggs and
    beat well. Sift flour, baking soda and
    salt 3 times and add to butter mixture
    with the nuts, mixing well.

2. Shape dough into 2 logs, 2 inches each
    in diameter. Wrap logs in foil and
    refrigerate overnight. Slice into $\frac{1}{2}$-inch
    thin slices and bake on an ungreased
    baking sheet at 400° for 6 to 8 min-
    utes until crisp. Cool on a cookie rack
    and serve with your best tea.

Mrs. Scates' Molasses Cookies

Makes 20 large or 30 small, depending on the size of your cookie cutters

In 1931 this favorite recipe was given to my mother by Mrs. Scates, wife of the Reverend Elmer Scates. These cookies are soft and moist; best eaten with a big glass of cold milk.

$\frac{1}{2}$ cup sugar
$\frac{1}{2}$ cup shortening
$\frac{1}{2}$ molasses
1 cup milk
3 to $3\frac{1}{2}$ cups flour
1 teaspoon ground ginger
1 teaspoon ground cinnamon
1 teaspoon baking soda

1. Preheat oven to 350°. In a medium bowl, cream sugar and shortening. Add molasses and milk and stir until well blended.

2. Combine flour (starting with 3 cups), ginger, cinnamon, and soda. Add to wet ingredients and mix until dough is firm enough to roll, adding a little more flour if it seems too soft.

3. In small amounts roll dough onto a lightly floured board or countertop to $\frac{1}{4}$-inch thick. Cut out and place on a greased cookie sheet. Bake for 10 to 12 minutes, being careful not to over-bake as the cookies should be soft.

Nana's Molasses Ice Box Cookies

Makes 3 dozen cookies

Nana Seaman was a petite lady, barely 90 pounds. Her home was always filled with many wonderful treats – this is one of them.

1 cup shortening
1 cup brown sugar
$\frac{1}{2}$ cup molasses
1 teaspoon vanilla
$2\frac{1}{2}$ cups flour (scant), sifted
1 teaspoon baking soda
1 teaspoon salt
2 teaspoons ginger

1. Beat shortening until creamy. Add brown sugar, molasses, and vanilla, mixing well. Add flour, baking soda, salt, and ginger, combining until well mixed.

2. Roll dough into 2 logs, wrap in wax paper and refrigerate until thoroughly chilled, at least 2 hours or best overnight. When ready to cook, slice very, very thin and bake in a 350° oven for 7 minutes until crispy. Cool on a cookie rack and store in a tightly covered container.

Soft Molasses Cookies

Makes 2 dozen cookies

My grandmother, Lucille Borges, was one of nine children; they lived in Waterford. As was the custom then, when Mrs. Frank Borges (Lu's mother) would make a dessert, many times she would put molasses in the mix to sweeten it. When the little brown jug was empty, the children would sit around in a circle on the floor. Each in their turn would take a stick and scrape the bottom and side of the jug to get the sugar and the residue of the molasses.

$\frac{1}{2}$ cup shortening
$\frac{1}{4}$ cup sugar
1 egg
1 cup dark molasses (Grandma's)
3 cups flour
$\frac{1}{2}$ teaspoon salt
$\frac{1}{4}$ teaspoon ginger
1 teaspoon cinnamon
2 teaspoons baking soda –
    dissolved in 2 tablespoons water

1. Cream well shortening and sugar in large bowl, add egg and molasses; beating and stirring with a large spoon as you add.

2. Sift together flour, salt, and spices, then gradually add baking soda and water. When well mixed, set in refrigerator (I chill for an hour or so. Makes it easier to handle when you roll it out.) Roll out a small amount at a time, a third of the dough, on to a well-floured board. The dough should be about $\frac{1}{4}$ inch thick; cut the cookies then put them on a greased cookie sheet about 2 inches apart.

3. Bake about 12 to 15 minutes at 350°. The cookies are done when the tops are firm to touch. You do have to watch so they don't burn on the bottoms as the molasses makes them burn easily. Remove with a spatula and cool.

Boston Herald Hermit Cookies

Makes 3 to 4 dozen bars
From an age-old clipping – still the best!

$\frac{3}{4}$ cup shortening
1 cup sugar
1 egg
$\frac{1}{4}$ cup molasses
$2\frac{1}{4}$ cups flour
1 teaspoon baking soda
2 teaspoons cinnamon
$\frac{3}{4}$ teaspoon ginger
$\frac{3}{4}$ teaspoon cloves
$\frac{1}{2}$ cup raisins
$\frac{1}{2}$ cup chopped nuts

1. Cream shortening with sugar until fluffy. Add egg and molasses and mix well.

2. Combine flour, baking soda, cinnamon, ginger, and cloves. Add dry ingredients to sugar-egg mixture and mix well. Stir in raisins and nuts and divide dough into 4 equal parts.

3. Shape each piece into a sausage shaped roll and place on 2 ungreased cookie sheets. Press each roll down slightly. Bake in a 375° oven for 9 to 10 minutes. Cracks may appear and dough may seem uncooked, but remove from oven. Cool for 15 minutes on cookie sheet. Cut diagonally into $1\frac{1}{2}$- to 2-inch bars and sprinkle with sugar while still hot. These store well in an airtight container.

Gumdrop Cookies

Makes 5 dozen
My mother-in-law, Marjory, was the first grade teacher many years ago in the Old Noank School, and was known for this cookie that she often baked for her students.

1 cup shortening
1 cup brown sugar
1 cup white sugar
2 eggs
$1\frac{1}{2}$ cups flour
$\frac{1}{2}$ teaspoon salt
$\frac{1}{2}$ teaspoon baking soda
1 cup coconut
2 cups oatmeal
1 cup spice gumdrops, cut up

1. Blend shortening, sugars and eggs until fluffy. Sift flour, salt and baking powder; add to butter mixture and mix well.

2. Add coconut, oatmeal and gumdrops. Form dough into 1-inch balls and place on a cookie sheet, about 2 inches apart. Press cookies flat with a fork dipped in cold water and bake at 375° for 10 to 12 minutes until crisp. Cool on a wire rack.

Clipper Chippers

Makes 3 to 4 dozen
These cookies are served aboard the cruise ship The Nantucket Clipper. The bakery chef graciously shared her recipe for this adaptation.

1 cup butter, softened
$\frac{3}{4}$ cup sugar
$\frac{3}{4}$ cup light brown sugar
1 tablespoon vanilla
1 tablespoon Tia Maria
1 tablespoon Frangelico liqueur
2 eggs
$2\frac{1}{2}$ cups flour
1 teaspoon baking soda
$\frac{1}{2}$ teaspoon salt
4 cups milk chocolate chips
1 cup walnut halves
$\frac{1}{2}$ cup pecan halves
$\frac{1}{2}$ cup macadamia nuts

1. Cream butter, sugars, vanilla, Tia Maria and Frangelico until light and fluffy. Add eggs and beat well.

2. Combine flour, baking soda and salt; gradually beat into creamed mixture. Stir in chips and nuts, cover and refrigerate overnight.

3. Drop batter by teaspoonfuls onto ungreased cookie sheet and bake at 325° for 10 to 13 minutes until browned.

Thelma's Dream Date Bars

Makes 24 bars
When we moved from Noank village to "up on the hill," our neighbor welcomed us with these yummy date bars. I copied the recipe on an envelope, dated 1959, which, after all these years I still refer to when baking the bars.

$\frac{1}{4}$ cup butter
$\frac{3}{4}$ cup sugar
1 egg
$1\frac{1}{3}$ cups Bisquik
$\frac{1}{2}$ cup chopped nuts
1 cup chopped dates
confectioners' sugar

Mix butter, sugar and egg. Add Bisquik, nuts, and dates, mixing well. Press batter into an 8-by-8-inch baking pan (batter will be very stiff) and bake for 25 minutes in a 350° oven. Cool for 1 hour before cutting into squares and sprinkle with confectioners' sugar.

My Sister's Molasses Whoopie Pies

Makes 22 pies
Filled with ginger crème – Whoopee Tina!

$2\frac{3}{4}$ cup flour
1 teaspoon baking soda
$\frac{1}{2}$ teaspoon salt
$1\frac{1}{4}$ teaspoons cinnamon
$\frac{1}{2}$ teaspoon ginger
1 cup ($\frac{1}{2}$ pound) butter or
   margarine, softened
$\frac{3}{4}$ cup sugar
2 eggs
$\frac{2}{3}$ cup molasses
$\frac{1}{2}$ cup milk

1. Sift flour with soda, salt, cinnamon, and ginger; set aside.

2. In a mixing bowl, cream butter and sugar until light. Beat in eggs until fluffy and stir in molasses. Add the flour mixture alternately with milk until well blended. Cover bowl and refrigerate mixture for one hour.

3. Drop batter by rounded tablespoons onto greased and floured baking sheets, spacing 2 inches apart. Bake in a 350° oven for 10 minutes until surface springs back when touched with your finger. Remove to a wire rack to cool completely.

GINGER CRÈME
$\frac{1}{2}$ cup ($\frac{1}{4}$ pound) softened butter
3 cups confectioners' sugar
2 to 3 tablespoons milk
$\frac{1}{4}$ cup molasses
$1\frac{1}{4}$ teaspoons ginger

Beat butter and sugar until creamy. Gradually beat in milk and molasses; add ginger and mix until crème is smooth and spreadable. Fill cookies and enjoy.

Almond Joy Macaroon Bars

Makes 24 bars
A bake sale favorite from Mystic Girl Scout Troop.

SHORTBREAD:
$\frac{3}{4}$ cup (12 tablespoons) unsalted butter
2 cups all-purpose flour
$\frac{1}{2}$ cup light brown sugar, firmly packed
$\frac{1}{2}$ teaspoon salt

Cut butter into $\frac{1}{2}$-inch pieces. In a food processor, process all ingredients until mixture begins to form small lumps. Sprinkle mixture in a 13-by-9-by-2-inch baking pan and press evenly onto bottom. Bake shortbread in a preheated 350° oven for 20 minutes or until golden.

CHOCOLATE MACAROON TOPPING:
4 large egg whites
1 cup sugar
1 teaspoon vanilla
$\frac{1}{2}$ cup all-purpose flour
1 7-ounce bag sweetened, flaked coconut
1$\frac{1}{2}$ cups semisweet chocolate bits

In a bowl, whisk together egg whites, sugar and vanilla until well combined. Blend in flour and coconut, mixing well. Sprinkle chocolate chips evenly over <u>hot</u> shortbread. Let chips melt and spread evenly over shortbread. Drop coconut mixture by teaspoons onto chocolate and spread evenly. Bake on the middle rack of the oven at 350° for 30 minutes. Cool completely in pan before cutting into bars.

Sail Away Bites

Makes 24 to 30
One of my baking inspirations when it was icy outside; using some of my favorite ingredients.

20 dried apricots, cut into $\frac{1}{4}$-inch pieces
1 11-ounce can Mandarin oranges, drained, juice reserved
1 cup ($\frac{1}{2}$ pound) butter or margarine
2 cups light brown sugar
1 teaspoon almond extract
1 egg
2 cups flour
2 teaspoons baking powder
$\frac{1}{2}$ teaspoon salt
$\frac{1}{4}$ cup slivered or finely chopped almonds (optional)

1. Place cut up apricots in reserved Mandarin orange juice to plump. Cream butter and sugar until fluffy, add almond extract, egg and beat well.
2. Drain the apricots, discarding juice and stir into butter mixture. Add the dry ingredients and gently fold in the Mandarin oranges. Spread batter in a greased 13-by-9-by-2-inch pan, sprinkle with almonds and bake at 350° for 25 to 30 minutes or until firm to the touch. Cool before cutting into squares with a sharp knife. These look very nice served in paper doily cups.

Double Chocolate Orange Brownies

Makes 2 dozen
Even better than a Tobler pull-apart chocolate orange.

1 cup ($\frac{1}{2}$ pound) butter or margarine
4 squares unsweetened baking chocolate
2 cups sugar
3 eggs
1 teaspoon pure orange extract
1 cup flour
1 6-ounce package semi-sweet
  chocolate chips

1. Melt butter or margarine with
    chocolate squares in a medium
    saucepan over low heat. Remove
    from heat. Gradually mix in sugar
    until thoroughly combined. Add eggs,
    one at a time, beating well after each
    addition.

2. Mix in orange extract and flour and
    spread batter in a lightly greased
    13-by-9-by-2-inch pan. Sprinkle
    chocolate chips over mixture, pressing
    down lightly. Bake at 350° for 35
    minutes, cool completely on a wire
    rack before cutting into bars.

Ginny's Hot Fudge Sauce

Makes 1 cup
**This recipe comes from a Westwood,
Massachusetts church cookbook of the
1950s. My mother never knew who the
"Ginny" was, but our whole family thanks
her. Wonderful served on Christmas Eve,
spooned hot over peppermint stick ice
cream alongside a plate of Christmas
cookies.**

$\frac{1}{2}$ cup sugar
2 tablespoons cocoa
pinch of salt
$\frac{1}{3}$ cup milk
1 tablespoon butter
$\frac{1}{2}$ teaspoon vanilla

Blend sugar, cocoa and salt in a small
saucepan. Add milk and butter; bring to
a boil and cook over medium heat for
3 minutes. Remove from heat and add
vanilla. May be served hot or at room
temperature. Refrigerate for up to
2 weeks.

Mom's Old Fashioned Fudge Sauce

Makes 1$\frac{1}{2}$ cups

1 cup sugar
4 tablespoons cocoa
1 tablespoon flour
$\frac{1}{2}$ cup half-and-half
2 tablespoons butter
$\frac{1}{2}$ teaspoon vanilla
pinch of salt

Mix sugar, cocoa and flour in a small saucepan. Add half-and-half and bring to a boil, stirring constantly. Boil for 2 minutes and remove from heat; add butter, vanilla, and salt. Serve warm over your favorite ice cream or cake. May be refrigerated for up to 2 weeks.

Mulligatawny's Favorite Dog Biscuits

Makes 6 to 7 dozen
The best for last, a tribute to man's best friend. These will last indefinitely (if your critter lets them).

2 cups whole wheat flour
$\frac{1}{2}$ cup rye flour
$\frac{1}{2}$ cup brewers' yeast
1 cup bulgur wheat
$\frac{1}{2}$ cup cornmeal
$\frac{1}{4}$ cup parsley flakes
$\frac{1}{4}$ cup dry milk
1 tablespoon kelp powder
$\frac{1}{4}$ cup warm water
1 cup chicken broth
1 beaten egg with 1 tablespoon water (glaze)

Combine dry ingredients in a large bowl. In a small bowl, combine dry yeast and warm water. Stir until yeast is dissolved. Add chicken broth. Stir liquid into dry ingredients, mixing with hands. Dough will be very stiff. If necessary, add a little more water or broth. On a well-floured surface, roll out dough to $\frac{1}{4}$-inch thickness. Cut with knife or cookie cutter into desired shapes (dog bones, of course). Transfer biscuits to cookie sheets and brush lightly with egg glaze. Bake at 300° for 45 minutes. Turn off heat and let biscuits dry out in the oven overnight. Store in airtight container.

Mystic Seaport Cookbooks

Seafood Secrets Volume I
Martini Bait, Put On The Pot, Luxurious Lobster, Light the Fire, and Top it Off, are only a beginning to the tempting chapters in our original collection of over 400 seafood recipes. From simple to elegant, these imaginative recipes can enhance cooking and dining experiences both ashore and afloat! This delectable repertoire of family favorites is amusingly illustrated by Sally Caldwell Fisher. Spiral bound, 9 1/4 inches by 8 inches, 256 pages, $16.95.

Seafood Secrets Volume II
An encore to the original Seafood Secrets, this book contains over 400 recipes from the sea, as well as fabulous side dishes selected specifically as those that complement the tantalizing recipes in the book. We've even included Bare Bones, a chapter containing recipes just for those fat-conscious folks, who want to enjoy neptune's magic in a low-fat manner. Again, Sally Fisher's whimsical illustrations are throughout the book, making this book our most enjoyable one ever. Spiral bound, 9 1/4 inches by 8 inches, 264 pages, $16.95.

Christmas Memories Cookbook
Block Island Turkey and Captain Cooke's Plum Pudding are only a sampling of the recipes in this collection. Recreate imaginative variations on classic New England cooking. Great for year-round entertaining and original gift ideas. Ample pages for "recording your" favorite holiday menus and recipes. Spiral bound, 9 1/4 inches by 8 inches, 272 pages, $16.95.

Global Feast
This book will transport you around the world with its unique collection of 350 very special family heirloom recipes. Hundreds of anecdotes, histories, family photographs, and illustrations. Spiral bound, 9 1/4 inches by 8 inches, 256 pages $16.95.

The Mystic Seaport All Seasons Cookbook
Compiled from recipes in the private files of Mystic Seaport Museum members, this exciting cookbook offers traditional as well as new and unusual ideas for entertaining throughout the year. Illustrated by Sally Caldwell Fisher, the cookbook is filled with tips, culinary lore, and a treasure of recipes pertaining to each season. Spiral bound, 9 1/4 inches by 8 inches, 248 pages, $16.95.

A New England Table
The pride of recipe collecting seems to be a New England tradition...from old cookbooks with faded and worn bindings, scraps of paper carefully tucked away over the years, or recipe cards passed on from mother to daughter. A look back to when good cooking was a way of life, this collection of over 450 recipes from friends and members of the Mystic Seaport community is a treasury of good food and tradition. The enchanting artwork on the cover is done by Carol Dyer. Spiral bound, 9 1/4 by 8 inches, 264 pages, $16.95.

Order Blank

Mail to: Mystic Seaport Store,
75 Greenmanville Avenue, Mystic, CT 06355
or call 1.800.331.BOOK (2665)

Please send me:

——— copies of A New England Table
        @ $16.95 ea.   ———

——— copies of Seafood Secrets Volume I
        @ $16.95 ea.   ———

——— copies of Seafood Secrets Volume II
        @ $16.95 ea.   ———

——— copies of Global Feasts
        @ $16.95 ea.   ———

——— copies of All Seasons Cookbook
        @ $16.95 ea.   ———

——— copies of Christmas Memories Cookbook
        @ $16.95 ea.   ———

                 CT residents add 6% Sales Tax ———

                    Packaging and Shipping
    ($5.95 for 1 book, add $1.00 ea. additional book) ———

                               TOTAL———

Please Send to:

Name ————————————————

Address ——————————————

City ——————————————————

State ———————— Zip ——————

___ Check ___ VISA ___ AMEX ___ MC

Exp. Date ————————————————

Card No. ————————————————

Signature ——————————————

All prices subject to change without notice.

Order Blank

Mail to: Mystic Seaport Store,
75 Greenmanville Avenue, Mystic, CT 06355
or call 1.800.331.BOOK (2665)

Please send me:

——— copies of A New England Table
        @ $16.95 ea.   ———

——— copies of Seafood Secrets Volume I
        @ $16.95 ea.   ———

——— copies of Seafood Secrets Volume II
        @ $16.95 ea.   ———

——— copies of Global Feasts
        @ $16.95 ea.   ———

——— copies of All Seasons Cookbook
        @ $16.95 ea.   ———

——— copies of Christmas Memories Cookbook
        @ $16.95 ea.   ———

                 CT residents add 6% Sales Tax ———

                    Packaging and Shipping
    ($5.95 for 1 book, add $1.00 ea. additional book) ———

                               TOTAL———

Please Send to:

Name ————————————————

Address ——————————————

City ——————————————————

State ———————— Zip ——————

___ Check ___ VISA ___ AMEX ___ MC

Exp. Date ————————————————

Card No. ————————————————

Signature ——————————————

All prices subject to change without notice.